Monmouth's Rebels

Peter Earle

Monmouth's Rebels

The Road to Sedgemoor 1685

ST. MARTIN'S PRESS
New York

Contents

Illustrations

Contemporary playing cards produced to celebrate the defeat of the rebellions of Monmouth and Argyll (*British Museum*)

James Duke of Monmouth (*Woburn Abbey, by permission of the Duke of Bedford*)

James II (*National Portrait Gallery*)

John, Lord Churchill (*National Portrait Gallery*)

Judge Jeffreys (*National Portrait Gallery*)

Bevil Skelton (*Mansell*)

Contemporary illustrations of craftsmen (*Guildhall Library*)

A selection of weapons (*Douglas Allen Photography*)

A present-day view of Sedgemoor (*Douglas Allen Photography*)

Maps

Introduction

My main aim in writing this new book about Monmouth's rebellion was to try to discover a little more about the sort of people who took part in this last purely English rebellion in English history. Previous studies of the rebellion tend to centre mainly on the biography, personality and sex life of its leader, the topography of the area in which the rebellion took place, the details of the course of the rebellion and its final defeat, and in particular on the fate of the captured rebels, a topic which has attracted great interest from sometimes shocked and sometimes frankly sadistic writers. Very little interest has been taken in what seems to me the much more important issue of who the rebels were and why they decided to leave apparently comfortable homes to risk their necks in what appears with hindsight to have been a rebellion with not much hope of success. This is an unbalanced approach. A rebellion is nothing without rebels. For this reason I have deliberately given much less space to the Duke of Monmouth and to gentlemen in general and far more space to the ordinary rebels than is usual in a book on this subject. In my view the Duke of Monmouth was chosen as a leader because he was available as a leader and not because he was the Duke of Monmouth. The rebels would have rebelled under another leader if there had been a suitable candidate around at the time. Those who love romantic stories about Stuarts may well be disappointed with my approach, but I hope that those who are interested in the nature of rebellion will approve of it.

To discover something new about the rebels was far harder than I had at first anticipated. They were drawn mainly from the Dissenters, a group for the most part literate and particularly noted for their habit of writing diaries. Since about fifteen hundred of the rebels were captured after the collapse of the rebellion at the battle of Sedgemoor I had hoped that at least one or two of them would have had papers on them which would give some clues to their character and motivation. But if such papers were seized after the battle, and surely they must have been, they have not survived. The only personal document taken from a rebel which survives today is the Duke of Monmouth's own pocket-book which tells us much about the leader of the rebellion but nothing about his followers.

There is also very little material on the lesser rebels in the form of informations or depositions taken down by government interrogators after the rebellion. The Government seems to have made no effort to discover why so many men were prepared to leave home to follow the Duke of Monmouth. Perhaps they were not interested. They were not social historians and no doubt thought that the repression which followed the rebellion would be sufficient to prevent a similar occurrence in the future. They have been proved right. Ever since 1685, the English have been unusually reluctant to rebel, however miserable their existence.

Given this general lack of direct documentary evidence about the rebels, I have been forced to approach my subject in a more roundabout way. What I have done is to adapt the source material and techniques used by local and demographic historians to produce a profile of the rebels of 1685. The results appear in a narrative and descriptive form in Chapter One and elsewhere in the text and in a more analytical form in the Appendix. My hope is that they will give the reader a much better and more accurate picture of the kind of people who were rebels than has been available in previous studies of the rebellion. I also hope that once we know who the rebels were the reasons for their decision to rebel will become more apparent.

My thanks are due to Blair Worden and Dudley Baines who very kindly read and commented on the text, to Jackie Baldick and Jackie Earle who cheered me up when I felt disheartened and to Joan Lynas who was, as always, a sympathetic and encouraging typist.

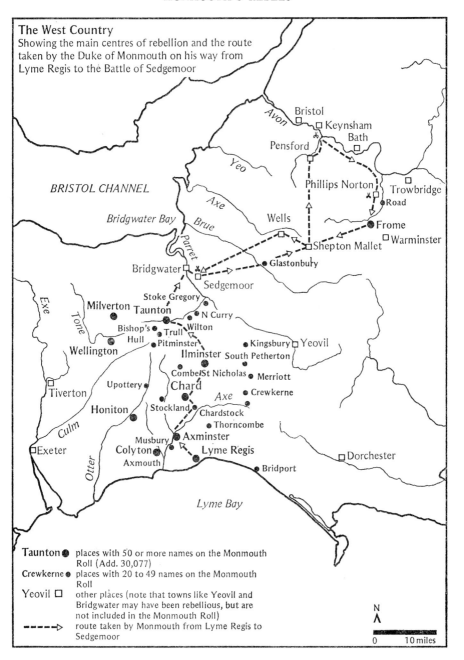

The West Country

Showing the main centres of rebellion and the route taken by the Duke of Monmouth on his way from Lyme Regis to the Battle of Sedgemoor

Bristol
Keynsham
Bath
Avon
Pensford
Yeo
BRISTOL CHANNEL
Phillips Norton
Trowbridge
Road
Axe
Wells
Frome
Warminster
Brue
Bridgwater Bay
Shepton Mallet
Parret
Glastonbury
Bridgwater
Sedgemoor
Stoke Gregory
Exe
Milverton
Taunton
N Curry
Tone
Bishop's
Hull
Wilton
Trull
Pitminster
Kingsbury
Yeovil
Wellington
Ilminster
South Petherton
Tiverton
Upottery
Combe St Nicholas
Merriott
Chard
Axe
Crewkerne
Honiton
Stockland
Chardstock
Culm
Thorncombe
Exeter
Musbury
Axminster
Colyton
Lyme Regis
Dorchester
Axmouth
Otter
Bridport

Lyme Bay

Taunton ● places with 50 or more names on the Monmouth Roll (Add. 30,077)
Crewkerne ● places with 20 to 49 names on the Monmouth Roll
Yeovil □ other places (note that towns like Yeovil and Bridgwater may have been rebellious, but are not included in the Monmouth Roll)
- - - -▷ route taken by Monmouth from Lyme Regis to Sedgemoor

N
Λ

0   10 miles

xi

One

His Majesty's Rebellious Subjects

The tall thin spire of St Mary's, Bridgwater, loomed out of the early morning mist, now slowly rising from the vast expanse of level moorland where the rebel army had made camp the night before. There were few signs of life on the moor. The great herds of cattle which normally pastured there had long been rounded up and concealed at the news of the approach of the rebels. Now all that could be seen between their own outriders and the low line of the Polden Hills to the north were a few scattered farms and villages, one or two windmills, some stunted trees and the great drainage ditches, known locally as rhines, which made the moor the valuable property that it was. For some of the rebels, for Thomas Godfrey, Thomas Gulhampton, for Walter Baker and his son, this flat green land was home and they pressed forward to identify the landmarks for their comrades. Here, on its little island rising some thirty feet from the moor, was their own village of Weston Zoyland, dominated by the great square tower of its parish church. This wide muddy ditch which they were now crossing was the Bussex Rhine which drained the waters of Sedgemoor into the river Parret, two miles to the south-west. Over there, some two miles to the north-west, surrounded by enclosed cornfields, was Chedzoy and beyond it Bawdrip, sheltering at the foot of the wooded Knowle Hill. And there, straight ahead to the west was Bridgwater, the home of many scores of the marching soldiers. But it is doubtful if many of the weary rebels paid much attention to the eager fingers of their guides, for they had been here before, a fact which dampened the spirits of the greatest zealot in their ranks. Disappointed and disillusioned, tired and hungry, they marched past their future graveyard with indifference and so made their way into the small Somerset port and set up their camp in the Castle Field.

What had gone wrong? It was almost exactly a fortnight since they had marched down this very same road on their way, as they thought, to London, the modern Babylon, thousands of determined men pledged to quiet the frustrations of a lifetime and destroy for ever the hated régime of popery, slavery and arbitrary government. They, the men of the West Country, were but the vanguard of this new army of the Lord. Their coming was to be the signal for all the oppressed to rise, crush their impious masters and dethrone the usurping King of England, the papist James II. Already they knew that the valiant men of Scotland were in arms, led by that great and godly nobleman, the Earl of Argyll, and the many Londoners in their ranks had assured them that the metropolis was only waiting for a sign from the west to rise in its turn. How could they fail? They had the numbers, the strength and the will to win. They were led by a great general, James Scott, Duke of Monmouth, and now by their own proclamation King of England, a man sent by the Lord to lead them, as their preachers told them, in order to be 'a deliverer for the nation and the interest of Christ'.[1] Was not his success and theirs actually foretold in a much-thumbed text from the Book of Ezekiel?[2] God himself was on their side.

What a mockery it all seemed now. For what had happened? Argyll had been defeated in Scotland and the Londoners had stayed at home. And they themselves had marched in a great figure of eight through north Somerset in almost continuous rain and were now back where they started with a royal army at their heels. They had done all that they had been asked to do but had achieved nothing at all. They had been to Glastonbury and camped in the ruins of the ancient abbey; they had crossed the Avon, looked at mighty Bristol, the second city of the kingdom, and then retreated; they had marched past the walls of the loyal city of Bath and been jeered at by its defenders; they had marched south down the borders of Wiltshire, increasingly aware of the growing royalist strength on their flanks. Finally they had set off from Frome and marched forty miles almost due west back to Bridgwater, away from London and glory and into a noose which the royal army and militia were daily tightening. What was to happen now? There was little choice. They must stand and fight or disperse and fly. There were really no other alternatives. It was enough to depress any rebel.

It was also rather depressing for the citizens of Bridgwater. No town had welcomed Monmouth and his army more readily in the early days of the rebellion. No pressure had been needed to persuade the Whig mayor, Alexander Popham, to proclaim Monmouth King of England. No effort had been spared by Monmouth's supporters among the leading citizens to make his welcome a memorable one. Most of the army's food and lodging for its one night's stay had been paid for by the town and, when they had set off towards Glastonbury on the following morning, the rebels had been enthusiastically cheered on their way. How different things were now. Bridgwater had heard the news of Monmouth's apparently aimless ramble round Somerset with a sense of increasing foreboding. It did not look as though they had backed a winner. Such foreboding increased when they heard that an order had been sent out in Monmouth's name, commanding the local constables and tithing-men to send into Bridgwater carpenters and labourers, spades and pickaxes, wheelbarrows and provisions. It seemed clear that the rebel army intended to stand a siege in Bridgwater itself, the last desperate move of a desperate and demoralized general. A siege could only lead to the looting and destruction of the town by rebel and royalist alike and the prospect of punishment for any who should survive the holocaust. The elder citizens knew what a siege was like; they had stood one in the Civil War, forty years before. But there was little they could do but hide their valuables and welcome the rebels. A small town with no garrison can hardly argue with an army of several thousands.

It was, then, with mixed feelings that the people of Bridgwater viewed the arrival of the rebel army as they marched, company by company, regiment by regiment, into the town on 3 July 1685. They might fear the future, but it was difficult to view the rebel soldiers without a feeling of pride, mingled perhaps with a little sadness. These were, after all, men like themselves who had left comfortable homes to uphold a cause that they too believed in, and it was sad to see them, gaunt, hungry and tired after their fruitless exertions.

They were a homely, familiar crowd, these five thousand men who made up the ranks of this last great rebel army to disturb the peace of southern England. They marched along the road in a plodding and stiff-jointed way, for most of them had long since left the sprightly days of youth behind and those who were still young shared the earnestness and determination of their elders. They were men who had thought hard and prayed hard before they decided to rebel. This was not the rebel army of popular imagination made up of smocked peasants urged on by Monmouth's fatal charms or of young apprentices who could think of no future beyond the exciting moonlight scramble to the rebel camp. Most of the rebels were husbands and fathers in their late twenties, their thirties and their early forties who had left their homes to fight because they thought it was their duty, the only way to make life tolerable and safe for the wives and children who had blessed them as they set out on their adventure.[3] Many of them were even older, men who had personally known a different England, an England free of popery and of that crypto-popery called the Anglican Church, an England in which true Protestants were able to practise their religion as their consciences dictated. Several of them were old enough to have fought as young men to create that England, men who had fought for Cromwell and Fairfax in the New Model Army, zealous men who could remember with pride the victories of the good old cause and the exciting discussions about the future of government and society which had followed those victories. Now they had taken up arms to fight once more, to try again to establish the leveller society of their dreams.

Many of them were true democrats, men who believed that 'there was no man born marked of God above another; for none comes into the world with a saddle on his back, neither any booted and spurred to ride him',[4] men who believed that shopkeepers, artisans and farmers like themselves had as good a right to rule the land as the greatest lord in the kingdom. There were some who went further, men who 'doe of their absolute power damn into ye pitt of hell all those that possesse five hundred pounds a year, [for] they are of ye rich that can't be saved.'[5] But such extreme radicals, though individually important in giving a truly revolutionary flavour to the rebel army, formed only a minority of those numbered in its ranks.

Most of the rank and file had no particularly exalted thoughts about political democracy. They wanted to be ruled by Parliament, not by the unfettered word of an absolute king; they would like that Parliament to be fairly elected and to sit each year, not just when the king chose that it should; but they would be happy enough if the men who sat in Parliament were the country gentlemen, the merchants and the lawyers who had always done so. They did not wish to overturn the social hierarchy nor to undermine the rule of property, for property to most of them was second only to God in their scale of values. Even many of the poorer rebels shared this conservative view of society for, poor though they might be now, their religion encouraged them to believe that they might improve themselves by their own efforts and that God would help them do so, for God helps those who help themselves.

They knew that God would help them now for it was in his name and for his greater glory that most of them had left their homes. It was religion, not politics or economics, that had sustained them through the disappointments of the campaign and it was religion which was to make them even now, after a week on the run, a formidable force which no royal soldier would dare treat other than with caution and respect. They were a pious and very earnest army, an army made up almost entirely of Nonconformists from the great bastion of Dissent in the three western counties of Somerset, Devon and Dorset, together with a few hundred men of similar religion who had managed to get past the royalist patrols from London and other parts of southern England to join them.

What sort of Dissenters they were is difficult to determine. Their opponents simply described them as fanatics, Anabaptists, sectaries or the Presbyterian crew, depending on the particular prejudice of the writer. This is unfortunate since Presbyterians and Baptists, for example, had very different views on both church and civil government and it would be interesting to know the relative proportions from the various sects. However, this is impossible. All we can say is that the most famous conventicles and those which drew upon them the greatest hostility from their Anglican neighbours, such as Paul's at Taunton, were Presbyterian meeting-houses. Paul's was said to be the largest conventicle in the whole West Country and such places must have produced many rebels and probably a particularly high proportion of local leaders, who were much more likely to belong to the structured Presbyterian church than any other. But there is plenty of evidence of rebels from the more democratic Baptist and Independent churches, and it would be foolish to assume that they were in a minority. The one group unlikely to be heavily represented was of course the Quakers. All the same, it is clear that some Quakers forgot their peaceable principles, as we can see from the case of Francis Scott who later publicly acknowledged his fault in taking up arms. 'Now this I doe freely acknowledg that whatever my end was I went out of the way of truth which I had long made a profession of and acted against the peaceable principall thereof and caused reproach thereunto and greived ye hearts of faithfull friends.'[6]

The fact that the rebels were mainly Dissenters meant that they were drawn from the most pious and moralistic section of the population. All sects have backsliders, of course, and we can find plenty of evidence of immoral behaviour amongst the members of Dissenting churches. But to be a Dissenter was to take a very positive view of religion. Few people would be prepared to accept the moral rigour of a Dissenting church and the civil and financial disadvantages of belonging to one, unless they were earnest in their beliefs. One small indication of the high moral tone of the rebel army can be found in the parish records of St Mary Magdalen at Taunton. The rebel army camped in and around Taunton for three days on its way from Lyme Regis, where Monmouth landed, to Bridgwater. All our evidence emphasizes the enthusiasm with which the rebels were greeted by the townsfolk of both sexes. And yet nine months later there was only one illegitimate child to be baptized, surely some sort of record for an army of several thousand men. As if to make sure that the exception should prove the rule the mother baptized the child Gustavus, after the greatest Protestant military hero of the seventeenth century.

For this army, too, like the Swedes and Scots who fought for the great Gustavus, were Protestant soldiers who marched to combat the spread of popery. Fear of the return of popery, of Jesuit plots and Irish massacres and the fires of Smithfield, had been a recurrent nightmare in the minds of earnest English men and women ever since the days of Mary Tudor. The restoration of the monarchy in 1660 had done nothing to dispel these fears. The returning Court was riddled with papists and with those fellow-travellers whom a mocking world called Church Papists, men who 'love Popery well but are loth to lose by it'. Indeed for many Dissenters the Anglican Church with its bishops and its surplices was nothing other than the Church of Rome in disguise, a belief which could only be strengthened by the determination of Charles ii's Parliament of Anglican gentlemen to take their revenge on the zealots who had so humbled them in the years of civil strife. The long period of persecution began with the passage of the Act of Uniformity in 1662 which led to the ejection of some two thousand Nonconformist ministers from their livings. This was followed by a series of measures designed to harry the ministers, to break up their religious meetings and to bar the members of Nonconformist congregations from those positions of civic responsibility which they had once occupied so proudly. Failure to comply with the law could lead to heavy fines and if the offender could not or would not pay, to prison. Who but the agents of popery would behave in such an intolerable way to true Protestants?

The vague fears, induced by nearly twenty years of intermittent persecution for conscience sake and coloured by enthusiastic reading of Foxe's *Book of Martyrs*, were made only too concrete in 1678 with the disclosure of the terrifying details of the Popish Plot. The Society of Jesus, encouraged and financed by the Pope and Louis xiv, were planning to murder Charles ii and put his brother James, Duke of York, a declared papist, on the throne in his place. The Jesuits were to be supported in their conspiracy by troops raised by the Catholic nobility, assisted by large contingents from France and Ireland. Once they were in power the Protestant religion was to be suppressed. So convincing was this story and so closely did it mirror the inmost fears of English Protestants that it was believed not only by the Nonconformists, but by nearly all Anglicans as well. Indeed at first no one dared to doubt the minutest detail of the plot, lest they too be thought a part of it. The reaction was immediate. Anglican and Nonconformist now stood together to defend themselves against the long-awaited threat. Many Catholics were arrested and many, especially Jesuits, were executed for their supposed part in the plot, after a trial which was little more than a mockery. Meanwhile a determined effort was made to stop the rot and make England once again a place fit for decent Protestants to live in. Two things needed to be done. The Nonconformists, the backbone of decency and the Protestant cause, must be given toleration and the Duke of York must be excluded from the succession to the throne. The long campaign, which had strong undercurrents of republicanism, was fought in every forum of public opinion; in the streets, the taverns, the meeting-houses, the Press and above all in the great talking-shop of Parliament, now purged of its cavalier majority by three successive elections held in the heat of the crisis. Hardly a contrary voice was to be heard and it seemed that the days of fear and persecution for the Dissenters were now over.

But, alas, it was not to be. The King was too powerful and too self-confident to be abashed by mere noise. Although at first he had been forced to follow the tide of public opinion, he knew that time would be on his side, time for many men to learn to doubt the fantastic details of the Plot, time for many others to get bored with the mass hysteria. After a while public opinion was not so one-sided and the King was able to act. It was noticed that no more Catholics were being brought to the gallows, though many more had been accused. And then, in March 1681, he removed the floor from under his opponents' feet by dissolving the last of the three Exclusion Parliaments. Now he and those who advised him could turn their attention once again to the Dissenters who had played such an important part in mobilizing the opposition to the Crown.

Historians are virtually unanimous in condemning the Popish Plot as the product of the fertile imagination of the man who exposed it, the moon-faced ex-Jesuit and ex-chaplain in the Royal Navy, Titus Oates. Few people would have accepted such an opinion in the 1680s, least of all the Dissenters whose innate belief in the reality of the plot was only strengthened by the fury of the Tory backlash which followed the Whig and Dissenter failure to teach the King how to rule. Persecution of the Dissenters which had lapsed during the three years of political excitement since the exposure of the Popish Plot in 1678 was intensified. Orders to enforce the laws against the Dissenters were sent out to Justices of the Peace throughout the country, orders which were obeyed with particular enthusiasm in two of the major concentrations of Dissent, London and the West Country. At the same time the King removed from the Whigs and Dissenters their last political platform, by remodelling the charters of the corporate towns from which they drew their strength in such a way that in the future only Tories were likely to be elected to the town governments.

It was now, faced by a future of continuous persecution and no possibility of airing their grievances at either the local or the parliamentary level, that the various opposition groups began to think of rebellion as an answer, indeed the only answer, to their plight and to the plight of the country. Only a rebellion could prevent England from becoming like France, a Catholic country ruled by an absolutist prince who was even now putting the finishing touches to that long campaign which would end his Protestant subjects' right to practise their religion. Fear of such an eventuality drew together earnest men of very different backgrounds and ways of thought. In particular, it was only such fears and frustration at their inability to do anything about it by constitutional means that brought the law-abiding, respectable Presbyterians into the revolutionary fold. In normal times they were by no means enamoured of the other Dissenters whom they, as well as Anglicans, were accustomed to call fanatics. This attitude is illustrated in a sermon preached at the Restoration by the Reverend

Ames Short, the Presbyterian minister of Lyme Regis. The return of Charles ii to his kingdom has freed us, he said,

from our feares and dangers of being harressed by the attempts of every aspiring, ambitious Adonijah, to make himself King. We need not now to feare the aspiring ambition either of a Cromwell or a Lambert. Nor need we now feare of being kept in bondage and slavery by an inconsiderable part of a Parliament, or a Phanatick Committee of Safety under the notion of a free State, or Commonwealth.

Later he went on to point out to his congregation, who no doubt agreed with him, that the accession of King Charles would free them 'from our soul-destroying and damning universall tolleration'.[7]

It was only when a man who could speak like this had been forced by even more intolerant men to become a 'factious preacher' whose congregation was 'a nursery of sedition',[8] that the Presbyterian leaders and opinion-makers in West Country towns might be persuaded to throw in their lot with Baptists and Independents who believed in a 'damning universall tolleration' or republicans who believed in 'a free state or commonwealth'. It took the Government some time to force the Presbyterians into such a degrading position, but ultimately they too became as factious as the next man, once they realized that they too could be repressed as savagely as could their social inferiors. Even then the Presbyterians had no wish to fight and it was only after the end of all possibility of a parliamentary improvement of their position that they were prepared to consider the possibility of rebellion.

Presbyterian, Independent and Republican all looked back to the period of the Civil War and interregnum for their inspiration, though the particular source of inspiration might be very different for each group. In this moment of crisis they could forget the differences and mutual recriminations of the past and join together to plot once more for the good old cause of God and religion, without being too specific about just what the good old cause was. This could be sorted out later when the present danger of slavery and popery had been removed. It is this retrospective attitude to rebellion which explains why so many of both the leaders and the rank and file in Monmouth's army were of the generation who could actually remember the events of the 1640s and 1650s or were brought up in their shadow. To the young men born after 1660 the cause which their fathers and elder brothers had fought for and still dreamed about was a dead cause, learned perhaps but never experienced, and so they shrank from the thought of dying for it. They were indeed a very different generation, less earnest and more worldly than their elders, less likely to risk life and estate for an idea. Obviously one should treat with caution contemporary comment in any age on the worldliness and lack of piety of the young. All the same the flood of criticism which came from both Anglican and Nonconformist pens on the decline of religion and the decline of intensity of feeling would indicate that this younger generation had certainly reacted against the piety and earnestness of their elders. Both church attendance and Nonconformity seem to have been in nearly continuous decline from the Restoration to the Methodist Revival. The men who fought for Monmouth were to be the last godly army in English history.

The same theme of retrospection also helps us to understand why rebellion was only seriously considered in two parts of the country, London and the West Country, and why it was only the West Country which actually did rebel in 1685. Many other areas, such as East Anglia, had Dissenting populations who would seem to have had just as much motive to rebel as the men of Taunton and Lyme Regis. They too had been persecuted and they too feared a papist king, but there was hardly a murmur of militancy from the great industrial and Dissenting city of Norwich. The reason may well lie in the different experiences faced by these regions in the Civil War. East Anglia had been a Puritan stronghold firm in its support for the parliamentary cause. But, just because it had been so strong, the region had not suffered the full rigours of civil war. Many men had set out to fight, but the war with all its horrors had never come to the towns and villages where they had left their wives and children. The Puritan population of the West Country had suffered much more and their direct experience, both of civil war and of victory, was to give them that edge of determination which was to lead them to revolt in 1685.

Towns like Taunton and Lyme Regis had been islands of parliamentary strength in a royalist sea. Both had been the victims of long and painful sieges by royalist armies, sieges in which their citizens had learned the lesson that they as well as those who volunteered as soldiers would have to fight if they wanted to win the day and see the victory of their cause. The people of Taunton still sang in 1685 the song that celebrated the relief of the royalist siege forty years earlier.

The cavaliers dispers'd with fear, and forcèd were to run,
On th'eleventh of May, by break of day, ere rising of the sun.
Let Taunton men be mindful then, in keeping of this day,
We'll give God praise, with joy always, upon th'eleventh of May.[9]

The very fact of the successful defiance of such West Country towns during the Civil War led to their harsher persecution in the Restoration period and thus hardened their resolve to rebel. Taunton lost its charter in 1660 and throughout the reign of Charles II was singled out as a centre of sedition, a fact which can have done little to make Anglican and Dissenter the good friends or at least indifferent neighbours which they were in other parts of the country. There was a vindictiveness about the persecution of the West Country Dissenters by their loyalist justices which is difficult to match elsewhere and makes it easier for us to understand why the men of Taunton and their colleagues in other towns and villages should have been so ready to emulate the exploits of their fathers and disperse the cavaliers once more.

Such an undertaking was being seriously discussed in the autumn of 1682. The lead was probably given by republican groups in the metropolis, but the idea of armed rebellion seems to have received a ready response in the West Country. The idea was for a multiple insurrection in London, Scotland, Cheshire and the West Country, possibly coupled with the assassination of the King and his papist brother. But lack of unity amongst the leaders and an inability to decide on either the timing or the ultimate object of the rebellion led to very little action and far too much talk. The taverns of the metropolis must have been buzzing with the innuendoes and the double-talk of the plotters. In the end the inevitable leak occurred and in June 1683 the so-called Rye House Plot was blown wide open by an informer.

The Government naturally concentrated its attention on the danger on its own doorstep and went to enormous lengths to try and uncover the organization of the proposed rebellion in London. But enquiries were also set in motion in the West Country. However, the loyalty and secrecy of the West Country rebels made it very difficult for the Government to learn very much about them, a problem which is naturally shared by the historian who relies on government sources for his information. The West Country Dissenters were described in 1685 as 'an enemy in our bosomes that is so secret, so cunning, so industrious, and haveing a cause that steeles them with courage even to desperatenesse',[10] perfect revolutionaries in fact. The only thing which could give them away was if a smile should appear on their normally gloomy faces. Then it was likely that they 'had some wicked designe afoot',[11] though what it was might be impossible to find out.

Local loyalists and Justices of the Peace were empowered to search for arms and attempt to discover who was actually involved in the proposed insurrection. The results of such enquiries were discouraging. The local gentry responded with enthusiasm to the opportunity to search Dissenters' houses, hoping of course that they might uncover a 'fat rebel' whose estate could be added to their own. They tried hard but found virtually nothing.

Rather more success was had through listening to gossip and drunken bragging. Several reports reached London about the Red Lion tavern in Taunton whose landlord, William Savage, was to be one of Monmouth's captains in 1685. In 1683 the story that was current was that free beer was available for a large number of men who, in return, were to be prepared to take up arms at a moment's notice.[12] In Bristol the republican club held at the Horseshoe tavern had a similar reputation.[13] But such information was of the vaguest sort and it would have been difficult to pin it down and make it the basis of a prosecution for high treason. When it is remembered that the Government had information that a thousand men were being raised in and about Taunton and a similar number in Bristol it is clear either that the potential rebels knew how to keep their mouths shut or that the whole thing was a complete fabrication, a supposition which seems unlikely in view of what was to happen just two years later. But in 1683 the only real evidence that men were being raised related to a man called Anthony Sandford, a former corporal in Cromwell's cavalry, who had boasted as early as 1681 that he 'hoped ere long to be a brave fellow and to ride a good horse again, as a gentleman by Taunton, Esquire Trenchard, would shortly raise a troop in which he was to be listed.'[14] John Trenchard, a Whig country gentleman and former Member of Parliament, was the man charged by the Rye House plotters to raise the men of the West Country, so the story seems quite plausible. Rumours of the existence of this troop of horse were flying about in the summer of 1683 but nothing was conclusively proved. Trenchard himself was a marked man in 1685 and fled the country before Monmouth's arrival so that he could not be charged with complicity in his rebellion.

Thwarted in their attempts to discover either arms or rebels, the local loyalists redoubled their persecution of the West Country Dissenters. The Justices of the Peace, ably assisted by thugs and paid informers, raided conventicle after conventicle, savagely fining or imprisoning those whom they were able to catch attending them. At the same time a determined effort was made in many places to smash the physical surroundings in which the Dissenters worshipped. No one was more rigorous in this pursuit than Stephen Timewell, the loyalist Mayor of Taunton, who was able to report to the Government in August 1683 that he had destroyed the main meeting-houses of both the Presbyterian and Baptist congregations in his seditious town.

I pulled down all the lasts and galleries in that great meeting-house called Poole [Pole's] in Taunton, with all the doors and gates, and likewise all the seats, pulpit and galleries of the Baptist meeting-house and burnt it together on the market-place. There were about ten cart loads. We were till three in the morning before it was all burnt; and we were very merry before it with the bells ringing all night.[15]

The image of Stephen Timewell and his loyalist friends dancing round their bonfire perfectly illustrates the chasm that lay between

Anglican and Dissenter in the West Country. Such mutual hatred could only be assuaged with blood.

For the time being such determined repression, which was repeated elsewhere, had its effect and Timewell was able to report that the Anglican Church was now full. But in the long run it was impossible to silence the really earnest Dissenters, sure as they were that God was on their side. And indeed, in 1683, just as the persecution in Taunton reached its peak, God was to let loose a terrible punishment on this town that had rejected his true believers. An appalling epidemic struck the town in the summer of 1683, an epidemic which was not to end until between ten and twenty per cent of the population had been buried.[16] No other sign was needed. The epidemic kindled a millenarian fire in the hearts of the Taunton Dissenters, which, added to their understandable desire for revenge, was to make them formidable enemies in 1685.

In the meantime the destruction of their meeting-houses merely served to take them away from under the eyes of their oppressors and to force them to seek spiritual consolation in hidden places where no man could know what they were plotting. Elsewhere in the West Country the same ardour could be found. It was in hideaways, such as the Reverend Stephen Towgood's 'church under the ground', out in the wilds in the hills above Axminster that Monmouth's rebellion was planned and men prayed for divine assistance for their cause. These secret conventicles were ideal for the plotter. Towgood had a regular membership drawn from as far away as Taunton, as well as from such comparatively nearby towns as Colyton, Chard and Lyme Regis. Most of these people travelled clandestinely to meetings every Sunday and thus had plenty of opportunity to disseminate information throughout the West Country. Even in the very worst period of the repression, at the end of 1684, Towgood still held services at night, but to ease the problems of night travel he normally held two services, one near Axminster on the evening of the Sabbath and the other near Chard towards dawn.[17] The names of those caught in conventicles confirm this evidence of the widespread membership of any particular congregation. At a conventicle held at St Gregory

Stoke in 1680, for instance, the names of eighty-six people from thirty-one different locations were taken. Between them they covered a high proportion of the whole future area of rebellion.[18] Such local networks could easily be linked through trading and family contacts with London and the Low Countries and thus be influenced by discussion in the metropolis or by the numerous exiled rebels living overseas. Many men in the West Country were linked with London through correspondence systems, such as that described by the informer James Harris connecting the radical Baptists of Taunton, east Devon and Dorset with the republican club held at the Salutation tavern in Lombard Street, London.[19]

It takes little imagination to realize the effect of the news of the death of Charles II in February 1685 on the men and women who were cowering from persecution in the hidden conventicles of the West Country. Now the worst had happened. What other future could they expect from his papist brother, but more persecution and a determined campaign to turn England into a papist country? 'And what could the poor people of God now expect, but as his brother, the former King, had made their yokes heavy, so this man would adde to their yokes; as his brother had chastised them with whips, so he would now chastise them with scorpions.'[20] By the time that Monmouth landed at Lyme Regis on 11 June the poor people of God were prepared to give their all for the cause. 'Now also they hoped that the day was come in which the good Old Cause of God and Religion that had lain as dead and buryed for a long time would revive again; And now was the soundings of trumpets and alarm for wars heard.'[21]

Who responded to the trumpet's call? Who joined this army of latter-day saints? We have seen that the rebels came mainly from the West Country, but in fact most of them came from a comparatively small area of the West Country, comprising east Devon, west Dorset and the whole of the county of Somerset.[22] This is partly a reflection of the effectiveness of militia units in preventing potential rebels from outside this area from joining the army. In particular there is no doubt that many hundreds of men from Bristol and Exeter would have joined the rebels if they had been able to. But it also reflects the fact that this particular area, with its heavy concentration of both Nonconformity and industrial workers, had been ever since 1660 the most factious and militant region in the country, with the possible exception of London. It was because he knew that he could raise an army on the way that Monmouth landed at Lyme Regis and marched via Taunton towards Bridgwater and Bristol. In this respect, if in few others, he had been well advised.

Within the area of rebellion it was the towns and villages with a large proportion of their population engaged in industry and commerce which provided most of the rebels. For Monmouth's army, which has often been described by historians as an army of peasants, was in fact an army consisting mainly of artisans and shopkeepers, the typical occupations of Dissenters. There were several hundreds of peasants, or rather farmers, in the rebel ranks but they were completely overshadowed by men from urban backgrounds or engaged in non-agricultural pursuits. The social composition of the army is also fairly clear. The rebels were overwhelmingly concentrated in the middle ranks of society. There were very few gentlemen and very few labourers or paupers. The typical rebel was a weaver or a shoemaker, a tailor or a woolcomber. But all occupations were represented. There were coachmen and sailors, cutlers and tanners, goldsmiths and brewers, blacksmiths and bodice-makers, as well as yeomen and husbandmen in the ranks of Monmouth's army.

We can learn a little more about the rebels if we look in rather more detail at one or two of the places which were important centres of the rebellion. The most rebellious place in Devon was the large village or small town of Colyton, a beautifully sited compact settlement on a tributary of the Axe, with the mixed agricultural and industrial occupational structure which was so typical of the larger villages in the West Country. Colyton was well known as a centre of Dissent, and the town provided at least eighty-six recruits for Monmouth's army, around a quarter of the total adult male population. This is a fairly high proportion when one remembers that there was evidence of a loyalist party in the town, that many men must have been too old or too sick to think of fighting and that all the men who did rebel had been taught obedience to the Crown and knew very well what to expect if they should fail. We do not know the occupations of all the Colyton men, but the evidence we have suggests a mixture of cloth- and leather-workers, yeomen and husbandmen, together with the usual collection of artisans such as carpenters, tailors and shoe-makers.

Two factors stand out when we try to determine why one Colyton man rather than another should have decided to rebel in 1685. The first is the extremely high age of the rebels. It is probable that three-quarters or more of the rebels were over the age of twenty-five, in other words were mature, responsible men who were more than likely to have a wife and children, even if none of them could emulate John Clapp, a mercer in his fifties, whose second wife Hannah had borne him ten children. Clapp himself was not exceptionally old for a rebel. Nearly a third of the Colyton men were over forty. The second point of interest is that it was unusual for more than one member of the same family to be a rebel. None of Clapp's sons joined him in his adventure. Indeed one can only assume from the evidence and the known size of families that in most cases it was deliberate family policy to have only one member in the rebel army. Most people like to hedge their bets and this policy would ensure that whoever won, the family and its possessions would for the most part survive. Who the one member would be depended on circumstances. It was not always the father or the son, the elder or the younger brother. Obviously, in most cases the choice would have depended on personal inclination. Not everyone has the guts or the motivation to rebel. But sometimes it was probably the result of a family decision and one must imagine a number of anxious discussions as the reality of rebellion loomed closer and families sought the guidance of God as to which of them should go out to fight. In view of the general age of the rebels it is quite possible that the situation imagined by Conan Doyle in his novel about the rebellion, *Micah Clarke*, had some basis in reality. Micah's father was an old Roundhead soldier and when he gets the word that the long-awaited rebellion is nigh he wants to go forth himself once again to do battle for the Lord. But when he tries out his sword he realizes that he is now an old man and so fits out his giant son, Micah, to go in his place. Micah does not have the same ideological motivation as his father but he is a dutiful son. *Micah Clarke* is fiction and Conan Doyle makes some serious errors in his story, but there is plenty of evidence of fathers fitting out their sons, and indeed their servants, for the rebellion.[23]

Such generalizations need not conceal the fact that the Colyton party included several young men and that a number of men went off to fight in the company of their sons or brothers. The youngest rebel from Colyton seems to have been John Abrahams, who was only fourteen when he left the town with his father to join the rebellion. John was married to the daughter of another rebel on 8 June 1685, only three days before Monmouth landed and long after Colyton had received advance notice of his intention to raise the men of the West Country. It was a long time before John Abrahams was able to enjoy a proper married life. He survived the rebellion, but did not return to start a family in Colyton until the mid-1690s, ten years after his marriage.

The leader of the Colyton rebels seems to have been Roger Satchell, a small landowner with property in Colyton itself and in Honiton. It was said of him that 'he always hated the name of a papist' and 'no sooner had he news of the Duke's being landed, but he sets himself to work to serve him, desiring all he knew to join with him, and was one of the first that went to him at Lyme and was with him to the end'.[24] One or two others in the Colyton party were quite well off, such as the husbandman Philip Cox who had lands to the value of £58 per annum. But most of them owned very little, except their own house and garden, and many had no real estate at all. They were not paupers, but they relied for their living on their own skills. For some, such as the young doctor Nicolas Thompson, such skill might earn him a good living. For others, such as the poor weaver William Clegg, life must always have been hard. When he was executed after the rebellion at the age of forty-six his worldly possessions were valued at only fifteen shillings.[25]

Two other Colyton men who were later executed have left us some idea of their motivations in joining the rebellion. They are more or less what we might expect. Joseph Speed, a poor shoe-maker in his forties who was 'somewhat encumbered in the world', could thank God that since the age of sixteen he had always had 'the checks of conscience' on him. His whole design 'in taking up arms under the Duke of Monmouth was to fight for the Protestant Religion which my own conscience dictated me to, and which the said Duke declared for'.[26] John Spragg, a mason, who was executed in front of his friends and neighbours in Colyton itself, 'believed that no Christian ought to resist a lawful power; but the case being between popery and protestantism, altered the matter; and the latter being in danger, he believed it was lawful for him to do what he did'.[27]

When we look at Taunton, the most rebellious place in Somerset, and indeed 'the sink of all the rebellion in the west', we find very much the same pattern as in Colyton. Taunton was a fairly large town by the standards of the day with a population of about six thousand. We know the names of three hundred and fifty men from the town's two parishes who joined the rebels. It must have been far easier to conceal the fact that one was out with Monmouth in a large, crowded town like Taunton but, even so, this figure represents nearly a quarter of the adult male population, the same proportion as in Colyton. In Taunton too we find the same comparatively high average age, with three-quarters or more of the rebels over twenty-five. Here too it was normal to find only one man from each family. Less than a fifth of the rebels from the large parish of St Mary Magdalen had a brother or a son in the rebel army, which just goes to show how exceptional was the woolcomber Thomas Bond who joined the rebel army with his three sons, Thomas aged twenty-eight, John aged twenty-six and the baby Philip who was only twenty.

Taunton was a great centre of the West Country cloth industry, famous for the production of serges and the cheaper Taunton cottons, a factor which was reflected in the composition of the rebels. Over two-thirds of all those whose occupations we know were clothworkers of one sort or another. Most of the other rebels worked in jobs associated with the town's role as the marketing centre of the prosperous agricultural region of the Vale of Taunton

Deane or else provided industrial, commercial and personal services for their fellow townsmen. Taunton was a far richer place than Colyton and there were some very wealthy rebels in the Taunton party, goldsmiths, merchants and even one or two gentlemen. But the gentlemen of Taunton were not the sort of gentlemen who flourished on long lineages, broad acres, dogs and port. They were men like the Presbyterian sergemaker and merchant John Hucker, who commanded a troop of rebel horse, or the republican landlord of the Red Lion, William Savage, whom we have already met. The wealth of most Taunton rebels, however, reflected the fact that so many of them were combers and weavers. They were poor, but not likely to be paupers unless there was a depression in the cloth industry which employed them. There had been serious unemployment in Taunton in the early 1680s, but by 1685 trade had recovered and there is no evidence that economic desperation was a motive for rebellion. The poor weavers from Taunton, like their colleagues from Colyton, fought because they hated the name of papist and their consciences told them to fight for the Protestant religion.

Such general observations may help us to imagine what the rebels looked like as they marched into Bridgwater on 3 July 1685. We can imagine that they were suntanned, weather-beaten and tired, since we know that it was summer-time and that they had marched a long way, often in bad weather. We can also be fairly confident that the typical rebel was a married Dissenting artisan in his thirties from a town or large village in the West Country. But they were now soldiers and it is as soldiers that we will meet them for most of the rest of this book. What sort of soldiers were they? What would the military connoisseur have made of this army of some five thousand men?

One thing that would surely have struck him was that Monmouth's army travelled light. Sir James Turner tells us in his *Pallas Armata* that an army of five thousand men would normally have some four hundred waggons.[28] Monmouth's baggage-train, which was under the command of his butler, had only forty. And most of these carried the wounded and the equipment of the rebel leaders, rather than food or ammunition, both of which were in very short supply. Another source of impediment to a seventeenth-century army was the large number of women who normally marched with the soldiers. After the Prince of Orange had sent the three Scots regiments in the Low Countries to help James II put down Argyll's rebellion, he ordered the English envoy to 'hyre a ship and send over into Scotland all the soldiers wyves that are left behinde and make a greate noyse here'.[29] But there seem to have been no women with Monmouth's army. The rebels left their wives behind when they left home to do battle for the Lord.

Women had an important function in a seventeenth-century army, doing much of the work which would now be done by such bodies as the catering corps, but they were rarely decisive in battle. Battles were won mainly by cavalry and guns and our sharp-eyed observer could hardly fail to notice that Monmouth's army was rather deficient in both these particulars. He had brought over with him an extremely good Dutch gunner. But this expert had to serve only four small iron guns, pitiful for an army of this size. The cavalry was not much better. One third of an army normally consisted of mounted men. Monmouth had less than a thousand, reflecting the fact that not very many real countrymen had enrolled under his standard. The weavers and shoemakers could not afford a horse. Many probably could not ride, unless they were amongst that select number of Monmouth's troopers who wore the stout buff leather coats of former Cromwellian Ironsides. Not only was Monmouth short of cavalry, but most of what he had was not much use. Two or three troops of cavalry were magnificently turned out and won much praise from the royalist patrols with whom they brushed but, for the most part, Monmouth's cavalry was of very poor quality, neither horse nor man being properly equipped for war, a pursuit which required rather different characteristics in a beast than those acceptable in the farmyard.

There remained the infantry, the core of the army and the only real hope for the success of the cause. They must have presented a rather bizarre spectacle to the uncommitted spectator. Some wore the red coats and white kersey breeches of the New Model Army, a sight not seen for quarter of a century and one which could only remind the viewer of the glories of the past, whether the current wearer was himself a grizzled veteran of Cromwell's days or the son or nephew of a New Model man. Others wore purple coats faced with scarlet which had been made in Holland specially for the rebellion.[30] Still others wore the yellow coats of the Somerset militia, many of whom had fled at their first contact with the rebels, stripping off their uniforms as they ran. But most of the rebels wore the sober, sensible clothing typical of the Dissenting artisan class from which they sprang. There were many tailors in the rebel ranks but there had been little time or money for sartorial display. For most of the men their only concessions to military flamboyance were the regimental colours fastened to their coats or a sprig of greenery in their hats. And whatever the clothing it was in poor condition now after so long marching in the rain and sleeping at night on the bare ground with no cover, while boots and shoes were in an appalling condition and many rebels had been reduced to marching barefoot.

The rebels' arms were as diverse as their uniforms and were in a similarly poor condition. Those who had been first to enlist when Monmouth landed at Lyme Regis had been the most fortunate and were equipped with the very best muskets that the age could afford, flintlocks with a much greater accuracy and reliability than the matchlocks still used by some of the regiments in the English royal army. But Monmouth had only brought over sufficient muskets to arm a quarter of his infantry and the rest of the men had had to fend for themselves. A man might have brought his father's New Model musket, together with his uniform and sword, when he left his home. Others had bought or even made weapons in anticipation of the rebellion, some of the richer rebels arming several of their fellows at their own cost. Once the rebellion had started it had been possible to augment such weapons by simply seizing what could be found, whether it was the stock of a Taunton gunsmith, the museum pieces hung above a loyalist fireplace, the weapons of a fleeing militia-man or the rusting pikes and muskets in a parish armoury. Arms from such sources could vary from up-to-date sporting guns commandeered from the local gentry to weapons of Elizabethan times, now likely to be more dangerous to the user than to his enemy. But all these sources were not sufficient to arm the whole rebel army. Many men had to march, and face the possibility of an encounter with a royalist patrol, armed with nothing but knives or hatchets, while the pikemen of several companies were equipped with scythe blades fixed to long poles, a formidable slashing weapon in the hands of a strong man, if not quite as effective as the standard pike in checking cavalry.

To say that Monmouth's army was a little shabby and not particularly well armed is not to say that it was necessarily ineffective. The rebels certainly looked like an army and not a rabble, despite their rather ragged appearance. They were all volunteers, all highly motivated men determined to win and well aware that a soldier is much more than a man in uniform. They were in fact drawn from exactly the same group in society which had made up the ranks of the New Model Army and no man in 1685 would have dreamed of underestimating such men, whatever they looked like. By the time that they marched into Bridgwater for the second time they looked and moved like soldiers. Scattered through their ranks were a large number of former regular soldiers who, even if now a bit long in the tooth, had not forgotten how to drill. Monmouth and the regular officers whom he had brought over from Holland had used these men to turn his raw recruits into something approaching the fearless automata necessary if he was to undertake the military manoeuvres of his day. On his first arrival at Lyme Regis the men who had flocked in to his colours had been divided up into companies and regiments and set to exercise for several days. Ever since, all the spare time available had been taken up in training them as soldiers. They had learned to march and make camp, they had learned to aim and fire their muskets, they had learned to carry and handle a pike. That all this had paid off had been clearly seen on the one occasion when the rebels had had a serious clash with the regular army at Phillips Norton, just south of Bath. Monmouth's men had lined the hedges and walls and returned fire with the coolness of veterans, and the royal army had been forced to retire.

No man who saw the faces of the rebels could help feeling that these were men who would fight and fight hard before they would accept defeat at the hands of the godless army which had been sent down from London to destroy them. 'Fear Nothing but God' was the motto embroidered in gold letters on several of the banners and colours that fluttered in the breeze above the glistening points of the shouldered pike and scythe blades. For many of the rebels this motto was literally true. They did fear nothing but God, a fact which gave them courage and determination which no mere mercenary army could hope to emulate. Their opponents knew this and treated them with caution. This was not a drunken mob to be dispersed by one charge of the militia. These were men who, once committed, would fight to the death for the sake of the cause which their banners proclaimed.

Or would they? One man had his doubts. One man felt in his heart that an irregular force could never stand up to the discipline and training of a royal army. Unfortunately, that man was the rebel army's leader who rode on his white horse in the midst of his hand-picked bodyguard. He had good reason for his doubts. How could James Scott, Duke of Monmouth, former captain-general of the English army, forget the greatest day of his military career when he himself had defeated just such a rebellious army composed of godly and determined men? How could he forget the day just six years before when he had led a royal army across the Clyde at Bothwell Brigg? What had bravery availed against the royal guns and the royal horse who hunted down the fleeing zealots with such ease? Were these men of the West Country, these men who had made him their leader and their king, any different from the Covenanters of Scotland? He feared not. No wonder that he had withdrawn from every opportunity of battle. When it came to the point he did not believe that his army, with its inexperienced infantry and motley horse, could win. He was no guerilla leader who could use the undoubted spirit of his men to do the unexpected. He was a regular army officer, a successful administrator with some experience of battle who knew what an army in the field could and could not achieve, and just now he felt that the army which he led could achieve very little. He felt cheated and afraid. He had set out from Holland in the firm belief that his cause was not just a popular one, but one that was shared by men of rank. Such a belief was not pure delusion. Five years before, in 1680, Monmouth had made a triumphal tour of the West Country. The leaders of the Whig gentry had thrown open their magnificent houses to entertain him and, everywhere he went, great crowds had welcomed him and cheered him as the figurehead of the popular, Protestant cause. In Holland he had been told that he would now be joined by these West Country gentlemen, born cavalry officers who would lead in their tenants and clients to his camp. He had also been told that his former friends in the Guards were still his friends who would take the first opportunity to desert to him with their men. He had thought that his campaign would be little more than a demonstration, that he would march to London at the head of a cheering army, 'with a switch in his hand'.[31] What a sad disillusion it had all been. Just one gentleman of distinction had joined him, at the head of 'a company of ragged horse'.[32] Not a single Guards officer had deserted his colours. Now he was left with an army in which he had little faith. He had done his best to turn it into an efficient force and certainly it looked better than it had a fortnight ago. If he could only have just one more month to train his infantry, just a few hundred really good cavalrymen, just a few more guns, then he might still have a real chance. But there was no more time. Bridgwater was the end of a long road. He had had his chance.

The fears and uncertainty of the rebel leader were not immediately obvious to those who saw him. James Scott, Duke of Monmouth, a tall good-looking man now in his mid-thirties, was an impressive figure, especially when seen from some distance, at once noble and military in his bearing, a natural athlete whose prowess at country sports had first endeared him to the populace who had seen him as their heaven-sent leader. His face bore out his claim to be the son of the late King Charles II and silenced most of those who attempted to slight his birth by remarking that his mother, Lucy Walter, had had many other lovers. There was the long nose and sensuous mouth of his pleasure-loving father, though there was little sign of his subtlety or hidden strength of character, while the good looks are marred for modern eyes by the petulance and femininity so beloved of Restoration painters. Close up he looked the weak and easily led man which he was. He was a man of moods, now eager, bright-eyed and erect in the saddle, with a kind word and a graceful gesture to all who approached him, now slumped with a look of the most hopeless melancholy. He would ride for hours with downcast eyes, speaking to no one, gloomily considering the hopeless mess that he had made of his life, pondering his mistakes and forever debating the loyalty of his nearest friends and comrades. Why had he, blessed by birth and the love of his father, ever drifted into opposition to the Court? Why had he not remained a happy, extrovert soldier like his half-brother the Duke of Grafton, who now waited only a few miles away ready to destroy him? Why had he ever made an enemy of his uncle, James, Duke of York and now King James II? Why, since he had made an enemy of that inflexible bigot, had he not stayed in the Low Countries happily hunting and making love to his beloved mistress, Lady Henrietta Wentworth? So many mistakes and now such a terrible future in store. No wonder that the Quaker John Whiting, who had seen him in Taunton, 'thought he look'd very thoughtful and dejected in his countenance, and thinner than when I saw him four years before.'[33]

Monmouth not only feared the defeat and disgrace which seemed in his ever more frequent black moods to be inevitable, he also feared the very men who had joined him in rebellion. Whom could he trust? In his pocket he had a little book where he had written down several things useful for the soldier on campaign.[34] Four whole pages were devoted to a formula by which he could determine whether a person would be faithful and keep his word. Did he use it frequently? If so, it can only have added to his doubts, since the formula was so designed that any particular person would be unfaithful one day and faithful the next.

Could he trust, for instance, the tall, rather stupid-looking man with the long thin nose, pursed mouth, bobbly eyes and general air of foppishness who rode at his side? Ford, Lord Grey of Warke, commander of the cavalry, was the only nobleman to join Monmouth in rebellion. He was a strange man to ride at the head of a godly army, a Restoration gallant of some resource, who had taken part in the planning of the proposed rebellion of 1683 in the interval between the abduction of his teenage sister-in-law and the scandalous trial at the Old Bailey which followed that crime. He was Monmouth's closest crony in the thoughtless good old days, before they had both got involved in the serious business of opposition to the Crown, and the pair had hunted foxes and women together through most of southern England. Perhaps he should have stuck to such pursuits. His complete ignorance of the military arts had been only too apparent in the first skirmish of the rebellion, in which the impression of Lord Grey which remained in most men's minds was the speed with which he had led the cavalry away from the enemy. Since then he had been given little opportunity to do much harm and had indeed been able to give a little courage to his vacillating friend, reminding him on one occasion of the likely effect on his reputation if he simply deserted his army and fled back to the arms of his mistress in Holland. All the same, few men in the army could trust or even respect Lord Grey and his command weakened an already weak cavalry.

Not all of Monmouth's officers were as incompetent or inexperienced as Lord Grey. They were a fairly heterogeneous collection drawn together from many sources and with a wide range of motivations for being in rebellion. Many of the best were old Cromwellians who had served in the New Model Army. Government sources suggest that there were still hundreds of New Model officers in London and several of these were able to join the rebels. Others came from exile in Holland and still more could be found in the West Country itself, men like the Baptist Captain Thomas Parsons of Membury in Devon, who had long been known to the Government as a potential dissident. Another source of trained officers of somewhat more recent vintage were the six Anglo–Scots regiments stationed in the Low Countries on permanent loan to the Prince of Orange. Several officers and men from the Earl of Bellasis's regiment, in particular, had been seduced from their duty by the promise of extra pay, their attachment to the cause or simply the prospect of a little excitement. Other adventurers had also come from the continent for a bit of fun or because they were friends of Monmouth or his adherents. Anton

Buys had planned to spend his eight months' leave from the service of Brandenburg in a tour of France and England. At Amsterdam he met Lord Grey, who suggested that he travel with him, since he had a ship ready which was going to carry an army over to England and then march to London. 'And so I would be able to take this opportunity to see the country and at the same time make my way to London.'[35] Buys had probably seen rather more of the country than he wished by now and had not been able to take a very important part in the campaign, since he spoke no English and very few of the rebels knew either French or German. He did get to London in the end – with an armed escort.

By no means all the officers had military experience. Anyone who was of any social distinction at all and was firm for the cause was likely to end up as an ensign, if not a captain. Many officers were lawyers, a profession which seems to have had more than its share of republicans and fanatics. Many were simply the wealthier inhabitants of the towns and villages of the West Country, men like Roger Satchell of Colyton or Samuel Key, a wealthy clothier from Ilminster, leaders who themselves persuaded their neighbours to join the rebellion and were naturally given command when they led their men into the rebel camp.

Monmouth and his immediate entourage had organized these officers and the men who flocked to his camp into something approximating to the well drilled armies with which he was familiar. Five regiments of infantry had been formed, each distinguished by a different colour. A quick survey of some of the officers in the various regiments should give us some idea of the strengths and weaknesses in the leadership of the army. The senior regiment which normally marched in the van was Monmouth's own. Their colour was red and they seem to have had the pick of the junior officers, at least five of them being former regular army officers who had been persuaded by one means or another to join the rebellion in Holland. These officers appear to have successfully imparted their skills to their men and the regiment had distinguished itself in every engagement in which it had fought. The Red Regiment had originally been commanded by Colonel Venner, at once a fanatic and an experienced soldier, a relation of the famous fifth monarchy man of the same name who had led a very bloody rising in London shortly after the Restoration. Venner shared his kinsman's views and was one of a number of men in Monmouth's army who expected 'the appearance of Christ's visible kingdom upon earth' in the very near future.[36] He had been wounded in the very first skirmish of the rebellion at Bridport and had since stayed on Monmouth's staff, one of his leading military advisers, a pessimist who thought that God had deserted the rebellion and who had only a few days previously advised his master to desert the cause.

Command of the regiment had devolved on a very different man, Nathaniel Wade, a cool-headed and very competent republican lawyer from Bristol who strongly opposed the proclamation of Monmouth as king. Wade had played an important part in planning the abortive rebellion of 1683 and had fled to Holland after its discovery. He was a man of no military experience himself, but had clearly inherited the skill of his father, a former major in the New Model Army, and he was one of the great military successes of the rebellion.

We know the names of several captains who commanded companies in the Red Regiment under Wade. None of them appear to have had much military experience but most of them, like Wade, had long been committed to the cause of rebellion. The oldest captain was Richard Goodenough, a former under-sheriff of London with a long history of opposition to the Government. He, too, had been very deeply involved in the proposed rebellion of 1683, when he had been commissioned to use his knowledge of the radical opposition in London in order to recruit leaders for the twenty divisions into which the city and suburbs were to have been split up. Dick Goodenough was also employed as paymaster-general of the rebel army, a task which was hardly full-time since there was very little pay to hand out. Both these men had been in the forefront when Monmouth's rebellion was planned in Holland, both played a very active part in the rebellion itself and both were to turn king's evidence after the event and betray their friends.

Captain Christopher Battiscombe was a much nobler man. He was a young lawyer of gentle birth from Dorset who had long been associated with 'the good old cause' but, though often inter-rogated, he never gave his friends away. He had been arrested in 1683, on suspicion of being connected with the Rye House Plot, but had managed to talk his way out of trouble, assuring his inter-rogators that the names written in his pocket-book, including that of Goodenough, were 'for remembrance of several businesses he had to do'.[37] Nothing daunted by this experience he remained an active plotter, flitting from England to the continent, and in June 1685 he had been sent ahead by Monmouth to raise the West Country gentry for the cause. In this, however, he had been almost totally unsuccessful. Yet another captain in the Red Regiment with a history of opposition to the Crown was Dick Slape of Taunton, like Battiscombe one of the very few gentlemen from the West Country to fight for Monmouth. He was the son of a royalist officer and had been loyal himself until the early 1680s, when he became a Whig, seduced it was said by Monmouth. He too was examined about his supposed involvement in the 1683 rebellion, being suspected of raising men in Taunton and its neighbourhood. Nothing positive was proved against him, however, and in 1685 he was available to command a company of a hundred scythesmen and musketeers.

The other regiments were officered by a similar medley. The White Regiment was commanded by Colonel Foulkes, a regular officer, who like Venner was an important military adviser to Monmouth. Foulkes, a former captain in the Earl of Bellasis's regiment in the Dutch service, was an old friend of Monmouth's and together with a junior colleague, Ensign Fox, had been the main agent in trying to seduce his brother officers and men from their allegiance. He managed to persuade quite a number of soldiers that he had a commission to raise a regiment for the Elector of Brandenburg's service.[38] Whether they really believed him, we shall never know. There was considerable sympathy for Mon-mouth's cause in these Anglo–Scots regiments abroad and the offer of a ready-made excuse, plus five guilders a week, seems to have been enough to add considerably to Monmouth's short supply of fit, well trained commissioned and non-commissioned officers.

The Yellow Regiment was commanded by Colonel Edward Matthews, a former Guards officer and by all accounts something of a tearaway. He was the son-in-law of Sir Thomas Armstrong, the distinguished old soldier who was described as 'Monmouth's evil genius' and who had been executed for his part in the Rye House Plot the previous year. Matthews had originally tried to dissuade Monmouth from the rebellion, but once committed he played an active part, travelling over in advance from Holland to try and raise support in London and Cheshire and also attempting to persuade his former colleagues in the Guards to desert their colours. After the rebellion Matthews managed to escape to Holland where he was described by a government spy as the leader of the 'ungodly' exiles in Amsterdam, a group who were principally distinguished by their drinking and nightly revels.[39] One of the majors in Matthews's regiment was the extraordinary Robert Perrot, a London brewer, fanatic and adventurer who had taken part in a scheme to steal the Crown Jewels, a scheme so audacious that the amused King Charles II had pardoned both Perrot and the leader of the raid, the even more extraordinary Colonel Blood.

The Green Regiment was commanded by Colonel Abraham Holmes, an old and gallant officer who had served under Cromwell. Holmes, who lived a retired life in the Dutch province of Friesland, had been reluctant to join Monmouth, not thinking he had much of a chance, but once engaged he showed all his old courage and ability. His regiment, particularly the officers, had suffered quite severely in the rearguard action at Phillips Norton. Three of his officers had been killed, including his son, and Holmes himself had been wounded severely in the arm and is reputed to have cut off what was left of the shattered limb with his own knife. If he was a fair example of the old Oliverians it is no wonder that the Government was so scared of them.

The last regiment to be formed, the Blue, was composed entirely of men from Taunton and Taunton Deane. It was commanded by an officer described by a local gentleman as 'that beggar old Buffett', another old Cromwellian officer who had made his way down from London.[40] He had at least two experienced officers to assist him, Captain Tompson, another man from the Dutch service, and Captain Robert Bruce, a Scotsman who had served fourteen years in the army of the Elector of Brandenburg. But most of the officers were local worthies from Taunton itself, such as Captain William Savage, the landlord of the Red Lion, and his son John.

A well informed observer who knew a little of the biography of this somewhat disparate collection of rebel officers ought to have been able to deduce something of the various motives which had led them to rebel. For some, like Grey or Matthews, the main point of the rebellion was simply to substitute the Duke of Monmouth for James II as King of England. Monmouth was the eldest son of Charles II, and though his claim to the throne was a little marred by his illegitimacy, it was rumoured that there existed somewhere a Black Box which contained evidence of his mother's marriage to King Charles. There is little doubt that such a resourceful man as Lord Grey would have been able to find something which looked very like this tantalizing box if the rebellion had been successful and there is also little doubt that such a man could expect to be extremely well rewarded once Monmouth was accepted as King of England. And if he failed? King James was not a young man and had no Catholic heir. There was a good chance that if a rebel officer could only escape from England, the King's successor would pardon him for his excusable Protestant zeal. In the meantime exile was not all that bad and there were few problems for a soldier of gentle birth who wished to earn his livelihood on the continent.

The motivation of many of the rebel officers went far beyond such a simple 'change of persons'. Many of them had a low opinion of Monmouth and had no wish to see him king, only following him because of the lack of any alternative popular leader more closely attuned to their cause. They would have preferred a man made of sterner stuff, such as the old republican hero the regicide Edmund Ludlow. But Ludlow, now nearly seventy, was happy as an exile in Switzerland and, when approached by the rebels, politely declined their invitation to return to England and lead them. Somewhat unrealistic approaches to other potential leaders, such as the sons of Cromwell and Ireton, had no better success and so they followed Monmouth who, even if he was made king, had such a weak claim to the throne that they felt they could control him with ease. For such men really had no wish to see any king in England. True republicans were few in the country as a whole, but they were well represented in the rebel army, especially among the old Cromwellian officers and the former Rye House plotters.

Others were less interested in a republic and indeed feared the 'mechanic tyranny' of a state controlled by the votes of artisans and farmers, the very men whom they now commanded. But they too looked back, to the world of the 1650s, a world where English soldiers and sailors were the wonder of Europe and a world where Englishmen were free to practise their religion as they wished. For a quarter of a century they had looked on in shame as England became a feeble satellite of France. For a quarter of a century they had suffered persecution for religion's sake. Now they could fight for England, God and the true Protestant religion. Many of the younger officers shared the views of these grey-haired, balding veterans. But, as we have seen, the motivations of Monmouth's officers were wide-ranging in the extreme. Some sought a change of persons, some a republic, some were fighting the same battle as the majority of the men who followed them, a battle against popery and intolerance. Such a diversity of objectives was bound to cause disunity and it had been virtually impossible to agree on a manifesto which would incorporate the dreams of all the rebels without alienating a large number of them. The only thing which held them together was their dislike of the present Government and their belief that constitutional ways of changing it no longer existed.

Such men must have caused Monmouth to have frequent reference to the magical formulae in his pocket-book. But one other group of rebel leaders may have given him even greater cause for alarm. These were the many Nonconformist ministers who marched with his army. Here again his memories of the Scottish rebellion which he had defeated in 1679 at Bothwell Brigg could have led him into a state of near panic. For it was common knowledge that one of the main reasons for the ease of his victory was the fact that the Scots ministers had spent so much time arguing with each other and with their godly followers about the nature of true religion that virtually no preparations had been made to check the royal advance. It would not take a very perceptive man to notice that there were similar disagreements in the camp at Bridgwater. All men might seek toleration but that was about as far as it went. There was little in common between the Scots Presbyterian minister Robert Ferguson, nicknamed the Plotter, who had come over with Monmouth, and the fanatic Anabaptist Sampson Larke of Combe Rawleigh in Devon, who rode with the cavalry, his sword at his side. Both might think they rode in a godly cause, both might hate the idea of an England ruled by a papist king, but on most other matters they would probably disagree. Presbyterian, Baptist and Independent had argued about theology, church government and civil politics in the 1640s and 1650s and they were still arguing now in the rebel camp.

Such disunity had not yet led to disaster, though it was clear that many of the rebel leaders despised and disliked each other. Those who were gentlemen despised the honest shopkeepers who rode beside them as their equals. Those who were godly had little respect for worldly courtiers and soldiers, such as Monmouth, Grey and Matthews. Those who were republicans felt cheated that they were now fighting just to install another king. Those who were soldiers despised those, such as Grey, who had shown so clearly that they were not. Those who were worldly had little time for the zealots with their long faces and pious words. It was a wonder that they still held together at all. But while they were alive and together and at the head of five thousand men they had hope. Once they dispersed they were doomed to exile, death or transportation and so they stayed together, to try once more to achieve their varied ends.

Two

All Quiet in Babylon

'All things are quiet here and in all parts of the Kingdom except Somersetshire. I hope in a little time we may say the same of that.'[1] His Majesty's principal Secretary of State, Robert Spencer, Earl of Sunderland, finished dictating his letter and gave it to the messenger. It was 4 July 1685. The confident tone reflected the news that Monmouth was now really on the run and that the *coup de grâce* might be expected any day. As the man who had been chiefly responsible in London for the complicated counter-measures which had been taken to contain and defeat the rebellion, he had some personal grounds for satisfaction. The business had really gone remarkably well, all things considered.

Sunderland, a career courtier now in his mid-forties, had good reason for his relief. He could look back on an unfortunate career as a politician in which he had supported one failed cause after another, not through any excess of ideological zeal, for he had little of that, but simply through a bad run of luck. He had the gambler's approach to politics, but the winning horse had not been easy to predict in the past few years and he had made some bad mistakes. Now that he had tied his fortunes to those of the new king he had no wish to see James defeated at the first fence by his bastard nephew. But it looked as if he no longer had to worry. Everything seemed to be going to plan.

His royal master no doubt saw things that way as well. Now a man of fifty-one, he had waited a very long time to come into his inheritance. For his whole life he had played second fiddle to his infuriating, if charming, brother. He had tried to curb his impatience, but he was a stubborn and self-opinionated man who disliked waiting for things and his frustration had had a marked effect on his appearance. Slowly the attractive, pleasant-mannered young man, the brave soldier and the bold lover, had turned into the embittered middle-aged monarch with the hard, indifferent eyes and cruel mouth who stares at us from Kneller's portrait. Those who were attracted by charm and gaiety were increasingly repelled by James, a man of grace but no humour. Long before he announced his conversion to Catholicism he had begun to lose friends. But his change of religion had crystallized this dislike and for many of the past twenty years he had been the most hated, as well as the most feared, man in England.

But now, in 1685, that was no longer true, at least among the men of rank, the men who mattered in the nation. It was his positive qualities and not his defects which they now noted. They contrasted his sobriety with his brother's debauchery, his passion for work and his love of detailed administration with Charles's indifference and laziness, his honesty and loyalty with Charles's double-dealing. And they liked what they discovered. Here was the king who could crush for ever the factious opposition which had so disturbed the nation for the past seven years. Here was a king who could rule a Tory nation as such a nation wished to be ruled, with authority, good sense and a proper understanding of the part that such loyal Tory gentlemen should play in such a rule.

From the very beginning King James had taken a deep personal interest in the rebellion and had worked very closely with Sunderland to organize its defeat. This was perhaps only to be expected. No one who had waited so long to be king could view such a threat with indifference. No one who enjoyed administration could have failed to enjoy the detailed logistic problems which had had to be solved day by day. But the motivation for his personal involvement went much deeper than that. For the King had a particular dislike of James, Duke of Monmouth, which went back a long way into the past. He hated this bastard upstart, with his good looks, graceful ways and easy popularity. James's nephew had begun to annoy him as early as the 1660s when the teenage favourite had successfully challenged his social position as the second man in the kingdom, mocking him at Court and even winning his women off him. Social and sexual rivalry hardened into political rivalry in the 1670s when the easy-going Monmouth, now distinguished as 'the Protestant Duke', slowly emerged as the figurehead of an opposition party led by the most resourceful politician of the age, the Earl of Shaftesbury. It soon became apparent that the main objective of this party was to exclude the Catholic James, Duke of York, from the succession to the throne and there were many in the party who felt that, once he had been disinherited, it was the Duke of Monmouth who had 'the fairest claim to the crown'. In the event King Charles rode out this political crisis with remarkable ease and James was to stand powerful and unchallenged at his side for the last two years of the reign, while Monmouth's foolhardy acquiescence in the plans of his adherents led only to the forfeiture of his offices and much of his father's affection and ultimately to exile. James might now feel secure, but there was always a nagging fear that Charles's love for his favourite son might lead him to forgive him and bring him back to London. As late as November 1684 Monmouth paid a secret visit to see his father. It was rumoured that, had he been successful in winning forgiveness, James, the nagging right-hand man who so annoyed his brother, would be sent away to Scotland, far from the centre of power. Monmouth's mission failed, as did a similar attempt at rapprochement shortly before his father's death. He remained in exile, embittered and unrepentant, certain that the only reason for his father's failure to forgive him had been his uncle's implacable opposition, certain too that the English people loved him and wanted him to return. That King James's dislike for his nephew was repaid in kind can be seen from the wording of the declaration published when Monmouth landed, a document which, although drawn up by Ferguson the Plotter, must clearly have had Monmouth's approval. 'Now therefore we do hereby solemnly declare and proclaim war against James, Duke of York, as a murderer, and an assassinator of innocent men, a traitor to the nation, and tyrant over the people.'[2] Here was a personal challenge which King James was only too happy to meet. Now he could quash for ever this upstart and put to an end his long career of insolence.

King James had no more love for the men who followed Monmouth than for their leader. He hated Nonconformists and republicans, two groups whom he regarded as identical, according to the French ambassador.[3] These men or their fathers had murdered his father, King Charles I, and had forced him, the most patriotic of Englishmen, into eleven years of exile and poverty. These were the men who had supported Shaftesbury and Monmouth in their long campaign to exclude him from the succession. Everything that they stood for was anathema to James, the most authoritarian monarch to sit on the throne of England in the authoritarian seventeenth century. He hated to share power even with a parliament of gentlemen, let alone a group of low-born, ranting tradesmen and mechanics. Such men needed to be taught a very severe lesson, to show them that such as they had no right to challenge the power of a divinely appointed king of England and no hope of success if they should try.

James was by no means content to leave such matters to the soldiers in the field and to his two Secretaries, Sunderland and the Earl of Middleton. Although his martial fame in English eyes rested upon his naval victory over the Dutch at the battle of Lowestoft in 1665, James was by training and inclination very much a soldier. When he had followed his brother Charles into exile in France after the Civil War, he had soon tired of the petty squabbles of the exiled Stuart court and had sought his living as a soldier of fortune. His military career had been sound, if not dramatic. He had been the pupil of the two greatest soldiers of the day, Marshal Turenne and the Prince de Condé. He had fought for the kings of both France and Spain. And in his last battle, the famous Battle of the Dunes in 1658, he had been brought face to face with the soldiers of the New Model Army, at that time in alliance with France against Spain for whom James was fighting. As an Englishman, even if they were his enemy, he found he could do nothing but admire the courage and fighting spirit of these phlegmatic men who so calmly resisted his charge. 'Not so much as one single man of them ask'd quarter, or threw down his armes; but every one defended himself to the last.'[4] Indeed they defended themselves so well that they won the battle. And now, twenty-seven years later, these men and their heirs were the adherents of Monmouth, a fact which led the King to treat the rebels with great respect. This was no time for foolhardiness. These men could be beaten, would be beaten, but it would take time and patience.

James could only be thankful that he had now been offered the opportunity. For the rebellion, as long as he succeeded in putting it down, was sure to play into his hands. Nothing would serve so well to put the men of property and influence behind him as a Dissenters' rebellion, especially one led by a bastard claimant to the throne who no doubt planned to reward his followers with the estates of his enemies. Nothing would serve so well to destroy the opposition to the Crown as the righteous punishment that might be meted out after the rebellion had been suppressed. But James had an even deeper motive for welcoming the rebellion. Fifteen years previously Charles II had told the French ambassador in London that he hoped the latest piece of repressive legislation would goad the Dissenters into rebellion and so give him a pretext to enlarge his army.[5] Now James had the chance denied to his brother. The threat to order and property persuaded his loyal subjects to give their blessing to a very rapid increase in the size of the royal army, an escalation in military power that James had no intention of reversing once the rebellion had been successfully quashed.

It was surprising that the English kings had had to wait so long before being presented with this opportunity. The Government had expected a rebellion from just such men who now marched with Monmouth ever since the Restoration. No one had expected that the proud and fanatical men of the New Model Army could have been disbanded with such ease. But, in fact, when the time came for each regiment to be dissolved the process had been carried out in remarkable calm. King Charles had made sure that he had enough money to pay the old soldiers their considerable arrears. Legislation had been passed to enable them to by-pass the apprenticeship laws and set up as artisans or in trade. Such precautions had paid off. Some of the old soldiers had been kept on in the new royal army. Some had been permitted to go into the service of allies such as the King of Portugal. Some had refused to make their peace with the restored Government and had gone into permanent exile. But most had simply disappeared quietly into the general ranks of the artisan and shopkeeping class from which they had originally been recruited. Every town had its old soldiers; London had thousands of them, but they kept remarkably quiet and offered little apparent threat to the Government.

Such a peaceful disbandment of such a potentially hostile body of men did not calm the fears of King Charles and his Government. They remained very watchful, though they were hampered by their lack of a regular police force. The Secretaries of State, who were responsible for the maintenance of domestic peace, had at their immediate disposal virtually no physical means of enforcing their will, save the small body of King's Messengers who spent most of their time scurrying round the metropolis and the country as a whole trying to locate and arrest suspected persons. The Government tried to make up for its physical weakness by building up an elaborate information service, so that trouble if it came would at least be expected and, if possible, prevented by arresting ringleaders before they had time to do much harm. A network of spies was established, both at home and abroad, to report on the activities of Dissenters, republicans, old Oliverians and other potentially subversive groups. The Secretaries of State also had a correspondence system which drew in loyalist gentlemen and minor government officials, such as customs and excise officers and postmasters all over the country. These men were encouraged to report regularly on the political situation and the activities of opposition elements in their particular localities. In return they received a newsletter from the Secretary of State's office which was eagerly awaited since it contained an edited version of the best pieces of news from the whole network of which they formed part. Finally the Government had a monopoly of the Post Office and thus was able to take advantage of the ingenuity of Sir Samuel Morland who had developed a new method of snooping which enabled the English 'to open letters more skilfully than anywhere in the world'.[6] This formal information service could easily be supplemented by making use of the Justices of the Peace and deputy lieutenants, men checked for their loyalty, whose business regularly involved the cross-questioning of a wide range of unfortunates, from sheep-stealers to pregnant servants, and who were quite capable of gathering political information.

Naturally, with so many people involved in the business of discovering plots, many plots were discovered. The Restoration period sees a good number of true or invented Nonconformist plots, often embroidered by the informant with elaborate Cabals and Councils of Six which must have made impressive reading for the Secretaries of State. None of these plots provided the Government with a serious challenge and when they were real they were easily put down. There were many people increasingly discontented with the new régime and increasingly resentful at the harsh experience of persecution for religion's sake. But they seemed to lack both the will and the necessary organization for a large-scale rising. Perhaps the words of William, Lord Russell, at his trial in 1683 tell the truth. 'A rebellion cannot be made now as it has been in former times; we have few great men.'[7] The great men of the past had all died, been executed, forced into exile or else had made their peace with the Government. There were certainly no great men to lead the plots of the 1660s and 1670s. But even great men need lesser men to follow them and there was little sign yet of mass opposition to the Government of King Charles. For many, of course, any settled government must have seemed preferable to the turmoil of the 1640s and 1650s, while persecution was not continuous and, until the 1680s, tended to hit the peaceful Quakers harder than the other sects. The situation was not yet ripe for rebellion. Meanwhile plots continued to be discovered and a continuous stream of suspected persons was brought up to London to be cross-examined by the Secretaries of State, the Privy Council or the King himself. Some were executed, some were imprisoned or exiled, but many were fed back into the system as spies determined to discover even more plots to earn their pardons.

The existence of this apparently poorly organized stratum of discontent and potential revolt in English society began to attract the attention of leading politicians. From the late 1660s the second Duke of Buckingham, an old playmate of King James and a remarkable scoundrel, began to dally with the republican elements in English society which had remained very quiet since the Restoration. He seems to have done little but encourage them, but towards the end of the following decade a more masterful hand could be seen at work as the great Earl of Shaftesbury built up all the opposition groups in England, disappointed courtiers, republicans, Dissenters and old Oliverians into one powerful party. This party had little in common, except fear of popery and of arbitrary government in general and in particular of James, Duke of York, but it did demonstrate to the Government the potentially dangerous situation that existed. The defeat of Shaftesbury in 1681 by the subtle King Charles only made the situation worse. For now the discontented, foiled of the parliamentary forum from which they had attempted to dictate to the King, seemed to have little choice but to acquiesce or rebel. The Secretaries of State redoubled their existing information service to meet the challenge of what by now seemed to be a genuinely revolutionary situation.

However, those informants of the Secretaries of State who had had such a good record of exposing non-existent plots in the past did not perform particularly efficiently in this new situation of genuine emergency. The Government was saved from rebellion, not as a result of the efforts of its own agents, but because the potential rebels had neither the unity of purpose nor the determination to rebel. When the Rye House Plot was exposed in June 1683 it came as a complete surprise to the Government, though active plotting had been going on since at least the autumn of the previous year, while only slightly less subversive discussion had been taking place for much longer. Although one must discount much of the somewhat hysterical information which was fed to the Government after the disclosure of the plot, there seems no doubt that a very considerable number of people were privy to the plans for the proposed rebellion and it seems astonishing that government informers were able to give no earlier notice of it. Still the plot, even if its apparently detailed organization in London, Scotland and the West Country was alarming, could be made to serve a very valuable purpose. Now was the opportunity to make sure that Lord Russell's words would be true and that there should be no great men left to make a rebellion.

The culling of potential leaders of rebellion was carried on with great vigour. Death had already removed the greatest of them all, the Earl of Shaftesbury, who had died a broken and defeated man in Amsterdam in January 1683. A fortunate murder, unconnected with politics, had also taken off the richest and most dedicated Whig gentleman in the West Country, Thomas Thynne, who had been assassinated by the agents of a Swedish nobleman who coveted his wife. But the Government could hardly rely on the amorous intrigues of foreigners to remove many of its opponents and so put forward all the forces at its disposal to pull in other suspicious persons. Once the plot had broken, witnesses were not slow to come forward and name names. The Government rapidly picked up many men who had been prominent in their opposition to the Crown in the last few years and almost as rapidly brought them to their trial on a charge of high treason. Two great men, William, Lord Russell, and Algernon Sidney were speedily tried and executed. The Earl of Essex was either murdered or committed suicide in prison. These were great losses for the opposition who had few leaders of rank and depended for the most part on men of character but lower status, such as the Baptist Captain Walcot, a great friend of the former republican leader, Edmund Ludlow, and an able henchman of the Earl of Shaftesbury, who was also executed for his supposed part in the Rye House Plot. However, the Government were unable to make a clean sweep of all left-wing aristocrats. Lord Grey managed to get his guards so drunk that he was able to slip away to the continent to wait and see what another day would bring. Other lords, such as Lord Delamere, a Whig magnate in Cheshire and a friend of Monmouth, were suspected but left free. Meanwhile the King was reluctant to bring Monmouth himself to justice, though witnesses implicated him as much as some of those who had been executed. He was permitted by his doting father to remain in a rather obvious hiding-place in the country and finally, after fluffing an invitation to make his peace with James, Duke of York, went into exile.

The Government had acted rapidly and ruthlessly but many

other men managed to get away, especially the leaders of the second rank, men who had organized the urban opposition to the Crown, men like Ferguson the Plotter who had worked very closely with the Earl of Shaftesbury, men like Richard Goodenough and Nathaniel Wade whom we have already met as officers in Monmouth's army, men like the one-eyed republican maltster, Richard Rumbold, the owner of the Rye House, who was to return to fight once more alongside the Earl of Argyll in Scotland. One or two men who had successfully evaded the clutches of the Government in the summer of 1683 were later captured abroad and returned to justice in England. Great was the Crown's relief when Sir Thomas Armstrong, the sixty-year-old soldier who was supposed to have led Monmouth into his evil ways, was cornered in Leyden and brought home to be executed without trial and have his quarters exposed in various prominent places. Another success was the capture of James Holloway, one of the leaders of the opposition in Bristol. After many adventures he was taken in the West Indies and brought home to be executed in his turn.

Meanwhile the Government tried hard to discover a little more about the local organization of the proposed rebellion. But once they got below the level of the supposed leaders they could find out very little. Many men had made it clear by their actions or their past history that they were not much enamoured of the Government and its policies. Factious ministers had preached sermons on notoriously revolutionary Old Testament texts, local politicians had signed petitions criticizing the Government, old Cromwellians were old Cromwellians and many people had been heard to say naughty things about the King and the Duke of York in their cups, or even sober. There was a gradual increase of the list of suspected persons who might be arrested for precaution in an emergency, but no real evidence of mass enlistment for rebellion could be found. Nor did the Government have much success in its search for any signs of material support for the proposed insurrection. A nation-wide search for arms was instigated and many weapons were found, some in rather suspicious places like the Buckinghamshire house of the Whig peer Lord Wharton, from which enough pistols, muskets, swords and armour to equip perhaps two dozen men were taken, to be deposited in the White Hart tavern in Aylesbury for safe keeping.[8] But this was hardly proof of any plot. Most gentlemen kept arms quite openly in their homes, often left over from the Civil War. These could be seized and sent to garrisons or used to arm the militia, but their discovery did not remove the possibility of a very much larger number of more modern weapons being hidden by the populace at large.

The financial connections of rebels were also hard to prove. One or two great London merchants of known Whig sympathies were massively fined, as was the very wealthy Whig gentleman John Hampden, the grandson of the great parliamentarian of the same name. Other rich men anticipated such action and fled the country to join the other exiles in the Low Countries. But the one legal action brought by the Government against a merchant specifically on the grounds of financing its traitorous opponents was a failure.[9] When Sir Thomas Armstrong was captured he had in his pocket a bill of exchange drawn on Joseph Hayes, a London merchant whose brother Israel in Amsterdam was known as 'the fountain which issues so much supply to these traitors who lurk abroad'.[10] This was an important case. If the funds flowing from the City of London to support the exiles in the Low Countries could be dried up, much future trouble could be averted. But the prosecution muffed the case and Hayes was acquitted, much to the joy of the London crowd. In any case it was difficult to prove such links, since most of London's legitimate overseas business was carried on with the Low Countries and it would have taken a very astute investigator to disentangle genuine commercial movement of money from the finance of traitors.

Despite such disappointments the situation in England seemed quiet enough in 1684, after the executioner's work had been done. The establishment of an autocratic, absolutist government and the continued persecution of the Dissenters went on unchecked. Was the Government now safe? To many it must have seemed that nothing could threaten it any more. But there were in fact great dangers, even if they were now well hidden. When James Holloway was brought to the scaffold at the end of April 1684 he was asked by the sheriff whether he thought that there were many people who would have been concerned in the rebellion if it had been successful. Holloway's reply must have shocked him. 'That we did think so; and if we should name every one that we thought would be concerned, I believe we might name three parts of London.'[11]

Such an estimate, even if clearly an exaggeration, had too much truth in it to be ignored by the Government. The fact was that hardly anyone, in the towns at least, had any reason to love the Establishment which worked so hard to persecute them and remove their civil liberties. A discontented populace might be separated from its potential leaders by the English Channel, but it remained discontented and who knew what new leaders, what new Cromwell or Lambert, might be thrown up in an emergency. The central Government and the Justices of the Peace remained extremely vigilant, keeping their eyes firmly on the long list of potential rebels, mainly in London and the West Country, whose names had been discovered in the massive investigation that had just taken place. The autumn and winter of 1684 were very quiet. It seemed that the all-out campaign against the Dissenters had had its desired effect. They seemed cowed now, tired of paying fine after fine for conscience sake, lost and bewildered now that their meeting-houses had been pulled down. Could the Government now relax, or was this the quiet before the storm? It was against this background of domestic peace that King Charles died, rather suddenly, on 6 February 1685. He seemed, in his own inimitable way, to have succeeded where his father and grandfather had failed and to have turned England into a loyal, subservient nation where the word of the King and his advisers went unchallenged. King James might well be pleased with his inheritance. But would he survive to enjoy it? Surely now that he actually was king those people who had striven for so long to bar him from the succession would act?

Neither the new King nor his Secretaries of State were taking any chances. Their immediate task was to secure the kingdom from the threat of any interference with the legitimate succession. As soon as he heard the news of King Charles's illness, Sunderland sent out a circular letter to the mayors of all ports ordering them to stop 'all passengers whatsoever from going beyond the seas' and likewise to hold all those coming in, till further notice.[12] Instructions were sent to lords lieutenants and commanders of garrisons to be on their guard. The Government did not control the manpower to ensure a complete clampdown and it was impossible to make sure that no one came in or out from small creeks or even considerable ports. The Mayor of Dover wrote to the Earl of Middleton complaining of his neighbour, the Mayor of Folkestone, to whom he had sent a copy of the Secretaries' instructions, 'but not with standing he permits boats dayly to goe to sea'.[13] Still, such measures were an obvious precaution and a large number of persons were held for questioning, but the only one of much interest to the Government was Monmouth's servant, John Gibbons, who was picked up off the packet boat from Flanders and said he had been dismissed by his master three weeks before. One poor man was given much trouble since his name was the same as that of one of the leading exiles, William Ayloffe. 'Dearest brother', he wrote from Dover, 'I need not tell you that we are all arrested here ever since ye sikenesse of ye deceased king, we are above a hundred persones we are not permitted to stir out of the house all our names are sent up to London and I wish that my name may not doe me any prejudice . . .'[14] However, he was eventually released.

There seemed in fact to be no cause for alarm. The proclamation of the new King went off with no trouble at all, indeed was welcomed with shouts of approbation and joy, possibly induced by the large quantity of free liquor which was dispensed for the occasion. And indeed who could find fault with such a king? Shortly after his succession he told the Privy Councillors that he intended to preserve the government 'in Church and State as it is now by law established. I know the principles of the Church of England are for monarchy and the members of it have shewed themselves good and loyal subjects, therefore I shall always take care to defend and support it.'[15] Who could doubt that he meant it? James was a man who was famous above all for keeping his word. That he was also a Catholic he made abundantly clear by openly attending Mass in the chapel of St James's Palace only two days after his brother's death. People muttered a little, but the nation remained quiet. There was no sign of any opposition to the new King, let alone rebellion.

Meanwhile King James got on with the business of running the country. He decided to call an early Parliament to meet in May and instructed Sunderland to make sure that it was a very loyal one, a task which the Secretary of State was well equipped to implement, especially now that nearly all the boroughs had had their franchises altered in the Tory interest. Sunderland wrote off to the local leaders throughout the country instructing them to take care that only 'persons of approved loyalty and affection to the Government be chosen'.[16] James made it clear that he expected this Parliament to give him plenty of money. This was what he meant by loyalty and affection. In return he would continue to keep in operation the laws which enabled the Justices of the Peace to persecute the Dissenters. This was what he meant by his promise 'to defend and support' the Church of England. It was understood, of course, that Catholics would no longer be considered as Dissenters. The machinery of repression was thus continued. James made no attempt to introduce toleration at this stage, an act which might well have prevented Monmouth's rebellion but would have alienated the good will of his Anglican and Tory supporters. But, as we have seen, it is quite possible that King James had no wish to prevent rebellion, once he had settled in to his inheritance. Only a rebellion could justify that large increase in the size of the royal army which was so dear to James's heart.

King James and his two Secretaries of State continued to keep their ears to the ground, to pick up the gossip of travellers and drunkards in order to find out if there was any talk of trouble. There was virtually none. It seemed as if a great blanket had been pulled down on English public opinion. Rather more news came to them from outside England, from the many places which might be expected to cause trouble or give help to those who wanted to make trouble in England. Scotland, in particular, was a worry. Ever since the Restoration the group of extreme Presbyterians known as the Covenanters had refused to accept the episcopal

Establishment which had been reimposed. Twice they had risen in revolt, the last time in 1679 when they had been defeated by an army commanded by the Duke of Monmouth, then still in his father's favour. Monmouth had treated the rebels in a remarkably lenient way after their defeat and had indeed successfully sought to make a party for himself in the northern kindgom. Since then the Covenanters had been cruelly persecuted, not least by King James himself who had spent some time in Scotland while his brother was coping with the Exclusion Crisis. No one would expect them to remain quiet if they were given the slightest encouragement. Such encouragement might well come from Scotland's leading nobleman, the Earl of Argyll, head of the mighty Clan Campbell, whom James had unwisely made his enemy and who was now in exile in the Low Countries. Clear evidence had come out in 1683 of a treasonable correspondence between the English rebels and all centres of dissidence in Scotland, the Covenanters, the Campbells and the fairly considerable number of Lowland republicans.

Ireland too could not be trusted to remain in peace. Much of the land was still held by officers and soldiers of the New Model Army who had been given or had bought it after the Cromwellian conquest in the early 1650s. These men and their descendants were nearly all Nonconformists and chafed uneasily at the Anglican Establishment which had been imposed on them. They were hardly likely to welcome a papist king who might well be inclined to encourage the Catholic majority whom Anglican and Nonconformist alike strove to keep in their place. Even in the King's farthest possessions in North America he could not feel completely in control. Puritan New England, in particular, had watched the course of English politics in recent years with great interest and who could tell what support in men or money might cross the Atlantic to uphold the true Protestant cause?

On the continent too there were many who felt sympathy for the English exiles and might well give them assistance if they should try to challenge the new King. The Dutch, in particular, could feel little love for the Stuart Court which had twice fought wars against them and had in recent years made common cause with their greatest enemy, the King of France. It was true that the greatest man in the United Provinces, the Stadtholder, William III of Orange, was himself half a Stuart, at the same time King James's nephew and the husband of his eldest daughter, Mary. But he posed the greatest question mark of all, for he himself had a claim on the English throne, a popular one since he was a Protestant. At the same time he had openly welcomed the Duke of Monmouth at his Court in the previous year, much to the annoyance of James, who had written him several avuncular letters requiring him to desist from giving public support to such a declared opponent of the Court. What William would do now was anyone's guess, but in any case he seemed to have very little control over the Dutch people, especially those who lived in the great trading city of Amsterdam. Most of the exiled traitors had settled in the Low Countries where they had for the most part been welcomed with open arms and many Dutchmen could be expected to give help or finance to a cause which was both Calvinist and republican. Other Protestants in such places as Switzerland and Brandenburg might be expected to feel the same, while in France it was said that ten thousand Huguenots, embittered by their own growing repression, were ready to sail to England to put an end to its rule by a papist king.[17] And who could say what the attitude of the great Louis XIV might be? He might well write nice letters to his cousin James, congratulating him on his accession to the throne and promising him financial support if he should need it, but for many years his main interest in English politics had been to foment division, so that Englishmen would be too busy squabbling with each other to interfere with his successful search for *gloire* and ever more territory.

It was not long before disturbing rumours began to filter through to the men at Whitehall from their agents abroad. For years now successive envoys at The Hague had tried to report on the movements of the considerable population of His Majesty's rebellious subjects who lived in the United Provinces and adjoining territories. This had always been the favourite haunt of exiles, an area of dense urban growth where it was easy to hide and not too difficult to make a precarious living, an area whose

Government was generally tolerant to all immigrants, be they royalist or republican, Catholic or Calvinist, and an area which was tantalizingly close to that England whither they all yearned so ardently to return, ideally at the head of a large, cheering armed band of followers. Ever since 1660 factious men who felt they could never make their peace with the restored monarchy had plotted and counter-plotted, schemed and dreamed of ever more implausible ways of returning triumphant to their homes, while successive envoys had tried to report to England the nature and the timing of the particular plot of the moment. It was never easy to acquire such information. The envoys retained spies in many of the great cities of the Netherlands, in Utrecht, in Rotterdam and Antwerp, and above all in the teeming commercial metropolis of Amsterdam. They were also fed a constant stream of information from amateurs, some genuinely loyal and disinterested, others hopefully trying to ingratiate themselves with a Government which they had offended in the past. But the information from any one of these sources rarely tallied with that from any other. Besides, the rebels and traitors themselves did little to help. They almost invariably had false names, false beards and false addresses. They moved from town to town and province to province with indecent haste. They fed into the envoy's information service a host of false news, just as improbable and just as difficult to assess as that which came from his own paid spies. All of this material, edited and assessed by the envoy, often a budding amateur detective himself, was sent over to England to be perused by a bewildered Secretary of State.

Early in April 1685 there seemed to be something out of the ordinary going on. All the rebels in the Low Countries were congregating in Rotterdam. Monmouth had been seen there. So had the Earl of Argyll. 'What designe those wicked people have in hand cannot easily be discovered, but there is something new a hatching amongst them.'[18] But what exactly was hatching? On 10 April the English envoy, Bevil Skelton, sent to the Earl of Middleton what was later seen to be some remarkably accurate information. 'It is whisperd about that Monmouth intends speedily to passe over into England and land in the west part of the Kingdome and that Mathews and those whoe are gone before are sent to prepare for his reception.'[19] Further letters repeated or amplified this information. The Government could hardly be said to have acted very fast. It was not until a fortnight later that a warrant for Captain Matthews's arrest was signed.[20] Perhaps the messenger was delayed at sea. But, in any case, who in England could know that this particular whisper was the true one? An equally strong rumour hinted that both Monmouth and Argyll intended to sail for either Scotland or Northern Ireland, and that ships, arms and a large body of Scottish exiles and mercenaries had been gathered together for the enterprise. Indeed no one could doubt the fact that the Scots were on the point of doing something, for they made virtually no secret of their preparations and the expedition was the common talk of the Low Countries. Skelton's efforts to get the Dutch to stop them sailing were totally ineffective and on 2 May they set sail for an unknown destination. Was Monmouth with them? Many thought so, many had actually seen him leave 'in a very meane seaman's habitt',[21] but no one in England could be absolutely sure. Nor was Skelton sure. It was reported that he had been seen in Liège on 11 May, 'but most people here think he has gone to England or Scotland.'[22] He had, in fact, disappeared.

Meanwhile, in England everything remained quiet. One or two people were picked up for speaking 'dangerous words', but the only serious trouble in London seemed to be in the city's two theatres where 'divers persons do rudely press and with evil language and blows force their way', without paying, 'to the danger of the public peace'.[23] There was no sign of anyone preparing for rebellion, the energy of fanatics and Dissenters being mainly devoted to the vain task of trying to combat the Earl of Sunderland's election machine.

In May things began to hot up a bit. Orders went out from London to Scotland and Northern Ireland to prepare a warm reception for the Earl of Argyll who was eventually to land at Tarbet to raise the standard of a Highland and Covenanter rebellion. Fresh information began to come in from the Low Countries. Monmouth had not sailed with Argyll. He and his adherents were themselves raising men and chartering ships for a rising in England. They seemed to have plenty of money. On 22 May Skelton wrote to the Earl of Middleton. 'I have informations from Amsterdam that there hath been of late bills drawne upon most of the marchants of that citty for vast summs and that from most part of the world, and all for the use of His Majesty's rebellious subjects. . . . All people are amazed and cannot guesse from whence they should have such supply.'[24] This was alarming news. It had been thought in England that Monmouth was broke. Money could buy men. Enough money could buy a whole army and the ships to carry them, and there were always plenty of foot-loose, mercenary, Protestant soldiers in Germany, Switzerland and the Low Countries.

In England the Secretaries of State set the machinery of containment into motion. Warrants were issued for the arrest of a long list of Rye House plotters, friends of Monmouth and West Country gentlemen known to have extreme Whig views. Some of the men were actually arrested, but many were able to get away, while many others were far beyond the reach of the King's Messengers, in Holland or already in Scotland with Argyll. At the same time orders were sent to deputy lieutenants and mayors of towns in many parts of England, but especially in the north-west and the West Country, to disarm 'all dangerous and suspected persons', a difficult task since, as we have seen, they did not know who fell into this category, except in very general terms. On 21 May the King gave his blessing to what he thought would be an astute piece of propaganda, the publication of *A True Account and Declaration of the Horrid Conspiracy against the late King, his present Majesty, and the Government.* This account of the Rye House Plot had been prepared under the supervision of the historian Bishop Sprat of Rochester, and would, James thought, remind his subjects of the folly of treason, a seasonable reminder, since 'it is but too evident that the same hellish plot is not entirely extinguished, but that diverse of the wicked actors in it are still carrying on new contrivances against the happy peace of our dominions.'[25] On the next day the King consolidated his goodwill by addressing the loyalist Parliament which Sunderland had successfully assembled,

assuring them of his love for the Church of England and reminding them of the absolute obedience he wanted from them. He then
went on to tell them of Argyll's landing in Scotland. 'I shall take
the best care I can, that this declaration of their own treason and
rebellion may meet with the reward it deserves: And I will not
doubt, but that you will be more zealous to support the Government and give me my revenue, as I have desired it, without
delay.'[26] Parliament responded with alacrity. No other English
king in the seventeenth century got what he wanted so quickly.
By 30 May the money bill had been read three times in both Houses
and passed without a single voice in opposition. In the next fortnight the King was to ask for yet more money and get that too.
Sunderland's talents in electioneering had not been wasted. But
this financial triumph did not answer the three key questions which
so worried the King and his advisers. When and where would
Monmouth land and how many trained soldiers would he bring
with him?

Would he land in Scotland and join Argyll? Or in Ireland?
Would he land in Cheshire where he was said to have such great
support? Or would he land in the West Country, the most
factious area of all, the area which had welcomed him so readily on
his tour in 1680, the area which had been ready to rise in 1683, as
those eagerly reading Sprat's book could find out for themselves?
No one knew. As late as 12 June, after Monmouth had actually
landed, the King wrote to the Prince of Orange giving his reasons
for thinking that he would land in Scotland or Lancashire or
Cheshire.[27] But the King could not afford to back these hunches.
If he sent troops to any one of these places and Monmouth did not
land there, it would be weeks before they could be transferred
elsewhere. The royal army was far too small for him to afford the
luxury of allowing a considerable part of it to be isolated. All he
could do was strengthen the existing garrisons and leave virtually
the whole of the army in and around London. London was
potentially the most dangerous place of all, full of old Cromwellian
soldiers only too keen to lead the factious elements in the metropolis to glory. London was also, of course, the centre of the road
system and the greatest port, from where troops could fairly

rapidly be sent to any other part of the kingdom. So the army remained in London and the King contented himself in early June with recalling officers to their regiments, issuing commissions to his faithful subjects to raise new forces to face the expected emergency and sending county magnates and militia officers back to their stations in the countryside.

In the West Country excitement rose to a pitch and then died down again. Deputy lieutenants and other local officials had been busy since the middle of May searching for arms and suspicious persons, but had found nothing particularly dramatic. Then on 30 May two letters from London had been seized, one addressed to Taunton and the other to Ilminster. The message seemed fairly clear. 'Freind . . . These are to advise thee that honest Protestants forthwith prepare and make themselves very ready . . . for they have notice here at Court that a certaine person will forthwith appeare in the West . . .'[28]

The Mayor and Justices of Taunton sent a general warning through the West Country 'to search the postes, coaches and carryers' and to check out all strangers, especially at Exeter Fair, a general meeting place which was notoriously difficult to control and where the rebels might design to rise first. At the same time militia units were despatched to Exeter and Taunton to keep the peace. Further excitements were to come. On 1 June a woman swore that she had heard about eighty horsemen pass in the night. Some thought this might be 'a rhomantique invention', but a general lookout was kept for the phantom horsemen. On 3 June Sir William Portman received a very alarming letter in London where he was attending Parliament. A very prudent man in Taunton wrote 'that he verily believ'd the dissenting party had some wicked designe afoot, for that their countenances and manners in conversation seem'd different of late to what they had bin.'[29] This was serious news, but still nothing happened. On 4 June the militia at Exeter were dismissed. There seemed no danger and no one wanted the fair to be disturbed unnecessarily. By the eighth the whole West Country had relaxed again. Even the eighty horsemen seemed to have been forgotten. London and the West Country were quiet, except in the prisons and guardhouses which were now slowly filling up with suspicious persons. The army remained in London and the Duke of Monmouth remained at sea, struggling to beat down channel into the teeth of an irritating west wind.

In Utrecht, Skelton's best spy sat down to write a fresh report on 6 June. 'The Duke purposeth to land and set up his standard at Lyme a small sea port in Dorsetshire where the Mayor of the towne and the tyde officers, or custome house officers shall befriend his landing . . . Their expectancy of assistance of landing is very great, and persons of great quality to engage.'[30] His sources must have been extremely good. Many of the men actually at sea with Monmouth did not know as much as this about their destination. But the letter was no doubt delayed by the same wind which delayed Monmouth himself.

The most inaccurate statement in the spy's letter was his estimate of the loyalty of the Mayor and customs house officers in Lyme Regis. For this he may be excused, since the corporation had been notoriously factious for most of the reign of Charles II. However, recently the charter of the town had been revised and Gregory Alford, a very loyal citizen of King James and a dedicated persecutor of Dissenters, was now the Mayor of Lyme. On the afternoon of Thursday 11 June he was interested to read, in a news-letter which had just arrived in the post from London, a description of three armed ships which had sailed from Holland a few days previously and were thought to be carrying the Duke of Monmouth to some destination in England or Scotland. He looked up from the paper and out to sea where three strange ships flying no colours had been lying all day and were now drawing closer into land. He began to feel rather uneasy, especially when several boats full of armed men began to pull towards the west end of the town. Mr Gregory Alford was not a very brave man, but in any case there was little he could do to stop them. He had no soldiers under his command. He did not even have any powder for the great cannon which was mounted on the seashore. He waited until he had seen the armed men actually land and then rode rapidly out of town towards Exeter, warning the country as he went. By midnight he was at Honiton, where he wrote a letter describing the landing of Monmouth and the seizure of the town but, since he had left before the town had actually been seized, he rather exaggerated the size of the invading forces.[31]

Mr Samuel Dassell, deputy searcher of the customs at Lyme, was a braver man than his mayor but then he was also a poorer man and in greater need of promotion. He also seems to have been rather foolhardy. He tried to make up for the deficiency of gunpowder in the town by taking some off a merchant ship that was lying in the harbour. By the time he had managed to do this, however, it was too late to do anything with it, as Monmouth's men were already running down the streets, cheered enthusiastically by the population of the port who cried out, 'A Monmouth! A Monmouth! The Protestant Religion', and flocked to their hero's side. Dassell still stayed in town to make absolutely sure that this really was the Duke of Monmouth and that he really had come to make war on the King, asking the rebels some very stupid questions for which he was lucky to escape without injury. Having seen the first recruits from the town enlisted, he then departed rather more discreetly with the Collector of Customs, Mr Anthony Thorold. Once out of town they managed to find a horse which they rode tandem to Crewkerne where they spread the news and then, better mounted, set out on the long ride to London. Here they knocked up their local Member of Parliament, Sir Winston Churchill, who together with his son John, Lord Churchill, escorted them to the royal chambers where they arrived at four in the morning of Saturday 13 June, just over thirty hours after Monmouth had actually landed. They told their story to the King, to the Privy Council and later at the bar of the House of Commons, received twenty pounds a piece and then no doubt went to bed exhausted. The long wait was over. After twenty-five years the Dissenters of the West Country had at last risen in rebellion.

The King got no rest after his early rising. The thirteenth of June was to be a very busy day, both for him and for the two Secretaries of State and an even harder one for their clerks who had to write out a vast number of letters at their dictation. The situation required very careful handling. Any rash move could lead to disaster. The King had at his disposal a regular army of about six thousand men, minute by continental standards, but in fact the largest army of any that had been seen in England since the threat of war with France in 1678. He also had militia units in every county who could be trusted to do police work, but whose experience of fighting real soldiers was nil. With such forces he had to be able to overawe a population which was potentially rebellious everywhere, and in particular contain the actual revolt in the south-west. But he must also keep sufficient forces in hand to deal with the very likely event of simultaneous rebellions in the north-west and in London. At the same time there was an actual rebellion going on in Scotland which the Scots army might not be able to contain by itself. It was all very tricky and James must have thought it fortunate that he had been trained by the great Turenne, even if he knew that Monmouth had as well. However, in the event of real danger, the King had two very important reserves on which he could call, the Irish army and the six Anglo-Scots regiments on permanent loan to William of Orange in the Low Countries. James had in fact already drawn on these reserves. A contingent of Irishmen and the three Scots regiments were already making their way towards Scotland, but such troops could of course be diverted to England if there was real trouble, or if Argyll was defeated.

The immediate decision that had to be made on the morning of 13 June was how many regular troops to send down to the south-west. If he sent too many it would encourage London and Cheshire to rise. Regular infantry could cover twenty miles in a day in an emergency, but they could not keep it up for long and on a long march an average of fifteen miles a day was all that could be expected. Cavalry and dragoons could of course move much faster. Lyme Regis was one hundred and fifty miles from London, ten days' march, and once the soldiers had gone as far as, say, Salisbury, six days out of London, it would be impossible for them to get back any quicker in the event of a metropolitan rising. These facts were, of course, also well known to Monmouth, a former captain-general of the English army. He knew he had ten days to train his recruits to face regular infantry, a fact which meant that if the King sent too few men, Monmouth might have some great success and the whole kingdom might rise.

The King's information was that Monmouth had landed with a hundred and fifty men and it was clear from Dassell's report that he could expect a considerable number of West Country men to flock to his colours. Even so he did not as yet pose a really significant threat. The rumours from Holland of a really large invasion force of foreign mercenaries were clearly nonsense. The soldier King rapidly digested all this information and gave his orders. They reflect the calculations of a man who knew exactly what he was doing. The militia of Devon and Somerset were given a watching brief. If Monmouth was weak they could finish the business themselves. If he was strong they could keep an eye on him and should at least be able to prevent too many recruits from joining him. But they could not be trusted to stand firm entirely on their own. In order to give them some very necessary stiffening the King ordered four troops of horse, two troops of dragoons and five companies of foot to march immediately for Salisbury. On the following day he sent Lord Churchill down after them to command. But great care was taken not to play into Monmouth's hands by weakening London. Orders were given to troops stationed in Kingston-upon-Thames and Chelmsford to march to Bow, Stratford, Highgate, Islington and Holloway to form a tight ring of armed men round the dangerous north and east sides of the City.[32] At the same time recruiting of soldiers and the general expansion of the army was given priority.

The news which the King was to receive in the course of the next week was both good and bad. The news from Scotland was very good. The royal army had been well prepared for Argyll's invasion, while the rebels had been weakened by their inability to agree where and how they were actually going to rebel. Within a few days of Monmouth's landing it seemed that King James need not worry much about danger from Scotland and in fact the rebellion was finally crushed on 18 June. Once the Government received this information it gave orders for the Irish contingent to be diverted to Chester and for the three Scots regiments from Holland to go to London. The news from north-west England and from London was also good. There was no real sign of any rising, though the general atmosphere of excitement in the metropolis boded trouble if Monmouth should have any real success. It was clear that the Londoners would rise if they felt absolutely certain that it was safe to do so, but that they were not prepared to take any risks, with their leaders in prison or fled and armed soldiers all round them.

The news from the south-west was not so good. Monmouth's army was much stronger than expected. He had marched out of Lyme on 15 June, brushed aside the Somerset and Devon militia with ease and was now headed towards Taunton where he could be expected to increase his strength considerably. It seemed likely that he would move towards Bristol, another factious town and a potential prize of enormous physical and psychological value to the rebel cause. If Monmouth captured Bristol everyone would take him seriously and there was no telling what might happen.

King James and his Secretaries went into action again. On 17 June the King wrote to the Prince of Orange requesting him to send the three English regiments in the Low Countries to London. On the same day he sent orders to the Duke of Beaufort, the greatest landowner in the west, to march into Bristol with the militia of the counties of Gloucester, Hereford and Monmouth, to overawe the factious population and strengthen the city's defences against the expected attack. The militia of all the counties in a great semi-circle round the area of rebellion were to move westwards to provide a second line of defence. On Friday 19 June a flurry of new orders for the regular troops were sent out. Three battalions of the Foot Guards, accompanied by cavalry and dragoons, were to march under the command of the Earl of Feversham to Bath and there liaise with the regular forces and militia already in the field under Lord Churchill. They were to be followed on the Monday by the great train of artillery escorted by another five companies of infantry from the Royal Regiment of Foot. The net was closing. Some of the gaps could be filled by the navy who had orders to guard the Bristol Channel and the Exe estuary, and to re-take Lyme now that Monmouth had abandoned it. Meanwhile London was not forgotten. The militia of Oxford-shire, Berkshire and Surrey was concentrated in Reading and

Farnham, ready to move east or west as occasion demanded, while the militia of the eastern counties was drawn in closer to the metropolis. As a final move the King sent out orders all over the country to seize 'all disaffected and suspicious persons, and particularly all nonconformist ministers and such persons as served against our royal father and late royal brother' and to hold them in custody till further notice.[33] The King was taking no chances. Many hundreds of people were seized under this order, far more than the regular prisons could hold. In London the halls of the great Livery Companies were used to supplement the gaols of the city, while one writer commented that so great were the numbers of disaffected persons that the whole country would have had to be one great prison for the order to be fully implemented.[34]

It was now just a question of waiting and keeping his nerve. Now that the army was in the neighbourhood of Bath, only a hundred miles away, the King could be much better informed of what was going on, often receiving letters on the day they were written. Sunderland was kept busy dictating letters of advice and encouragement in reply. The news was almost entirely good. Every effort that Monmouth made to break out of the net was foiled in turn. He was frightened away first from Bristol and then from Bath. Finally on 27 June he turned his back on London and marched out of Frome to the west. He was on the run. Better make sure he did not go too far. The Cornish militia were brought up to the Tamar. Exeter was strengthened. The net was tightened. King James and his two Secretaries could relax a bit.

So could the King's loyal subjects in London. The three weeks since the news of Monmouth's invasion had reached the city had been a time of great excitement in which rumours and false alarms and a general feeling of panic had made life almost too hectic for many Londoners. The news which filtered through to the Court and thus to the city at large was generally fairly favourable but there were items which could cause alarm. The wholesale desertion of the Somerset militia, the proclamation of Monmouth as king at Taunton, the apparent inability of anyone to stop him as he marched towards Bristol had all been very worrying for

London loyalists, surrounded as they were by a jostling population of fanatics and bragging young apprentices. Nor was what
came from the Court the whole of the news. Many Londoners had
relations or servants in the West Country, in the militia or the
royal army, who fed them other information, often less reliable
and more sensational. Monmouth had ten thousand, twenty
thousand, forty thousand men. He could have twenty-two
thousand more from London whenever he sent for them. Nothing
could stop him. The West Country militia had gone over to the
rebels *en masse*. Four hundred and five officers from the royal army
had deserted to their former commander. So the rumours built
up.[35] Many of them found their way into newspapers and news-
letters. A correspondent from Dartmouth wrote to the Earl of
Middleton complaining of the disheartening news available in the
one coffee house in the town. 'If ye publick news-letters be such
elsewhere, as they are at Dertmouth Coffee-House they may help
to make ye people, already crazy, then starke mad. The last posts
brought such a one as mentioned ye Duke of Albemarle's being
slayne; ye flight of 1500 men from their colonell . . .'[36] As late
as the 1 July, five days after Monmouth had marched away from
Bristol, the London *Observator* was telling its readers that 'there
was a hot discourse upon Saturday last that the Duke had taken
Bristol; kill'd 3000 of the King's men, and lost 2000 himself; but
that they went so fast over to the Duke that he march'd a hundred
men more, after the battel, than he did before'.[37] Such sources
were naturally fed by the rebel propagandists, a very able group
of men, who did their considerable bit to make the picture as
black as possible and so maintain the state of tension in the
metropolis. Much could be made of Argyll's rebellion, so far
away in Scotland that real news arrived long after the fake news
of his great successes had been disseminated through the not very
critical population of London.

We can get a very good idea of the general impressions of an
intelligent man in London at this critical time from the despatches
of the Tuscan minister, Francesco Terriesi. He was naturally in
close touch with the Court and received the news of the reports
from the royal commanders in the West as fast as anyone. But, as

an agent for Italian merchants, he was also in close touch with the city and was a keen observer of the mood of the London mob. This mood alarmed him. In his opinion the vast majority of the population were fanatics dedicated to the destruction of the monarchy whom the forces of law and order could not possibly control in the event of mass insurrection. Even before Monmouth's landing there had been a mood of anticipation and exhilaration in the city which was only intensified by his arrival and the apparent failure of the King's forces to contain him. Now the war cry, 'A Monmouth, A Monmouth', operated like a charm on the populace, a drum-beat in their ears which reminded them of the prophecy that Monmouth had been sent by God to rid them of popery, slavery and arbitrary government. This prophecy was supported in their minds by a revolutionary text from Ezekiel:

Remove the diadem, and take off the crown; this shall not be the same: exalt him that is low, and abase him that is high.

I will overturn, overturn, overturn it: and it shall be no more, until he came whose right it is; and I will give it him.[38]

The civilized Tuscan might mock a people who believed a text was true, just because they were able to spell out the words in it, but he was truly alarmed by the reiteration of the two refrains, 'A Monmouth' and 'overturn, overturn' in the mouths of the populace. All that was needed to persuade them that God really was on their side was one victory by Monmouth in the west. Then they would rise. Meanwhile they waited, virtually no business was carried on and debtors refused to pay their debts, since who knew what would happen to creditors on the Day of Judgment.[39]

In fact Terriesi exaggerates both the numbers of the Dissenters and republicans and the intensity of their commitment to Monmouth. In London, particularly, it had been difficult to generate quite such an emotional response to his leadership. He might be respected as a military leader. He might be considered as a useful link between the urban opposition and the aristocracy and gentry. But the man who could shock even Restoration London could hardly be seen as a Messiah. Monmouth was known too well in London to arouse the same degree of enthusiasm as he received in the West Country, a fact which can be illustrated by the very different comments of two clergymen who were both firm for the good old cause of religion. The Reverend Stephen Towgood, minister of an Independent congregation in Axminster, saw Monmouth as 'a deliverer for the nation, and the interest of Christ'.[40] Matthew Meade, a minister from Stepney, was later bitterly cursed by the exiled rebels for dissuading the men of London and Wapping from joining 'such ungodly deliverers as Monmouth, Gray and ye rest of their party, sayeing that God will cause delivrance and ruine Babylon in his own way by a holier generation'.[41]

Nevertheless, the excitement was real enough and so were the fears of the courtiers and the well affected who could not believe that Monmouth would have been so rash as to land with so few men, had he not assurance of a general rising. It was clear too that such a rising would not simply be a rebellion against the King, but a very real challenge to the whole order of society which gave them their privileges. All the same, most men were in no hurry to commit themselves. If Monmouth won they had no wish to be numbered among his active enemies. But, as the days went by and the gradual containment of the rebellion became more obvious, such men rushed forward to offer their services to the Crown and then lost themselves in the delicious pleasures of raising a troop of cavalry, ordering uniforms, buying horses and practising a few sword thrusts in front of the mirror.

Soon there were so many new troops of horse and companies of foot that new fears began to replace the fear of Monmouth. Men who had hidden their valuables and discreetly barricaded their windows against the threat of city violence now began to fear the very royal power which had been developed to defend them. Why was the King so slow to move in and destroy the rebels? Muttered criticism could be heard of the military policy of the King and his commanders in the west.

It will be high time that somewhat be attempted upon the rebells by the King's forces, [wrote Bishop Fell] for it is an unaccountable thing that they should be suffered to ramble up and down for several weeks without any notice taken of them, or so much as a single troop falling upon their rear. Whatever bystanders think of it, neighbor princes will imagin that we ar a very easy prey to an invading army, who cannot make head in three weeks time, to a desperate man who landed with only an hundred and fifty with him.[42]

What was the cause of the delay? A whispered answer was soon going the rounds. The King was in no hurry. He had no wish to waste this opportunity to expand the forces at his control. Worse still was the news that the King was using the weapons seized from the Dissenters to arm the Catholics. Old fears which had lain dormant for a few years now sprang to mind, fears of a popish plot, an Irish massacre, the stuff of nightmare. Soon after Monmouth's landing, the King had tactfully declined an offer from the Spanish ambassador to send over up to six thousand veteran soldiers from Flanders to quash the rebellion.[43] But he did nothing to allay these new fears, for they were true. The King was indeed arming Catholics, though not necessarily with the archaic weapons seized from the Dissenters.

On Sunday 5 July the Duke of Monmouth sent two last emissaries to try and raise the Londoners in his support. It was far too late. London was now a cowed city, the prisons and the great Livery Halls packed with Dissenters, the streets full of armed men and business nearly at a standstill. In the whole country hardly a man dared move out of his house, unless he was very well known to be a loyalist going about his lawful business. The London Dissenters had waited for a sign from the west. Monmouth had waited for a sign from London. But no sign had come. All was quiet in Babylon.

Three

The Envoy Extraordinary

'I am soe tyred with sitting up and writing every day and every night of late not having had time almost to ease or sleep that I scarcely know what I have said.'[1] Perhaps the writer, Bevil Skelton, His Majesty's Envoy Extraordinary at The Hague, did not want to know what he had said in the long, distressing letter which he wrote to the Earl of Middleton on the last day of May, 1685. He had just had to report the complete failure of all his attempts to get the Admiralty of Amsterdam to arrest Monmouth's frigate, the *Helderenburgh*. 'After the timely notice I gave of the ship Heldernberg [sic] being designed to carry armes to the rebells and to transport severall of them into some part of His Majesty's dominions, they have not regarded my repeated complaints and desires, but have clear'd the ship which is readie to sayle.'[2] No wonder Skelton was nearly in tears. He would have cried out loud had he known that on that very day all three of Monmouth's ships had set sail from the island of Texel at the mouth of the Zuider Zee. It was the climax of two months of the most bitter frustration and disappointment.

Skelton, a former soldier who had served King Charles II in various diplomatic capacities in Germany and Austria, had arrived at The Hague towards the end of March 1685. His main task was to persuade the Dutch authorities to banish the numerous English and Scots traitors who had taken refuge in their territories and to prevent any attempt by them to cross the seas and set up the flag of rebellion. His failure was complete and, as a result, he has had a very bad press from historians who have seen him as utterly incompetent and have for the most part accepted the verdict of his contemporary Gilbert Burnet who described him as 'the haughtiest, but withal the weakest, of men'.[3] He certainly emerges from his letters as a rather pathetic figure, very sorry for himself, very earnest in his attempts at self-justification and very insistent in apportioning blame to others. But he was a loyal man who tried his best to do his duty, and one can only feel sympathy for the man who had the misfortune to occupy this particular post at this particular time. It seems unlikely that anyone else would have done any better.

The main problem was the extremely unhelpful and obstructive attitude taken by the Dutch themselves. They were supposed to be the allies of England and thus of King James, the lawful King of England, but this fact was certainly not apparent to the outsider. The Dutch would do nothing on their own initiative to hinder the rebels. Many went out of their way to help them, giving them money and shelter and warning them in advance of any action to be taken against them by the Dutch authorities or of the latest move by Envoy Skelton. This general attitude towards the rebels was true of all towns and all provinces of the Netherlands, but by far the worst offenders were the magistrates and citizens of Amsterdam whose behaviour on several occasions brought Skelton to the verge of apoplexy. The city was traditionally republican and Calvinist and thus had a natural antipathy to King James both as a king and as a papist. During the whole period of the build-up to the rebellion and during the rebellion itself the people of Amsterdam openly showed their enthusiasm for the cause, printing inflammatory broadsides and pamphlets for circulation both in the Low Countries and in England, lending the rebels money, selling them arms and equipment and providing an impenetrable cover for them in their traditionally hospitable town. Skelton reported the mood in Amsterdam after Monmouth had landed. 'It is publickly sayd in theire streets, upon theire exchange and in theire coffee howses that they ought to assist those goode people whoe are gone to fight for the Protestant cause, adding scandalous discourses of his Majesty's person, and if any man shall dar to contradict them, he shall runne the hazard of having his braines beate out.'[4]

The general behaviour of the citizens of Amsterdam was quite intolerable for so-called allies. Skelton thought it would be better for King James if they had been declared enemies. However, no one could really expect such notorious enemies of monarchy to behave in any other way. What gave rise to more misgivings then, and ever since, was the behaviour of King James's nephew and son-in-law, William of Orange, Stadtholder of the seven provinces, Captain and Admiral General of the military and naval forces of the republic and indisputably the most powerful man in the country. Here surely was the man who could stir the Dutch to behave like good allies rather than undeclared enemies. And yet throughout the critical period of preparation for the rebellion the Prince of Orange was to play an extremely enigmatic role. Outwardly he was full of respect for his royal uncle in England and only too willing to do his best to carry out his many requests. But that best seemed very half-hearted both to James in London and to Skelton at The Hague. It was difficult to believe the assurances of a man reputed to have the best intelligence service in Europe that he knew nothing of any preparation for rebellion or that he did not know the whereabouts of Monmouth and other rebels. Everyone else in Holland knew these things. It was difficult to believe that a man with such power and drive as William could be so slow in getting things done in his own country. Weeks or months went by before English demands for executive action were actually put into effect. What was William up to?

The verdict of history has depended very much on the political outlook of the historian, since William was far too clever a man to leave any record on paper of his assistance or friendship towards the rebels. Whig historians have tended to give their hero the benefit of the doubt. But Tories, and other writers who are not committed to the Whig interpretation of history have suggested that he was deliberately trying to get the best of all possible worlds. William had one great aim in life, which was to contain the apparently unlimited expansionist ambitions of his neighbour King Louis xiv. His hopes of doing this depended very heavily on harnessing the potential military and naval strength of England to his cause. But could such hopes be realized while the francophile papist James II was King of England? It seemed doubtful but, in any case, it was obviously a wise policy for William not to offend James too much. Hence William ultimately acceded to all James's requests and actively offered to help put down the rebellion which had so unhappily been planned under his own unseeing eyes. On the other hand Monmouth's proposed expedition offered many possibilities. If he was very successful then England would be ruled by a group committed to the Protestant cause and thus likely to fight alongside William against France. If he was fairly successful then King James might well find it difficult to contain the rebellion with his small army and thus find it necessary to request the assistance of the six Anglo–Scots regiments in the Low Countries. And, if he did, who would be a more appropriate man to command not only them but the whole English army than King James's nephew, the Prince of Orange, a military hero and a loyal Stuart? And who could say what might happen once the same determined man commanded the armed forces of both England and the Netherlands? And if Monmouth failed and paid the price? It would be sad of course, since he was a likeable man of about William's age, like him a keen huntsman and a social asset at his Court. But it would wonderfully simplify the problem of the succession to the English throne. The Protestant party in England had always been weakened by a split between those who supported the legitimate succession and those who supported the Duke of Monmouth. But, with Monmouth dead, there could be no doubt that King James's eldest daughter, Mary, the wife of William of Orange, was the only possible claimant to the throne. There could also be little doubt whom the Protestants would invite to settle the kingdom should the headstrong King James take his centralizing and catholicizing ambitions too far. And so the Prince of Orange took rather a long time to implement the many requests which his uncle made of him. He was also to discover some rather surprising gaps in his intelligence service. Whether he also patted his friend James Scott, Duke of Monmouth, on the back and wished him well we do not know. It seems quite likely but, if he did, he certainly left no record and Monmouth himself kept his mouth shut.

Both William himself and the city government of Amsterdam had a marvellous built-in excuse for delay, an excuse which generations of Dutch statesmen and governments were to find extremely useful. This was the extraordinarily complex Dutch constitution, a constitution which was as unintelligible to the foreign contemporary as it is to the modern student. Time and time again Skelton was to discover that William was not able to do something without reference to the States General or some other body or person, while the magistrates of Amsterdam could have a regular field day by referring to the Estates of Holland, the States General or William himself decisions which it seemed to the outsider they could perfectly well have taken by themselves.

It was into this strange and rather Kafkaesque republican world that the as yet comparatively innocent Bevil Skelton came to take up his post in March 1685. His first task was to identify just who 'His Majesty's rebellious subjects' were. There were plenty of them. Providing the main social distinction amongst the English contingent were two rather bizarre *ménages à trois*. The Duke of Monmouth, depressed by his recent expulsion from the social pleasures of the Spanish Netherlands, grieved at the loss of his father and apparently set on a quiet life in the country, had set up house with his mistress Lady Henrietta Wentworth and her mother, Lady Philadelphia. Lord Grey, broke and actively seeking a military command in the service of the Elector of Brandenburg, was living with his mistress, who was also his wife's younger sister, and the complaisant Mr Turner who had been introduced into the household as her husband. Moving rapidly down the social scale there were the 'four rivals',* republicans and Rye House plotters – Rumbold, Nelthrop, Goodenough and Wade – very active and very rebellious subjects of His Majesty.[5] Even more active and more rebellious, if that was possible, was the Reverend Robert Ferguson, 'a tall lean man, dark-brown hair, a great Roman nose, thin-jawed, heat in the face, speaks in the Scotch tone, a sharp piercing eye, stoops a little at the shoulders; he hath a shuffling

---

* 'Rivals' for the hand of the 'young lady' (Monmouth). Spies and rebels alike disguised real situations in this rather transparent way. In this case it is the fortune which the young lady is likely to inherit on the death of her uncle which is of interest.

gait that differs from all men, wears a periwig down almost over his eyes, about forty-five years of age.'[6] Most of the time of successive envoys at The Hague seemed to have been spent in the frustrating game of searching for Ferguson but, despite his appearance, he was never caught by anyone, however clever the trap that they thought they had set for him. He seemed to live a charmed life.

These seven important rebels were just the tip of the iceberg. There were potentially rebellious Englishmen of one sort or another all over the Netherlands, some who had fled from England for political or religious reasons, some who simply chose to live in Holland because they found it a tolerant and congenial place to live or because they were in business there. Skelton had to keep his eye on all these people. There were officers who had been cashiered from the English regiments in the Dutch service at King James's request, such as Captain Foulkes and Ensign Fox. There were great Whig merchants who had fled from London after the Rye House Plot, such as Sir Patience Ward and Sir Thomas Papillon, now living quietly in Utrecht and apparently planning to stay some time, since they had recently had coaches made for them. 'These two think that the others are only building castles in the air, and that all their schemes will only bring about their own loss; as for them, they want nothing other than to live quietly here.'[7] So wrote Skelton's efficient spy from Utrecht. Not all the rebels were as quiet as Ward and Papillon or the great philosopher John Locke, former secretary to the Earl of Shaftesbury, who also lived in Utrecht. There were fanatics, like the Reverend James Hogg, who kept a conventicle in Utrecht and was thought to be as dangerous as Ferguson.[8] Even worse was Ferguson's brother who called himself Willoughby, a man who saw it as his mission to assassinate King James. A special weapon had been made in Amsterdam for the purpose, not a pistol, 'nor any invention to fire with powder, but like a bow and arrow so that it will make no noise', and small enough to hide in a specially made pocket.[9]

Then there were the Scots exiles, far greater in number than the English and settled in all the ports and riverine cities from

Hamburg to Flanders. Many of them had been there a long time, but more recent recruits included many Covenanters who had fled after the battle of Bothwell Brigg in 1679. Amongst them could be found Balfour, the arch-fanatic, one of the men who had murdered the Archbishop of St Andrews in his coach and the anti-hero of Sir Walter Scott's novel *Old Mortality*. Exile had not changed his savage nature. When a loyalist English soldier reproached him with his crime in the streets of Rotterdam, Balfour drew his pistol and threatened to shoot him on the spot, 'calling him all the names imaginable'.[10]

On the whole the Scots were a much more distinguished group socially than the English. Here were many respected members of the Lowland gentry, men with good, solid Scottish names like Fletcher of Saltoun and Erskine of Carnock. Here too was the great Archibald Campbell, ninth Earl of Argyll, living quite comfortably on his family estates in Friesland but not likely to want to live there for long.

To help him watch all these people Skelton seems to have had an assistant and a clerk, three or four professional spies and a few amateurs, some well meaning but hopeless, some distinctly suspicious like the so-called Henry Hemmings who pointed out how easily Monmouth might be shot as he travelled from place to place. Skelton, who seems to have felt a genuine horror at the very idea of assassination, rejected this easy solution to his problems and concluded in any case that Hemmings had been sent to spy on him by the rebels.[11] In an emergency Skelton could call on other officials in the English service, such as the consul in Amsterdam, Henry Bull. But this might not be of much help since Bull was described by a senior Dutch official as a broken goldsmith, a fool and 'a selfe ended knave' and even Skelton called him 'a very timorous heavie fellow' who was frightened by the rebels and dared not do his duty.[12] One can conclude that Skelton was quite incapable of doing the job he had been sent to do unless he had the active assistance of the Dutch. But this he was unable to expect.

Skelton's attempts to implement King James's request that the leading rebels be banished make sad reading. It was hardly an unreasonable request to make in the circumstances. In his very first letter home, on 27 March, Skelton told the Earl of Middleton that he had not much confidence that the traitors would be expelled unless the King spoke 'very sharply' to the Dutch ambassador.[13] James who was very good at speaking sharply, did so and also wrote a number of sharp letters on the subject to William of Orange. A month later, on 21 April, not much progress had been made. Skelton reported that 'if His Majesty were to require the banishment of any of his rebellious subjects out of these provinces it would be complyed of, as long as they are named' and 'a few of the most notorious villaynes amongst them will be delivred up'.[14] By 5 May things really seemed to be going quite well. The States General had agreed to banish the rebels. A week later Skelton was expecting that in a few days the proclamation for the banishment of the rebels would be published. Even the deputies of Amsterdam had made no difficulty in giving their consent. Yet another week passed and Skelton was still hoping that in a few days the proclamations would be published. At last, on 26 May, they really were printed, just five days before Monmouth set sail for England. But no rebel was ever banished, for nobody in the Netherlands was able to locate a single one of the eighty rebels whom Skelton had listed, despite the fact that many of them were very well known in Amsterdam, Utrecht and Rotterdam. Strange to say they had all completely disappeared.[15]

Meanwhile the rebels had been plotting away for all they were worth, quite oblivious of their worthy envoy's efforts to get them banished. Skelton and his men worked hard to penetrate their designs. Report after report was sent back to London, complete with enclosures from the spies in the major trading cities. The movements or supposed movements of the leading rebels, their mistresses and servants were charted; every change of pseudonym and every change of plan was faithfully chronicled. There was nothing very much wrong with Skelton's information network. But the fact that he knew fairly well what was going on did not help him very much, since he was quite incapable of doing anything to stop the rebels from plotting, buying arms, borrowing money, hiring ships or anything else that they wanted to do.

Despite the fact that Skelton regularly fed him with information, it was weeks before William of Orange would officially believe that Monmouth was planning a rebellion. As for the city government of Amsterdam, they blandly told Skelton after Monmouth had sailed that they had been 'assured that the Duke of Monmouth had not a thought that was contrary to his dewtie'.[16]

The historian does not have to rely on Skelton's reports for his knowledge of what the rebels were doing, for many of them have left accounts of their activities during these hectic weeks of preparation. Most of these accounts were extracted by the Government after the rebellion and have that particular flavour of men talking fast to save their lives but, for all that, the picture is clear enough. There was general agreement amongst the leading rebels that the sudden death of Charles II made it imperative that they act quickly before King James was able to consolidate his power. Few of the exiles had any very recent knowledge of public opinion in England and they were quite happy to disregard or disbelieve any news which ran counter to their preconceived ideas, such as the peaceful acceptance of the new King and the generally apathetic mood of a population who were happier to wait and see what would happen rather than to risk life and property to make something happen. The rebels preferred to argue from first principles. If the country had been on the verge of rebellion in the early 1680s when the succession of James was merely a vague threat in the future, it seemed obvious that now that he was really king the whole English population was simply waiting for someone to give them a lead. Information from England which denied such a revolutionary situation was ignored, whilst optimistic information often deliberately fabricated by men determined to commit waverers on both sides of the Channel was accepted quite uncritically. A realistic appreciation of the situation was in any case quite impossible, in view of the general clampdown by King James's Government and the dangerous and slow communications between England and the Low Countries. As a result both the English and Scots expeditions were to set sail in a mood of self-inspired optimism, but with only the vaguest promises of support from their supposed friends across the sea. It is little wonder that they were rather disappointed by the general lack of active enthusiasm for their cause.

Most of the exiles were agreed that the rebellion should take the same form as the proposed rebellion of 1683, a multiple and if possible simultaneous insurrection in Scotland, Cheshire, the West Country and London. But such a complex plan was of course much easier to discuss than to put into operation. The Scots saw few problems. Although they had differences of opinion on many matters they were agreed on the essentials. They had the men and the money, they had a leader and they seemed to have no doubt that their arrival in their homeland would spark off a major rebellion. They wanted to be off as soon as possible and resented the delays and doubts of the smaller, weaker, poorer and apparently less committed group of English exiles. They were prepared to wait a bit in the interests of co-ordination, but not for long. If the English refused to get a move on they would do the business by themselves.

The English were quite unable to see things in such a simple light. They dared not move before they had at least some assurance of support at home. They could not move before they had raised some money to buy arms and hire ships to carry them. And they were reluctant to move without the Duke of Monmouth, their best hope of stirring up widespread popular support. It took some time to persuade him. At first he seemed to prefer the quiet life in his love-nest to the challenge of rebellion. Then he seemed determined to sail with Argyll, much to the latter's dismay. Then, after a show of interest in the English venture, he seemed to settle into a gloomy pessimistic mood which appeared to reach bottom about the second week of April, a fact which attracted the attention of Skelton's spy in Rotterdam who reported on 14 April that the rebels, who had gathered there for meetings since the beginning of the month, had now all dispersed and 'tis sayd that they are very ill sattisfy'd with the Duke of Monmouth's conduct'.[17] Optimistic letters from England cheered Monmouth up in the course of the next week and from then on he played a fairly active part in planning his expedition with the other English rebels.

Monmouth's final commitment to the cause solved the problem of leadership, or rather ensured that there would be a leader, but it did not of course solve the problems of money or co-ordination and support in England. The exiles had early notice that they could expect popular support in the West Country, although there remained a doubt as to the attitude of the local gentry on whose support Monmouth placed great reliance.

What support could the exiles hope for from the other two areas, Cheshire and London? The concept of a Cheshire rising which appears in all plans for rebellion in these years seems to have been little more than a vague idea in the minds of various local aristocrats, such as Lord Delamere, who tended to equate the county's enthusiasm for Monmouth as an athlete and jockey with a desire to die for him. The rebels seemed to think that these lords need only snap their fingers to raise ten or twenty thousand men. Maybe the lords thought so too. Lord Delamere certainly behaved in a rather odd way at the time of Monmouth's rebellion, absenting himself from Parliament and flitting suspiciously off to Cheshire in disguise, and he was rather lucky to be acquitted at his later trial. But Cheshire never did rise and never really looked as though it would rise. All the same Monmouth believed the myth and messengers were sent to stir the Cheshire lords into action.

There remained London, the key to the success of the whole rebellion, the potential source of both the money to finance it and the men to fight in it. There were two very obvious difficulties in organizing a rising in London. The city was very closely under the eye of a Government which had many informers and many soldiers ready to arrest a long list of potential rebels at the slightest hint of any trouble. And these potential rebels had no really committed leaders, since those who had been most active in the past were either dead or in the Low Countries with Monmouth. These difficulties were compounded by the fact that two of the men that Monmouth relied on to stir up the Londoners were themselves not very happy about the proposed rebellion. The Reverend Matthew Meade who was expected to raise the dissenters in the East End refused to give his support to the ungodly Monmouth. Major Wildman, a republican who had been plotting against successive governments since the 1640s, was somewhat more enigmatic. He distrusted Monmouth, suspecting him of double dealing after the Rye House Plot and also suspecting him of seeking his uncle's crown, an ambition which of course was anathema to the committed republican. He also did not think that the time was ripe for rebellion. Despite these misgivings, Wildman seems to have been incapable of doing no plotting at all and his habit of phrasing his remarks in an ambiguous fashion may well have deceived some of Monmouth's messengers into believing he had promised more than he really had. The exiles certainly felt that Wildman had badly let them down, though he in fact never committed himself either financially or in person to the rebellion and was prepared to do no more than pass on messages, sound opinion and offer a vague assurance that London would rise if there were great successes elsewhere. This, though realistic, was hardly encouraging and the exiles in the Low Countries either reinterpreted Wildman's reported remarks in a way that seemed more satisfactory to them or else believed what they read in other reports which were more optimistic, such as that written by Monmouth's equerry, Captain Edward Matthews. Such self-deception may have persuaded them that London was ready to rise but it did not produce any money. For, despite reports both in London and the Low Countries that the exchanges were clogged up with the remittance of cash by London ministers and merchants, Monmouth received virtually no money at all from London and had to borrow what he could in the Low Countries. This was very little, despite the friendly help of his mistress and her mother who pawned their jewels to help him, and Monmouth was to land at Lyme Regis with practically nothing left in his exchequer.

While Monmouth's messengers had been making their way between England and Holland with virtually no interference from either the Dutch or the more watchful English authorities, the Scots had got fed up with waiting. They had hired three ships and towards the end of April were openly loading them with supplies and ammunition. This was really a bit much; the Scots expedition was the talk of the whole Low Countries. Skelton saw the Prince of Orange who promised to make the Admiralty of Amsterdam do their utmost to seize the ships. The people from the Admiralty were very helpful and ordered their water bailiff to go with Consul Bull to search and, if necessary arrest the ships. But then the bailiff discovered that the ships were lying outside the Admiralty's jurisdiction. What Bull must do was to write to Skelton instructing him to get a written permission from the States General. Bull and Skelton complied. On 1 May Bull was back at the Admiralty, who were still a little worried about taking any action in the absence of any 'more certain' information. What was Consul Bull going to do if he had made a mistake and the ships were full of innocent men? And in any case there was no law against exporting arms in peacetime. Still, they could hardly ignore a signed order from the States General and indeed were kind enough to send two men to help Bull, though unfortunately they did not just at that moment have any ships to assist him. So Bull had to set off with two men in a hired yacht to arrest three ships full of armed desperate men. He tried hard, considering what a timorous fellow he was supposed to be, even sending his man to follow them as far as the Vlie. Here orders were given to the customs searchers to seize the arms, 'but the searchers, finding that what armes were aboard had paid duty, did not concern themselves', especially when they were told that the ships were bound for Königsberg and Danzig. Skelton and his men had failed again. The Prince of Orange was very sorry about it all.[18]

Monmouth had been expected to follow the Scots in a week or ten days. There was however a delay of twenty-nine days before he set sail and forty before he landed in Dorset. This gave King James plenty of time to pull in suspects and prepare himself for the rebels' reception. It also ruined any chance of the two rebellions splitting the King's forces in any meaningful way, though in fact James did not need to send English troops to put down the Scots rebellion in any case. All chance of surprise was thus lost as the month of May was frittered away in ill-co-ordinated efforts to get the necessary men, money, arms and ships together. To tell the truth the English rebels were only a little better at organizing their expedition than Skelton was at preventing it from sailing. Some delay was caused by the need to wait for encouraging news from England. More was caused by Monmouth's insistence on using up most of his limited funds in hiring a thirty-two-gun frigate to give him some protection against the English ships which were lying in wait for him off the Dutch coast. The money would have been better spent on a faster, smaller ship and many more arms. But at last everything was ready and Monmouth sent off his final messenger, the old Cromwellian cavalry officer John Jones, on 22 May. Jones was to report to Captain Matthews in London and tell him that Monmouth was sailing the following day and that the general rendezvous was to be at Taunton in Somerset.

Monmouth's confidence was somewhat premature. Even now he was to be delayed, this time by the weather, though not by the Dutch authorities despite promises that the scandal of the Scots expedition would not be repeated. It was not till 29 May that the rebels boarded their three ships. On the following day Commissary van der Block of the Texel Admiralty set out to try and arrest them, but when he arrived at their former berth they had already sailed and, as it was low water, he was unable to follow. When the tide rose he took a pilot's boat and managed to catch up with Monmouth's frigate. He then arrested her. Unfortunately the rebels took not the slightest notice and there was nothing for the Commissary to do but disembark and report to Skelton that he was sorry that he had been unable to stop the ship.[19] On the same day Skelton's agent Captain Slater had been hopping up and down with frustration on the island of Texel, complaining that if he had had any assistance at all he could have caught 'ye whole knott of rogues' at once. The rogues, however, were not bothered. Thirty of them, 'very gentilely clad' came to have a look at him, 'and are so audatious, and secure in their enterprize, that they openly affront us and laugh at us, and come by crowdes into ye house where I am and looke into my chamber.'[20]

The Prince of Orange was very sorry about this as well. Now that the rebels were gone he was keen to make amends. There had been some delay since King James had first requested the assistance of the three Scots regiments from the Low Countries on 22

May. Prince William had not been sure that the States General would agree.[21] Then Skelton had had difficulty getting credit to pay and equip them, 'for the factious rogues here have spread reports that all is in confusion in England, and disheartened those that before were readie to furnish me with whatever I wanted.'[22] But on 5 June they were all ready and were reviewed by Skelton and the Prince of Orange himself at Rotterdam. 'I never saw a better body of men in my lyfe, which the Prince of Orange was also pleased to declare, and besides that, they are old experienced soldiers, they are all new clad from head to foote'.[23] It was a shame that King James had refused William's kind offer to command them in person, but the King thought the rebellion of Argyll 'not considerable enough for you to be troubled with it'.[24]

As Monmouth struggled down channel against contrary winds and handed out commissions to his motley collection of officers, he must have wished that he, too, had the services of such fine regiments, 'a body of old good men' as King James had called them when he first requested their assistance. There were old men and good men waiting for Monmouth in the West Country, but they were not quite the same as these disciplined veterans from the Low Countries.

Four

The Hornett of Fear

'My deare Lord . . . To heare your alive is some satisfackcion, but when I consider ye dangere your in, ye worst friend I have will pitty me . . . Your soe good and so deare to me that noe outher thoughts than theses can posable have an exces.'[1] Christopher Monck, second Duke of Albemarle, a reformed rake in his early thirties, must have been a little cheered to receive such a loving letter from his wife on the last day of June 1685. His life had not really been in much danger, despite regular reports of his death at the hands of the rebels, but he had certainly had rather a miserable time since early June when he came down to Devon to command the county's militia, and he needed cheering up. All his life he had been overshadowed by the enormous reputation of his father, George Monck, naval and military hero and the maker of the Restoration. Now he had been given the chance to win glory himself, as the man on the spot who could snuff out the rebellion of his former friend and partner in devilry, James Scott, Duke of Monmouth, in one whirlwind campaign. But somehow it had not worked out like that and when the glory did come it was to be others who gained it.

It should have been easy enough. Albemarle had been trained as a soldier and was, even now, the commander of the King's Guards, a coveted position which he had gained at Monmouth's expense, after the latter's disgrace. As Lord Lieutenant of Devon he could bring at least four thousand men of the local militia into the field and could expect to co-operate with his colleagues in Dorset and Somerset to produce an overwhelming force of say ten thousand trained men to crush Monmouth before he had even left

Lyme Regis. The potential advantage in numbers must have been at least four to one. And yet, when it came to the point, it was not quite so easy as that. The 'trained' soldiers of the militia were only required to train for a few days a year, a requirement which was rarely implemented and, when it was, largely consisted of getting to the muster, being counted, having a few drinks and going home again. The weapons of the militia were kept in a similar state of readiness. When the Wiltshire militia mustered at Devizes it was found that the locks of most of their muskets had been eaten away by rust. But, even if the muskets had been fit to fire and the men fit to fire them, they would still have been little use, since there were no bullet moulds to make the ammunition.[2] Military training and up to date military equipment were in any case not particularly relevant to the main function of the militia, which was to act as policemen rather than as soldiers and to use the butts of their muskets rather than the muzzles. Militia men had been very useful in assisting the Justices of the Peace break up the conventicles of the West Country and bully those found attending them. But there was a world of difference between an unarmed Dissenter worshipping with his wife and children in a conventicle and an armed Dissenter in open rebellion. Such men were not going to stand by and be clubbed on the head.

Albemarle was well aware of the limitations of the forces he was commanding. He also knew that many of his men sympathized with the rebels, drawn as they were from the same area and the same class as the militia who were to oppose them. Were they not Protestants too, and was this not a Protestant cause? He was therefore reluctant to move too fast when the news of Monmouth's landing was brought to him at Exeter. An attack on the rebel camp might lead to a humiliating defeat. What he could do was to use the militia as a police force to prevent the rebels recruiting from the major part of his county. In this he seems to have been extremely effective. It was really quite easy to stop a handful of men, usually unarmed, from passing through the militia lines. There seem to have been no rebels at all from west and north Devon and there is record of only three from the mighty city of Exeter with its large population of Dissenting clothworkers.

Others who tried ended up in the city's gaols and workhouses under guard. Similar activity by the militia of Dorset and Wiltshire kept the rebellion extremely localized. The militia of Dorset were even able to beat off a fairly considerable raid on Bridport by the rebels, despite the fact that it was night-time, they were not too well prepared and most of their officers were still in London at the Parliament. The failure of his men to overwhelm the militia at Bridport seems to have been sufficient to discourage Monmouth from attacking Exeter, a move which if successful would have given his rebellion a great psychological boost, as well as providing him with a magnificent base and a considerable haul of recruits and arms. Perhaps it was unlucky that he did not try Exeter first, since the Dorset militia seems to have been made of sterner stuff than their brothers of Devon. But Monmouth was not to know this as yet. Later the whole West Country militia were to come in for universal condemnation, but in these early days their patrols were successful in their vital role of containing the rebellion. Some rebels got through of course. Several of the patrols consisted of men favourable to Monmouth's cause who asked few questions. In any case it was difficult to stop an armed man on horseback. But only in Somerset and in the parts of Devon and Dorset within easy reach of Lyme Regis were the militia totally unable or unwilling to prevent men reaching the rebel camp.

The policy of caution and concentration on the arrest and examination of 'all stragling and suspitious persons, who shall be found travelling up and down', was in accordance with instructions from London.[3] At the first news of Monmouth's landing Sunderland had written to Albemarle that the King was sending regular troops to his assistance. Meanwhile the King had full confidence in him and he was to 'do as you shall see cause.' Slightly less confidence was shown the next day when the King had had time to think a little more about how much faith he should place in the loyalty of the West Country militia. 'He [the King] thinkes fit, that in ye meane time, as long as ye D. of Monmouth stayes in Lyme, you should forbear to attempt any thing against him, except upon great advantages . . . and in case he should march out of Lime towards Taunton, or elsewhere into ye countrey, His Majesty would have you to attend his motions and take any fitting ocasion to attack him, which His Majesty leaves to your discretion.'[4] The following day, 15 June, before Albemarle could have received this letter, Monmouth did march out of Lyme, 'with much dread and terror, to the amazement and wonder of many what the Lord had brought'.[5] Here was surely Albemarle's 'fitting occasion to attack' Monmouth in a blaze of glory. Untrained troops are notoriously vulnerable on the march. Albemarle passed the news through to his colleagues in the Somerset militia stationed at Crewkerne and Chard and both the Devonshire and the Somerset militia marched towards Axminster to intercept and destroy the rebel army. The race for Axminster was a close one. First to arrive were the scouts of the Somerset militia. But they were chased out by the vanguard of Monmouth's army who had doubled their speed for the last few miles. The town was quickly occupied, cannon brought up to guard the roads down which the two militia armies were advancing and the hedges and walls lined with musketeers.[6] The threat was enough.

The Lord eminently appeared, filling this New Army with wonderful courage, and sending an hornett of fear amongst those that came to oppose them, so that a dreadfull consternation of spirit ceized on them . . . some ran away with amazement, some were so stricken with terrour that they were even bereft of their reason, and like distracted persons. Others threw away their weapons of war, and would take them up no more; and many watched opportunities to leave their colours and old officers, and came and joyned with this new company.[7]

This somewhat colourful description of the wholesale flight of the militia might be suspected of bias since it was written by a rebel preacher from Axminster. But what he wrote was essentially true, as can be seen if we read 'the shamefullest story that ever you heard',[8] an almost hysterical account of the same events by an officer in the Somerset militia. The Duke of Albemarle's dreams of glory vanished in a moment. His men might be good policemen, but they had just proved that they were certainly not good soldiers. He sat down to write his report. When the messenger arrived in

London, the watchful Florentine minister noted that the news must be extremely bad since the King went to Council after supper and stayed there till half past eleven.[9] King James now knew that it was going to take rather more than the militia to defeat the Duke of Monmouth.

What remained of the Devon and Somerset militia, which was rather more than the quotation above suggests, were reorganized and rested after their long cross-country run. Once again they reverted to their original role of screening the area of rebellion. They never had to fight again. No one would have trusted them. But they remained effective in limiting the rebellion and in occupying Monmouth's deserted quarters in the wake of his march. As a result Monmouth was never king of very much of the West Country. Meanwhile some real soldiers were getting quite close to the rebel army

John, Lord Churchill, was another young man in search of military glory. He was pleased when he was instructed to command the regular troops sent down to stiffen the militia. It was his first important independent command; he was a West Country man and knew the area well and he could look forward to considerable material advancement if he was successful. And it should not be difficult to defeat a ragged bunch of rebels, even if they were commanded by the Duke of Monmouth. Churchill, as a regular army officer, knew Monmouth well and had often served under his command. He had once saved the Duke's life in a daring exploit at the siege of Maestricht, twelve years earlier. But he had little sympathy with his rebellion, Protestant though it was, and laughed at Monmouth's crude attempts to suborn him. Churchill was a realist, not the man to support a rebellion which seemed doomed to failure. He was also very much a servant of the Duke of York. The first steps on his long, long climb to the peaks of English society had been greatly assisted by the fact that his elder sister, Arabella, was the Duke of York's mistress. Since the fortunate day of the Duke's first infatuation, Churchill had risen fast in his household and in the English army, a loyal and devoted servant who could expect to do very well for himself now that his master was king.

Churchill did not have very many men under his command as he rode hard for the West Country, but they were very good men for the job. Riding with him were four troops of the Earl of Oxford's Regiment of Horse Guards, known from their uniforms as the Blues, and two troops of Churchill's own regiment, the Royal Dragoons, less than four hundred troopers altogether. These dragoons, 'footmen on horseback', had a history which must have seemed a little ironical to Monmouth when he heard that they were on their way to fight him.[10] They had originally been Monmouth's Horse under his own command in the service of France. They had continued to serve under him in Scotland during the campaign which ended with the destruction of the Covenanters at the battle of Bothwell Brigg, a campaign in which they had demonstrated that they knew exactly how to deal with rebels. After that they had served in the English outpost of Tangier until it was evacuated in 1684 and now had become the Royal Dragoons, crack troops who could fight equally well on foot or on horseback, just the sort of men to inflict on the rebels that same 'hornett of fear' which they had inflicted on the militia.

Regular infantry was also on the way. Marching as fast as they could in the wake of Churchill to reinforce and encourage the militia were five companies of the Queen's Regiment of Foot under Colonel Percy Kirke, about five hundred men. Moving rather more slowly were five companies of Trelawney's Regiment, under Churchill's younger brother, Charles, who were escorting the artillery from the garrison at Portsmouth. These were all men to fear. They were the two foot regiments which had provided the garrison of Tangier, the one place where English soldiers got continuous experience of active service in a series of savage skirmishes with the Moors. They had acquired in Africa a violent contempt for civilians and enemies alike and had had to be kept on a tight leash when they were recalled to England in 1684. King Charles had given up Tangier because it was too expensive to maintain this outpost which he had received as part of the dowry of his queen. But he had not been mindless of the very valuable stiffening that troops bred in such an active station could give to his small, rather inexperienced and largely ceremonial army. Dissidents might think twice before they pitted middle-aged weavers and shoemakers against Kirke's Lambs.

Churchill met the Duke of Albemarle at Axminster just three days after the ignominious flight of the militia. His troopers and their horses were exhausted after the ride, but it was clear that they would not be able to rest for long. For Churchill had very soon discovered that Kirke was marching to reinforce militia units which no longer existed. Some regiments and companies were soon to be re-formed, but many men had gone home and many others had joined the rebels. An exaggerated report which Churchill passed on to London stated that the equivalent of a whole regiment of the Somerset militia had joined the ranks of Monmouth's army. The general situation was not too promising. The whole area seemed exultant at the rebels' early success, eager to supply them with food and lodging and determined to give no help at all to the militia or the regular soldiers. Until Kirke arrived and until the Devonshire and Somerset militia could pull themselves together, Churchill had only his own mounted escort and fifteen hundred infantry from the more dependable militia of Dorset, whom he had picked up on the way, to combat a confident rebel army which was now five thousand strong. Churchill wrote to the King describing the situation and asking for regular reinforcements as quickly as possible. Meanwhile, even if he was unable to attack the rebels head-on, he felt confident in the eventual success of the King's forces. While he waited for the reinforcements to arrive, he would cause the rebels considerable annoyance and prevent their countrymen from giving them any further assistance.

While Churchill consoled the disappointed Albemarle at Axminster, Monmouth marched into Taunton, twenty-two miles away, to receive a tumultuous reception. The church bells rang, crowds thronged the streets crying 'A Monmouth, A Monmouth', schoolgirls presented their Protestant duke with banners embroidered from their petticoats and a whole new regiment was added to Monmouth's army, made up of those many hundred Taunton men who had been waiting so long to rebel. It was here, in Taunton, that Monmouth was finally persuaded by a group of his supporters, led by Ferguson, to make himself king. It was thought that this would make the rebellion more respectable and possibly attract some gentlemen to support the cause. The republican opposition to this breach of Monmouth's previous promise not to seek the crown except at the hands of Parliament was brushed aside and two days after his arrival in Taunton Monmouth was proclaimed King of England by a Bristol clothier called Joseph Tiley. Monmouth now proceeded to behave in a suitably regal manner, issuing proclamations, summoning such disrespectful subjects as Christopher, Duke of Albemarle, and John, Lord Churchill, who happened to be in arms against him, touching people for the King's Evil and kindly allowing his adoring subjects to kneel before him to kiss his hands. The women and children loved the show as indeed did most of the men, even if some of the old republicans in Monmouth's army might turn their heads away in disgust. But even they were happy, confident that this was one Stuart king whom they could control with ease. They had good cause to be happy. This was the highest point of their rebellion. All the rebels, whether they were monarchists or republicans, Presbyterians or Baptists, were jubilant at their victory over the combined forces of the militia. After a week in arms they were now convinced that they were real soldiers, able to take on anything that the pretended king in Whitehall or his 'treasonable convention', masquerading as a parliament at Westminster, might send down to the West Country to oppose them.

The initiative lay clearly with the Duke of Monmouth. What would he do now? Churchill expected him to turn back, attack his pitiful forces and then destroy all that remained of the royal opposition in the west. Then he might really be the commander of the army of forty thousand with which London gossip credited him. This is clearly what Churchill would have done in Monmouth's place. But Monmouth was no Churchill. He wasted three days in Taunton in pointless ceremonies, three days in which the royal reinforcements could march fifty miles nearer to the West Country. He discussed the situation with his leading adherents in a council of war, the first that he had held since he landed at Lyme Regis. They decided to maintain the momentum of rebellion by marching on towards Bristol, picking up recruits as they marched. This would have been a good plan if he had set off a bit earlier. Bristol was full of potential rebels and had not yet been reinforced and strengthened by the Duke of Beaufort with his own loyal men from the Welsh Marches. This was done while Monmouth stayed in Taunton. By the time that he set out on the first stage of his march, on Sunday 21 June, Kirke had joined Churchill, and the King had received the reports from Churchill and Albemarle and had acted on them. Six more troops of cavalry and dragoons were riding hard for Bath; two battalions of the First Foot Guards under Monmouth's half-brother, the Duke of Grafton, were already on the second stage of their march to the West Country; a battalion of the Coldstream Guards was setting out the next day and there were more to come, including yet another regiment which had fought under Monmouth's command in France, the famous Royal Scots, at this time known as Dumbarton's Regiment after their colonel. Whatever the cause of Monmouth's delay in Taunton, whether it was vanity, indecision or *raison d'état*, the delay was to prove fatal to the success of his rebellion.

On 21 June, the second Sunday of the rebellion, Churchill attended divine service with his officers in the parish church of Chard where he listened to a sermon preached by the Duke of Albemarle's chaplain on a text from Romans 13. 'And they that resist shall receive to themselves damnation.'[11] The Reverend Robert Ferguson had hoped to preach to the rebels on the same day in the magnificent church of St Mary Magdalen in Taunton and had borrowed the Vicar's gown in readiness. But Monmouth now realized that he had waited too long and the army set out before Ferguson could revel in his hour of glory. Nothing daunted, he preached to the army as it marched towards Bridgwater from the suitably martial chapter twenty of the Book of Deuteronomy. 'Hear, O Israel, ye approach this day unto battle against your enemies: Let not your hearts faint, fear not, and do not tremble, neither be ye terrified because of them; for the Lord your God is he that goeth with you, to fight for you against your enemies, to save you.'[12] The long running battle had started.

Time alone would show whether Ferguson was right and God really did support the rebel cause.

Churchill felt confident in his role as the agent chosen to inflict damnation on his master's enemies. He must have been delighted by Monmouth's delay and by his decision to march towards the place where the two jaws of the royal army could be expected to snap shut, rather than to attack the militia units which still lay undefeated and untested on the flanks and to his rear. He was less delighted with another piece of information which arrived together with the news of the welcome reinforcements from London. He no longer had an independent command. On 18 June the Earl of Sunderland wrote to the Duke of Somerset, Lord Lieutenant of Somerset, to tell him that the King had appointed Lord John Churchill to command his forces in the west. But the next day King James changed his mind and decided that Louis Duras, Earl of Feversham, a naturalized French Huguenot who was in command of the fresh troops sent down from London, should be the commander-in-chief of all the King's forces in the West Country with the rank of lieutenant-general and that the local lords lieutenant as well as Churchill should co-operate with him in that capacity. As some consolation Churchill was promoted to brigadier. Feversham's appointment has often been criticized, though much of such criticism rests on a somewhat anachronistic comparison of the Frenchman's military competence in 1685 with that of Churchill at the peak of his fame as the Duke of Marlborough some twenty years later. King James would have had to have been a remarkable visionary to have foreseen that. Other writers have suggested that Churchill was superseded because he was a West Country man and a former friend of Monmouth's and so was not completely to be trusted, a suggestion which is given further anachronistic support from the fact that Churchill did betray his master, King James, only three years later. The truth is that most regular army officers were former friends of Monmouth, many were West Country men and many were to betray King James in 1688. But the King had no good reason to suspect them now and the truth is probably that the King quite simply thought that Feversham was more suitable than Churchill for the appointment. Feversham, a nephew of King James's hero, the great Marshal Turenne, had as good a military reputation as Churchill in 1685. He was also an older man who had served the King, as Duke of York, even longer than had Churchill. He was also in command of by far the larger of the two parts of the royal army. The possibility that he was also lazy and a glutton, as many critics have maintained, would not have seemed particularly relevant in the circumstances. Nor was the fact that he was born a Frenchman of any great significance. Seventeenth-century armies were normally cosmopolitan. The fact that Louis Duras, Earl of Feversham, should hold a high rank in the army of King James was no more surprising that that King James himself should once have held a high rank in the army of the King of France. Naturally neither Churchill, nor Albemarle, welcomed Feversham's appointment. Both wanted any glory that was going for themselves. Churchill's first reaction was to sulk a bit. 'My Lord Feversham', he wrote on 22 June, 'has sole command here, so that I know nothing but what it is his pleasure to tell me ... I see plainly that the trouble is mine, and that the honour will be another's.'[13] The Duchess of Albemarle expressed her mixed reactions to the news in her delightfully illiterate way. 'I am in som hopes I shall see my deare soon, being the King has noe servis for you and his Magistyes think fiting to put thouses ouver you you have soe long comman[d]ed, which is my Lord Ferfuersham and Churchill, too much beloe you in evuery surkamstance as to exspreuances [experience].'[14] But neither man showed any inclination towards disloyalty. Albemarle waited with the reorganized Devon militia on Monmouth's flank at Wellington. Churchill was much closer. Before he had even heard of the appointment, he had made contact with the rebel army. He was never to lose it.

Churchill's immediate task was to get his dragoons and cavalry troopers to snap at Monmouth's heels as he marched through the rain from Taunton to Bridgwater and then over the Polden and Mendip hills on his way towards Bristol. No man dared straggle from the ranks or go too far in search of food or provender, lest he be picked up by the royal cavalry patrols. 'We were all this day alarmed in the rear, by a party of horse and dragoons,' wrote Nathaniel Wade of the rebel march on 24 June.[15] Such close attention, with little hope of retaliation, played havoc with the nerves of the rebel infantry, already tired and footsore after their long march, and it does not seem to have done much for the confidence of Monmouth himself. Meanwhile, Churchill's patrols could ride as they wished in the surrounding countryside, pillaging the homes of those known to be in the rebel army, bullying those who had stayed at home and preventing any further recruits or supplies from reaching the rebels. Soon they held that part of Somerset in the neighbourhood of the rebel line of march in a blanket of fear. The Quaker John Whiting has left a vivid description of the arrival of one such patrol at the village of Long Sutton. 'And there came the Queen's Guards (as they said) under the Lord Churchill, into the parish, and terror march'd before them (for one could hear their horses grind the ground under their feet, almost a mile before they came).' They then ransacked the house of one Captain Tucker who was out with the rebels, 'cutting and tearing the beds, hangings and furniture to pieces, shaking out the feathers, and carrying away the bedsticks and what else they could, letting out the beer, wine and sider, about the cellar, setting fire to a barn . . .'.[16] Such behaviour might not make the people of Somerset love their lawful king, but it was on the whole sufficient to keep them quiet in their homes and stop them from supplying the rebel army. Later they were to be more positive in their allegiance when they discovered that supplies carried to the royal army would actually be paid for at King James's express command. Monmouth could no longer pay even if he had wanted to, since he had run out of money and there was no more forthcoming unless he could capture Bristol with its overflowing customs house.

The obvious way to stop Churchill's wolf-like attention would have been to destroy the dragoons and horsemen who provided the bite. When Monmouth left Taunton he had three times as many mounted men as Churchill and, even when the latter was reinforced, he had twice his numbers. But in the very first cavalry skirmish of the campaign, in the countryside south-east of Taunton, Monmouth discovered that even his very best troopers were no match for the regulars. Eighty of Churchill's troopers and a similar number of rebels 'charged very bravely' at each other but, although the commander of the royal patrol was killed by a shot in the brain, it was the rebels who ran away, leaving several dead and wounded on the ground. 'These were all in armour, and their carbines and pistolls were all with double barrills.'[17] If they were so well armed they probably had horses to match, but few of Monmouth's troopers were equipped like this. Fewer still would have the nerve and experience to charge straight at a royal patrol of equal strength. A few days later near Langport, a small royalist patrol scattered a rebel patrol of twice its numbers. And so it was to go on. Churchill's men could harry and raid at their will. But they could not stop Monmouth's army marching towards Bristol.

The men who could stop Monmouth and put an end to the rebellion were the regular infantry now marching down the Great West Road. On 22 June when Monmouth marched out of Glastonbury on the road towards Bristol, only twenty-seven miles away by the most direct route, the Foot Guards under the Duke of Grafton were still only marching from Reading to Newbury, with over sixty miles still to go before they reached the western metropolis. Monmouth had plenty of time if he knew how to use it. King James had foreseen this time-lag and had given orders for the bridge over the river Avon at Keynsham, half-way between Bristol and Bath, to be destroyed. It would be almost impossible for the rebels to attack Bristol across the Avon from the Somerset side and they might well lose two days repairing the bridge and crossing to attack the city at its weakest point on the Gloucester-shire side. Even so, the rebels still had time in hand to take the city by assault or to march away from the royal army to Gloucester and so up towards Cheshire, thus escaping the net which was rapidly being drawn around them and opening up a new phase of the rebellion. Fortunately for the royalists Monmouth did not move as fast as he might, nor did he take the most direct route. But it was a close-run thing, much closer in fact than the royal commander-in-chief, the Earl of Feversham, seemed to realize.

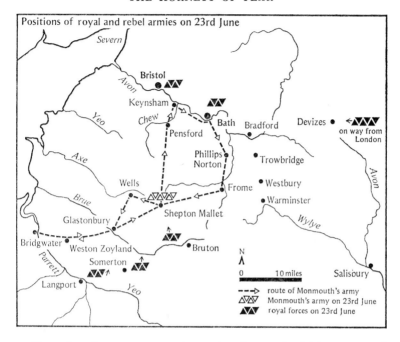

Positions of royal and rebel armies on 23rd June

Feversham's most urgent duty when he received his command was to find out for himself what was going on in the West Country. Riding hard with a mounted escort he reached Bristol in three days and reported back to his master on 23 June in a very confident letter. 'I can assure your Majesty that they have lost the opportunity of seizing anything worth having, if they had ever had it, and I cannot believe that the business can last more than ten days.'[18] Bristol was 'in a great ferment', but the city's defences had been strengthened under the energetic supervision of the Duke of Beaufort. 'We have been upon our guard, being fully satisfyed that their eye was mainly upon this city,' wrote a correspondent of the Bishop of Bristol; 'if the Duke of Beaufort had not been timely sent hither, and assailed himself with all prudence and diligence ever since it had certainly become a cheap and easy prey to them.'[19] The city's garrison was made up of the militia levies of the Welsh Marches and Gloucestershire under the Duke of Beaufort, together with half the remaining Somerset militia, now much heartened by the arrival of regulars. The loyal city of Bath had a garrison made up of the other half of the Somerset militia, which would shortly be reinforced by three troops of regular cavalry and dragoons down from London and a large contingent from the Wiltshire militia under the Earl of Pembroke. Monmouth's army was at Glastonbury and the reports that Feversham received about their equipment made him chuckle at the thought of what would happen when the regular infantry, now at Marlborough, should arrive. Churchill's men were at Langport, eight miles south-west of Monmouth. Churchill's brother Charles, with the artillery from Portsmouth, was close by at Somerton. Further regular cavalry patrols under Colonel Oglethorpe were at Bruton, eight miles to the east of the rebel army. Feversham felt confident that any move that Monmouth might make could easily be covered by his men. All sorts of rumours about the rebels' intended movements were flying around. They were headed against Bristol or against Bath; they were going to go straight through the middle towards Gloucester; they were marching towards London or towards the royal infantry at Marlborough. The fact was that Monmouth was moving into a trap and did not know which way to run. Feversham felt sure that he could defeat him now, with the cavalry alone, but assured his master that he would not attack without the infantry, since it was so near. There was no point in taking any risk.

Monmouth was in fact in Shepton Mallet, nearer Bristol than Glastonbury, when Feversham wrote this letter. The next day he marched to Pensford, 'within five miles of Bristol, where we met with nothing remarkable, but that we perceived a great fire in or near Bristol that night'.[20] It turned out to be a ship burning in the river. The same night Monmouth sent Captain Tiley ahead with a troop of horse to take possession of Keynsham and to repair the bridge over the river Avon. As Tiley moved in a troop of militia horse who were guarding the village rapidly moved out and hurried off to spread the alarm. It seems extraordinary that Feversham had not placed a stronger guard at this key point. A few musketeers or a single gun could have made the repair of the bridge into a very hazardous operation. As it was, Tiley carried out his work without any interruption at all. By dawn the bridge was mended and the whole of the rebel army had crossed over into Gloucestershire before noon. The plan was to carry Bristol by assault that same night. But, since it was raining and there was no shelter on the north side of the river, Monmouth ordered all the army, except for a few cavalry patrols, back across the bridge to Keynsham village where they could rest in comfort and prepare themselves for the most terrifying of military manoeuvres, the storm of a city by night.

The day that Monmouth marched from Shepton Mallet to Pensford, Feversham, in blissful ignorance of how close the enemy was, had ridden from Bristol over to Bath to inspect the defences. At midnight he was informed of the real whereabouts of the rebels by Colonel Oglethorpe, the commander of his scouting patrol. Feversham now acted fast. Within four hours all the cavalry under his command had ridden the thirteen miles back to Bristol and had taken up their station in a meadow near the south gate of the city, where they were to be kept on their guard with constant alarms from Monmouth's cavalry patrols. The scene was set for a battle in the outskirts of Bristol between the rebel army and Feversham's cavalry. Despite the weather the situation must have seemed bright enough to anyone less despondent than Monmouth. Bristol, with its long republican and Dissenting tradition, could be expected to rise in his support and keep the militia garrison fully occupied. The burning ship was said to be the signal that they were ready. Feversham did not have all that many cavalry at Bristol, although both Churchill and Oglethorpe were riding free somewhere south of the Avon. And the royal infantry were still a long way away to the east. Here was Monmouth's great chance for a decisive battle with the odds on his side. But the battle never took place.

Towards evening, when the nerves of the rebels must have been stretched to breaking point at the thought of what the night might bring, two apparently unco-ordinated attacks were made by the royalist cavalry on the rebel camp at Keynsham.[21] From the west came Captain John Parker who had swum the Avon from Bristol with some two hundred and fifty of Feversham's troopers, ridden along the south bank of the river and then charged in on the rebel cavalry. From the south came Colonel Oglethorpe with a hundred men from his scouting patrol. Confused fighting followed in the narrow lanes of the village. Many rebels were killed or wounded before Parker and Oglethorpe retired with the loss of a few men, including three or four of Oglethorpe's troopers who were taken prisoner after being carried away by the rebel horse in the crowd. One of these men, Hatton Wolrich, was later 'condemned to death by Monmouth's pretended Council of War, but fortunately escaped'.[22] These prisoners were able to do their king very good service by convincing the Duke of Monmouth that the King's army, some four thousand strong, was at hand.

The cavalry skirmish at Keynsham on 26 June is hardly one of the greatest events in the history of warfare, involving as it did some three hundred and fifty royalist troopers who rushed into the village, fired off their pistols, slashed around a bit with their swords and then rushed out again. But it sounded the knell of Monmouth's rebellion. Faced with the unconfirmed, and in fact untrue, information that the whole royal army was close by, Monmouth lost his nerve, gave up his attempt on Bristol and even his dinner and sneaked away in the middle of a miserable night along the south bank of the Avon with no other immediate aim than to pick up some probably mythical recruits in Wiltshire. Two days after Feversham wrote his letter to the King, his description of Monmouth as a muddle-headed rambler who did not know which way to turn had come true.

The rebel army marched 'very hard' to Bath, but then drew up before the town and sent forward a trumpeter to summon the garrison of five hundred militia to surrender to their lawful king. However, as Nathaniel Wade tells us, this was 'only in bravado, for we had no expectation of its surrendry'.[23] The town's answer was to shoot the messenger dead on the spot. Monmouth then set off over the hilly country to the south of Bath and camped for the night in the village of Phillips Norton,* 'the foot all in the field', tired, wet and thoroughly fed up after the long day's ignominious retreat from the outskirts of Bristol. There was little rest for the

* Now known as Norton St Phillip.

rebels who were constantly aroused by false alarms that the royal
army was upon them.

The royalists had a slightly more leisurely day. Early in the
morning it was discovered that Monmouth had 'marched away in
the night, it being a miserable rainy night, leaving behind them
some horse and arms, and fifteen pair of boots we found under the
bed in a room they were going to supper in, for we found the
cloth and plates and napkins laid very decently when we came this
morning to the town'.[24] Feversham rode off back to Bath with his
cavalry along the north bank of the Avon and that evening he was
at last able to take command of the greater part of his army, as
Churchill and Kirke arrived from the south-west with the forces
under their command and Grafton led in his guardsmen after
their long march from London. Feversham now had about two
and a half thousand regular troops under his command, about half
Monmouth's numbers. The only forces still missing were the main
artillery train from London escorted by Dumbarton's Regiment
of Scotsmen who were still three days' march away to the east.
Next morning, 27 June, the Earl of Feversham paraded his army
in front of Bath and then set off to find if the Duke of Monmouth
was still at Phillips Norton. 'We shall follow the rogues very
closely at the heels,' wrote one of Oglethorpe's officers, 'and it
will not be long, I hope, before we overtake them to their utter
confusion, for they tell us that his subjects grow very weary of his
reign, and that the last night's business has cruelly frightened
them.'[25]

A night patrol had already been sent ahead to find out what
Monmouth was doing, but Feversham was not satisfied by their
account that they had 'heard the rebbells were in the towne
marching or preparing to march'. He wanted real information,
not hearsay, and the only way to acquire that was to go on
advancing until 'they had been shot att'.[26] Captain Hawley with
forty-five grenadiers were sent forward as an advance party for
this purpose, followed closely by five hundred foot and most of
the cavalry and dragoons under the Duke of Grafton and Colonel
Kirke. Sure enough Hawley's men were 'shot att' and after a while
they may have wished that they had acquired their information

like their predecessors by hearsay. 'Captn. Hawley's men all most all cutt of but 14 left Lord Newburg shot in to the belly but not ded and several horsis killed.'[27] Monmouth's men might be on the run but they had certainly not lost their fighting spirit.

Monmouth had been just about to leave for Frome when the regulars arrived, but he had taken the precaution to leave the approaches to Phillips Norton from Bath well guarded and it was this rearguard under Captain Vincent who gave Hawley such a warm welcome. In this sort of situation the often melancholy and hesitant Monmouth was quick to think and quick to act and many royalist officers noted his active presence in the fighting that followed. Nathaniel Wade with the Red Regiment was brought up on Vincent's right to attack the leading companies of Grafton's infantry who had been following hard on Hawley's heels. 'The regiment being much superior in numbers, we fell with a good part of them into their rear; so that they were surrounded on all hands, save the left flank, by which way, through the hedge, many of them escaped.'[28] Then up came the veteran Colonel Abraham Holmes with the Green Regiment, 'and after about an hour's dispute, having made them retire from hedge to hedge, he gained the furthermost hedge next the field; the King's foot, together with a party of horse that had likewise entered the lane, retiring to the King's army, who were drawn up in the ploughed field about five hundred paces from the hedge'.[29] This party of horse was commanded by Lord Churchill and did a good job of covering the royal vanguard's retreat from what must have been an extremely uncomfortable position. The Duke of Grafton was as uncomfortable as anyone. He had his horse shot under him and was nearly cut off and taken prisoner, only escaping by leaping on a wounded horse, after chivalrously refusing an offer by a sergeant-major of the Blues to give up his own. The royalists scrambled back to safety as best they could but, all the same, Feversham lost many men in the hand-to-hand fighting in the hedgerows and fields to the north of the village. He would have lost a good many more if Monmouth had been able to follow up this classic piece of infantry tactics with a really well co-ordinated cavalry charge. But Monmouth, as we have seen, did not have the cavalry who could be trusted to do this. All he could do was bring up all the rest of his infantry to line the hedges and order two of his cannon, guarded by scythesmen, to cover the lane leading towards the royal army and place the other two on a small hill to the right of the lane. Soon the King's cannon, which had been held up by the steep and muddy roads, were also in a position to support their infantry and the skirmish ended with the gunners of the two armies cannonading each other through six hours of continuous rain, a duel which led to no great loss on either side but which demonstrated that, in artillery as well as cavalry, Feversham was immeasurably stronger than Monmouth. But, in infantry, there was little to choose between the regular guardsmen and the Taunton weavers. A fortnight of rebellion had taught them to fire fairly straight and to obey orders. No one had ever questioned their courage.

Monmouth and his officers were in two minds whether to follow up their success, while their men were in such good heart. The question was finally decided by the withdrawal of the royal army from the field. 'We had no mind to pursue them,' wrote Wade, 'because we had no manner of confidence in our horse.' Feversham, after his initial discomfiture, had deployed his army in a strong enough position, making good use of the hedges and ditches to give cover to his infantry, but decided after consulting his colonels that there was no point sleeping on the ground without tents in the very heavy rain and so retired to Bradford-on-Avon, a place which covered the roads both to Bristol and London and which was only seven miles from Devizes where the main train of artillery, infantry reinforcements and tents for three thousand men were expected the following evening. The royal army rested in Bradford for the whole day following the skirmish at Phillips Norton. They probably needed the break. As Feversham explained in an apologetic and not too confident letter to the King, the men who had marched down from London had had no rest for nine days and had walked straight into a battle, while his cavalry had been on the move virtually the whole time.[30] Old soldiers might be thankful for Feversham's care of their comfort. No one likes sleeping on the ground in the rain without tents and in the immediate presence of the enemy. But the royal army was no longer on the heels of 'the rogues' and they never did 'overtake them to their utter confusion'. Monmouth had regained the initiative by his spirited rearguard action at Phillips Norton. He also had no tents but his men marched on. Two days later Churchill wrote a letter to his wife which summed up the situation. 'We have had abundance of rain, which has very much tired our soldiers, which I think is ill, because it makes us not press the Duke of Monmouth so much as I think he should be, and that it will make me the longer from you, for I suppose until he be routed I shall not have the happiness of being with you, which is most earnestly desired by me.'[31]

Feversham's decision to rest the royal army gave Monmouth a chance to rest his own men who, in the week since they had left Taunton, had spent an exhausting and ultimately dispiriting time trekking up and down over the hills and along the valleys of the Mendips. The rebel army slipped out of Phillips Norton late in the evening after the fight, leaving great fires burning in an attempt to fool the royalist cavalry patrols that they were still there and then marched due south to Frome, 'in a miserable rainy night, up to the knees in dirt, almost to the destruction of our foot'.[32] A militia man, who had never been near the rebel army, reported in a letter to the Earl of Abingdon that 'wee have persued them from place to place that thay are quit tired out, soe that thay are forst to incampe and not move'.[33] Tired they were, but at this moment no one was pursuing them or forcing them to do anything. They were still a formidable undefeated army who seemed to have many options open to them. They could slip past the royal army and head across Wiltshire to Salisbury Plain and so towards London. They could double back and have another go at seizing Bristol. They could stay where they were and tempt Feversham to attack them in a prepared position.

Monmouth did none of these things. He seems to have spent most of his time in Frome in a mixture of sulk, fear and desperation, constantly expecting a knife in his back from someone tempted by the £5,000 reward that had been offered for him dead or alive, quarrelling with his lieutenants, complaining at the bad

faith of the royalist officers who had not deserted to him at
Phillips Norton as he had confidently expected, complaining at
the failure of the country gentlemen to ride into his camp, complaining at the non-appearance of the phantom horsemen from
Wiltshire who were said to be so eager to join him. It was in
Frome, too, that he heard two pieces of extremely bad news, the
complete collapse of Argyll's rebellion in Scotland and the offer
by the King of a free pardon to all rebels who laid down their
arms and returned to their obedience. Many of the haggard men
in the rebel camp might welcome such an offer after the disappointments of the past few days. Monmouth would have accepted it like a shot, had he been included in the King's offer.
What hope was there now? The royal army united, no rising in
London, Argyll defeated, his cavalry not to be trusted, his treasure
chest empty; why, oh why, had he not stayed in Holland with
Henrietta? It was in a mood of such complete despondency that
Monmouth actually considered deserting from his army and
making his way with his officers to some port to escape overseas.
The men could throw themselves on the mercy of the kind King
James. Lord Grey and others dissuaded him from such a base
suggestion, 'and resolutions were taken by him to stick by his
army', but the whole business can have done little to increase the
confidence of the rebels in their broken reed of a leader.[34] In the
end Monmouth stayed too long in Frome to do anything but
retreat back where he had come from, justifying his feeble
strategy by an unconfirmed report from a character called Thomas
Phook that an army of clubmen, ten thousand strong, were
waiting in the marshes below Axbridge, ready to join the Duke if
he should come to them. The fame of the clubmen of West
Somerset, uncommitted peasants who had banded together to
protect themselves from both sides in the Civil War, was a local
legend, but this particular army proved, like the Wiltshire horsemen, to be pure myth. One hundred and sixty men, not ten
thousand, was the total addition to the rebel army from this
source. On the morning of Tuesday, 30 June, Monmouth marched
out of Frome due west on the road to Bridgwater.

Reporters from both the royalist and rebel armies suggest that the decision to move west, and not east, had been forced on Monmouth by Feversham. Monmouth had made no secret of his intention to continue his march towards London, sending messengers ahead to Warminster to prepare his quarters and arrange for food to be ready for the army. The small Wiltshire market town was in a frenzy of excitement, as men searched their hearts to determine where their loyalties lay. They need not have bothered. Monmouth's preparations were far too obvious for Feversham's scouts to miss. Colonel Oglethorpe reported back to headquarters and on Monday, after their day's rest at Bradford-on-Avon, the royal army marched the twelve miles south to Westbury, some four miles north of Warminster, ready to attack the rebel army as it moved out of the enclosed hilly country on to the open plain. This was one battle which Monmouth wanted to avoid. In a country of stone walls and hedges he was a match for the royal army, as had been seen at Phillips Norton. But it took little imagination to see what would happen to his inexperienced infantry when faced by a royalist cavalry charge in open country. Seasoned pikemen in squares could check a cavalry charge but the rebels were not seasoned pikemen and they had very few pikes. One wonders if Monmouth had ever really meant to continue his march to the east. If he had it is difficult to explain his long delay in Frome and the transparency of the advance notice he had given in Warminster. If the plan was a feint it was a good one. On the night of 30 June Monmouth's army slept in Shepton Mallet, 'at free quarters, money being short'.[35] Feversham, having discovered Monmouth's change of direction, slept in Frome. The royal army which had been so close on the rebels' heels at Phillips Norton was now eleven miles away, nearly a full day's march. Monmouth had gained a little more initiative, though how he would use it was anyone's guess.

Feversham, who had been so confident when he first arrived in the West Country, seems to have been shaken a bit by the affair at Phillips Norton. The rebels were rather better soldiers than he had anticipated. He wrote to the King from Westbury early in the morning of 30 June, reporting Monmouth's decision not to move into Wiltshire and his march towards Frome. He would, he said, march straight to Frome and follow the rebels as near as possible. 'If I can ever catch them up I will never leave them again.'[36] But, in fact, he stayed a whole day in Frome and did not resume his pursuit of the rebels till 2 July when he marched to Shepton Mallet, a town which must have been getting a bit fed up with armies camping there for the night. The gap between the two armies had now nearly doubled, despite the fact that Monmouth had gone out of his way to Wells where he had captured some arms, ammunition and money which had been carelessly left there by Colonel Kirke.

The truth was that Feversham had no wish to get too close to the enemy too soon. What would happen if the rebels turned round and decided to fight in a place that suited their particular strengths? 'I do not believe that the enemy could beat us, although we have very little infantry.'[37] This was true enough. Feversham had six battalions of less than two thousand men altogether, of which the sixth, the Royal Scots, had just joined him after escorting the train of artillery. Monmouth might not be able to beat these men, but he could do them much damage in the right circumstances. It seemed much better to let Monmouth march ahead, to deploy the cavalry to make sure that he did not turn off north and head for Bristol again and wait for him to go to ground. 'Why risk honest men when we can assuredly ruin him in another way, and very easily.'[38]

Delay suited Feversham admirably. If the business went on long enough he would get infantry reinforcements. Those from Holland 'would be better than any other.' Meanwhile the rebel army was getting smaller every day, as disillusioned men slipped off in the night to go home or accept the King's pardon. The further the rebels went back into Somerset the nearer most of them were to home and the easier it was to desert. Discipline seemed to be breaking down as well. Reports of pillage and rebels drunk on plundered liquor became more common. The constant search for horses, food and arms took on a more sinister colouring as the hungry rebels became desperate and the country people lost their initial eagerness to help the cause. In Wells the spirit of the Puritans of old had come to the fore as rebels ran riot in the cathedral, damaging the organ and some of the furniture, stabling their horses in the aisles and stripping the lead off the roof to make bullets. 'Which was taken as a prelude,' wrote the Tuscan minister in London when he got the news, 'the beginning of the ruin of Monmouth and the dissolution of his followers.'[39] It was said that Lord Grey had drawn his sword to protect the high altar from desecration by his own troopers. Such behaviour could only split the already divided rebels even more.

At last, on 3 July, as the royal army set up camp in the ancient capital of Somerset at Somerton, Feversham got the information that he had been waiting for. His spies returned from Bridgwater, ten miles away, 'with an account that the rebells were in the towne, and had made a barricade on the bridge, planted 2 pieces of their cannon att the cross, 2 in the castle, and one at the Southgate.'[40] Monmouth had gone to ground. Would he run, would he fight or would he stand a siege? Whatever he did it was desirable that the royal army should be a little closer to him. Feversham rested his troops in Somerton on Saturday, 4 July, and then on Sunday morning marched down to the level moorland and so to Weston Zoyland, some three miles away from Bridgwater across the moor. Here,

my Lord Feversham, after he had viewed the ground, ordered our foot to encamp, behind a convenient ditch that runs from Weston into the moor, which they did in one lyne, leaving room between their tents and the ditch to draw up. On the left of our foot were our canon, fronting the great road that comes from Bridgwater to Weston, and in the village which was covered by our camp, were our horse and dragoons quartered.[41]

Patrols of cavalry and dragoons were posted out in front of the royal infantry, beyond the ditch. Everything seemed quite safe and well ordered and 'we went securely to sleep.'[42]

Five

A Weekend with the Family

'I find by the enimes warant to the constables that they have more mind to gett horses and sadells, then anny thing else which lookes as if he had a mind to break away with his horse to som other place and leave his foot entrenched att Bridgwater.'[1] Lord Churchill's assessment of the rebels' next move does little honour to the Duke of Monmouth. Would he really desert his infantry? Those who had heard him propose to desert his whole army in Frome might not find it difficult to believe. It was certainly a possibility, and the cavalry patrols were instructed to keep their eyes open for any movement by the rebels out of Bridgwater, although it did not seem possible for Monmouth to go far in any direction without fighting. Instructions from King James and Feversham had drawn the net tight and Monmouth's kingdom had now been restricted to the sweep of country bordered by Exmoor to the west and the Blackdown Hills to the south. The militia garrisons had disappeared smartly from this rebel-infested territory at the news of Monmouth's return, but they had not fled very far. They now lay just out of reach like jackals ready for the kill. Soon they were reinforced by their comrades from both north and south. The Duke of Beaufort in Bristol had been ordered on 30 June to 'send out some of your militia horse under good officers to hinder the countrey from sending in provisions to the rebells, to keep more men from joyning with them, and to take up their straglers. This His Majesty would have done without engaging their army, but at such a distance as to be out of danger, and yet so as to give them trouble.' Later, when the news of Monmouth's fortification of Bridgwater reached London, Beaufort was told to send 'some parties as neare that place as may be' and molest the rebels by such 'meanes as you shall think proper'.[2] The Duke of Albemarle had got permission to come out of Exeter, whose defences he had strengthened, 'to put a stop to the rebells' if they should try to make their way into Devonshire. King James's regular forces, it was promised, 'will not be above a day or two at most behind.'[3] Two days could be a long time in war. Could Albemarle even now earn the glory which had eluded him at Axminster? His friends hoped so. Fulke Grosvenor wrote to Albemarle from Somerton, explaining that he did not dare ride over to join him, lest his hasty departure from the royal camp be construed as cowardice, 'a bare shift or pretense to wigle myselfe out of danger'. He wished the Duke good hunting. 'I heartily pray that Perkin* may steare his course towards your Grace, that you may have the greatest share in ye hour of his distruccon', and not those 'who designe it undeservedly for themselves'.[4] Everyone thought that Monmouth must either run or fight. The only question was which way would he run and whom he would fight first, Beaufort's men, Albemarle's men or the royal army.

The one thing that few people believed that Monmouth would really do was to stand a siege in Bridgwater. What future was there in that, now that the King's great guns had joined the royal army? How long would it take for them to burn the town down with red-hot shells or to pound to bits the new fortifications which the local pressed men and the rebel soldiers were hurriedly throwing up with the pick-axes and spades that Dick Goodenough had ordered to be brought into the town on 'His Majesty's' business? Bridgwater was surrounded by a tidal ditch and was difficult to storm, but it had only taken General Fairfax eleven days to force the royalist garrison in the burning town to surrender in the summer of 1645. Would it take the Earl of Feversham any longer? If it did, time was on his side. What were the rebels going to eat if they faced a long siege? Monmouth had ordered the local popula-tion to bring in all the corn, provisions and cattle that could be spared, 'with all speed imajonable'.[5] Feversham had ordered them

* i.e., Monmouth, after Perkin Warbeck, another pretender who had invaded the West Country.

not to do so, 'on pain of death'.[6] Whom were they likely to obey?
Feversham now had cavalry in plenty to enforce his orders, not
only the regular troopers, but militia horsemen, who liked nothing
better than 'threatening and terrifying the poor people in a dreadful manner',[7] and a horde of gentlemen volunteers who, now that
it seemed safe to do so, had ridden down from London to join in
the fun. Meanwhile, still more regular infantry was on its way. On
the night of Saturday, 4 July, the Dutch envoys in London had
seen the three Scots regiments from the Low Countries, those 'old,
good men', march through the town to Hyde Park, their way lit
by flaming torches. Here they were reviewed by the King and
Queen who 'were very pleased to see them pass.'[8] The following
day these eighteen hundred men, the finest troops that the Prince
of Orange had ever seen, were ordered to set out from Hounslow
Heath to reinforce the royal army in the West Country.[9]

It is possible that these last reinforcements boded more harm
than good for the King's cause. The regiments were recruited
from Scotsmen in the Low Countries and the recruiting officers do
not seem to have been too careful whom they took, looking more
for a soldierly bearing than for ideological purity. As a result,
many of the Scots exiles who had fled after the battle of Bothwell
Brigg could be found in the ranks of the three regiments. Such
men, the most fanatical of all King James's subjects, were natural
supporters of their former conqueror, the Duke of Monmouth.
Monmouth was said later to have relied on the mutiny of the
Dutch regiments. They certainly seemed more likely to mutiny
than the Guards, for whose arrival at his camp in the dark of night
he had waited so disconsolately at Phillips Norton. Several of the
Scotsmen were heard to drink the Duke of Monmouth's health
when they were in London.[10] The evidence against most of them
was not sufficient to convict, but three were found guilty at a later
court martial. Two were hanged. The other was whipped standing
with a rope about his neck beneath the gallows in the presence
of all three regiments.[11]

Monmouth could certainly have done with some recruits,
especially recruits who were such seasoned soldiers as these. The
army which marched into Bridgwater on Friday, 3 July was

perceptibly smaller than the army which had marched out on the 21 June. Disappointment, fear and death had taken their toll. Perhaps two hundred men had already died for the good old cause, picked off by patrols of dragoons, cut down in cavalry skirmishes or killed in the one real battle so far, at Phillips Norton. Many had been wounded, such as Robert Sandy, one of the men from Colyton, who had been struck at Norton 'with some heavy cuting instrument on his head at two places; on the hinder parte a piece of his skull was cut off and left hanging by the flesh as bigg as a five shilling piece and ye brayne left naked, only a thin skin to keep it in, on ye foreparte was a large wound out of which I took severall pieces of skull.'[12] The military doctors of the day could patch up the slashes made by sword and pike, as long as they were not too serious, and this man was cured. But there was little hope of recovery for a man at all badly wounded by a dirty musket bullet. There was little hope anyhow for a wounded rebel, unless he fell in the midst of his own men, for the royal surgeons had orders not to treat them. Then there were the prisoners, not very many so far, though those who had been taken were to find that the King's soldiers were not too tender in their methods of interrogation. John and William Slade of Ilminster, father and son, were captured at Wincanton and suspected of being spies. 'Ye soldiers to make them confes burnd their hands to the bone so that the flesh did mortifie and fall a way in pieces.'[13] There would be more of this sort of thing later but, for the moment, such losses paled into insignificance besides the constant drain of desertion.

From the very beginning men who had decided in advance that they would fight for Monmouth and the cause had lost their nerve or recovered their senses. When Monmouth landed at Lyme Regis, one hundred and sixteen men, over a third of the adult male population of the small town, had come forward to enlist in the rebel army. But, within three days, nineteen had changed their minds and refused to march out of the town with the rebels.[14] Other desertions were to follow. John Swayne, a fuller of Lyme Regis, later confessed that he took up arms with Monmouth when he landed and marched as far as Taunton, 'but saith from Taunton he returned home to Lyme again, and hath ever since laid hidden for fear.'[15] William Collins also left the rebel army at Taunton, in order so he said to go and visit his sick grandfather.[16] No doubt many others deserted and have left no record, but their numbers were more than made up by new recruits as Monmouth marched into Somerset. By the time that he arrived at Bridgwater, ten days after his disembarkation, his army was probably at its peak size of some seven thousand men, nearly three times as large as any regular troops which could conceivably have been sent against him in the immediate future. But from then onwards he was to get less recruits and more desertions, particularly after he turned away from Bristol on 26 June. This was the first real sign that the rebel leader might not be the great general he had been taken for and that the rebellion itself might be an ignominious failure. Retreat in the rain is hardly good for morale and the drain of desertions became serious, to become a flood when the news of King James's offer of a free pardon reached the rebel army. No efforts were spared by the rebel leaders to prevent this information leaking through to the rank and file. But to no avail. The proclamation was read out in Frome market place, the day after Monmouth marched out.[17] The rebels must soon have heard of it from the countrymen who still brought provisions to the army. If, by some chance, the officers were still able to keep their men in ignorance, it was not to be for long. The day before the army marched into Bridgwater one of the rebel soldiers, a Taunton blacksmith, brought a copy of the proclamation into the camp. Next day, at roll-call, it was found that a thousand men had slipped off in the night. The blacksmith was caught and condemned to be hanged, but the damage had been done. The army which Monmouth led into Bridgwater was barely five thousand strong, still about twice the size of the royalist army, and no doubt including the most devoted and determined of the rebels, but a dwindling force for all that.

What was Monmouth to do with his dwindling army? He had at one time thought of returning to Taunton, the scene of his greatest triumphs, but a deputation of leading citizens had come to his camp and begged him 'not to go thither, for that a siege would undoe them, they haveing suffered very much already'. The Duke was said to have replied that 'they had done well not to have sent for him so earnestly to come to them from Lime.'[18] The same thing was to happen in Bridgwater. Wade said later that the fortification of Bridgwater was 'only to secure our quarters, and amuse the world, intending nothing less than to stay there'.[19] Maybe this was true, though a local clergyman, the royalist Rector of Chedzoy, Andrew Paschall, heard a rather different story when he came out of hiding and started asking questions a few days later. 'He was about to fortify that place [Bridgwater], and to that purpose summoned in pioneers, but the townsmen disapproving it, he desisted and dismissed the countrymen.'[20] What was Monmouth to do? No one wanted him any more. No one would rise in support of him. The royal army lay to the east. Militia units stiffened with regulars lay to the west, the north and the south. His officers would not let him run away. Monmouth discussed the future with his council of war all Saturday. It was not till Sunday morning, when he received notice of the march of the King's army from Somerton towards Weston Zoyland, that he finally made up his mind. He would start all over again, march from Bridgwater to Keynsham Bridge and then maybe take another look at the defences of Bristol or march to Gloucester and so 'take the formerly intended course into Shropshire and Cheshire.'[21] The waggons were got ready for the move.

There were no very important duties for the rebel soldiers, once the plan to fortify Bridgwater had been abandoned. Much of the weekend was taken up in family reunions which must have had the same sort of poignancy as those fleeting visits home made by men from the trenches in the First World War. Many of the Taunton men walked or rode the eleven miles home to see their families. How many would ever see them again? Some of the veterans might not mind too much, happy to die nobly now in a good cause rather than live out a miserable old age in receipt of charity or poor relief. They could kiss their wives and daughters, shake hands with their old friends and march proudly back to the rebel camp. Other rebels were the sort of men who could take life as it came, win or lose, like John Littlejohn, still unmarried at the age of thirty and the only one of seven brothers to go out with Monmouth. A few drinks, a laugh and a wave and back he went to death or glory. Others might find the life of a soldier preferable to a crowded home, like the locksmith Thomas Jennings, the father of six children under the age of nine who returned home to find his wife pregnant with the seventh. But most of the men had much to live for, new-born babies to bring up like John Poyntington and Thomas Rowe, new wives to enjoy like Robert Verrier, William Ash and Moses Hutchins, all of whom had got married just before the rebellion.[22] How could they bear to go back to the camp? How appalling must have been the temptation to stay at home and hide until the whole beastly business was over. But, despite these temptations, there is little evidence of desertion during this last weekend of the rebellion. Most of those who were going to desert had already done so and the men who were left were the diehards who were more afraid of deserting their friends and the cause than of death itself.

Many men did not have to go home to see their families. Bridgwater was packed with women and children who had come to see their loved ones one more time. 'Some observed that there were, as they judged, a thousand women came into Bridgwater before the fight to take their leave of their husbands and other relations in the rebellion, who were thought not to have added, however zealous for the cause, to their courage.'[23] But there were no families to say goodbye to the men of Devon and Dorset or of those parts of Somerset beyond the lines of the militia and the royal army.

These men found plenty to do that last weekend. There were arms to fix, some of them never much good but much worse now after so many days marching through the rain. There were drills to perform, one last chance to learn just how to stop a royalist cavalry charge with a pike. 'Pikemen take heed. Advance your pikes. To the front, charge.' There were sermons to be heard as the many preachers in the rebel army found one more Old Testament text to justify the good old cause of God and religion and to bolster up the courage of the men who were to fight for it. There were drinks to be drunk and good stories to listen to, as the old soldiers boasted once again of their former exploits with Fairfax, Lambert and Cromwell. There were sights to be seen, some not very encouraging, such as the ease with which Captain Coy of the

Royal Dragoons cut his way through a stronger party of rebel horse who had tried to intercept him; some rather more fun like the demonstration by an inhabitant of Bridgwater of a machine, 'which could discharge many barrels of musquets at once'.[24] Then there was the never-ending task of searching for food, drink, arms and horses. Parties of rebels went through the surrounding villages like locusts, but they found very little. They had eaten or taken nearly everything already. The house of William Clarke of Sandford, near Bridgwater, 'was seaven times in a day search'd by the rebells, and at last by them plundered of all. The edimenta and bibamenta, sadles, bridles and armes went at first, but at length Dick Goodenough would have made mee a usurer against my will, and most uniustly threatned to plunder mee of all I had left if I would not lend his king £200 but ... I had not the money nor could not borrow, soe the paymaster left mee in great ffury.'[25] All in all, it was quite a busy weekend.

When the Taunton men returned to Bridgwater, sad but still determined after their visit home, they were soon made aware of a new spirit of excitement in the rebel camp. The news that was passing round was enough to excite any man. Monmouth was going to fight. At three o'clock a spy, a farm labourer called Godfrey, had come into the rebel camp with a full description of the dispositions of the royal army at Weston Zoyland. This was mere routine, but Godfrey had further news. The regulars had taken little trouble in preparing their defences, confident that the rebel army was now done for. In particular their fearsome array of guns was separated from the army and could give it no support. This was interesting. Even more so was the information that Godfrey knew a roundabout route to the royal camp which would avoid both their cannon and their outposts and enable the rebels to make a surprise attack on their unguarded flank.

Monmouth was all ready to leave for the north when he received this news. His army was drawn up in a meadow outside the town, ready to begin the march to Keynsham Bridge as soon as it should get dark. But Godfrey's information changed all that. Here surely was one last chance to turn his miserable rebellion into an overwhelming success. He climbed the tower of St Mary's, Bridgwater, and surveyed the royal camp through a 'perspective glass' to check Godfrey's information. He knew the ground that lay before him well. He had marched along the road from Bridgwater to Weston Zoyland twice and for the last two days his men had roamed the moorland to his front, searching the villages for arms and supplies and rounding up the few remaining cattle that were pastured there. There, on his right, was the great road from Bridgwater to Weston Zoyland and there, sited astride it, was the royal artillery, on the extreme right of the royalist position. A long way to the left of the guns, in front and to the left of the village of Weston Zoyland, was the royal infantry. He could even recognize one of the regiments stationed on the extreme left of the royal line. He could hardly forget them, for they were Dumbarton's Regiment whom he had once commanded. These were the men whom the rebels, marching in by Godfrey's roundabout route from far to the left of the royal army, would encounter first. Monmouth was worried. 'I know these men will fight,' he muttered to his aides. 'If I had them, I would not doubt of success.'[26] All the same, it looked as though Godfrey's information was correct.

How much Monmouth could really see from the tower of St Mary's is difficult to say. The view is now obstructed. But a historian can use a little licence to fill in some of the details. The village of Weston Zoyland was protected on the west and north by a wide ditch called the Bussex Rhine which curled round in front of the royal position, about half a mile in front of the village itself. The ditch held more water than usual, since it had been a wet summer, but it was not impassable, either for horse or foot. It is often said that Monmouth was unaware of the existence of the Bussex Rhine, but this seems extremely unlikely in view of the amount of time that he had spent in the neighbourhood. Feversham's six infantry battalions had set up their tents on the sloping ground about 'a hundred yards behind the ditch', giving plenty of room for them to deploy if they were attacked by the rebels. Dumbarton's Regiment of Scotsmen under Colonel Douglas was on the far right of the royal army, the left to Monmouth as he looked at them from Bridgwater church. Then came the three

battalions of guardsmen, one of Coldstreamers commanded by
Colonel Sackville and two regiments of what are now known as
the Grenadier Guards, under the command of the Duke of
Grafton. On the royal left were the two Tangier regiments, the
five companies of Trelawney's commanded by Colonel Charles
Churchill and on the extreme left of the infantry the five companies
of the Queen's commanded by Colonel Percy Kirke. There was
then a five hundred yard gap between Kirke's men and the royal
guns pointed down the Bridgwater road, providing adequate
defence against any attack from that direction but giving no
support to the royal infantry whatsoever. It was obvious that
Feversham did not expect an attack by the demoralized rebels and
was reluctant to move the guns on to the soft ground of the moor.
The royal cavalry and dragoons were all billeted in the village
itself, resting after 'their perpetual marching'. Feversham had no
reserves, except fifteen hundred men of the Wiltshire militia, who
were billeted in the villages of Middlezoy and Othery, two or
three miles away to the south-east. These were the only militia
whom Feversham was prepared to trust anywhere close to him.
All the rest, except for one very fine regiment of Oxfordshire
horse, had either been sent home or had been posted to places
where they could do no possible harm to the royal army in the
event of mutiny or desertion.

Feversham agreed with Churchill that Monmouth would
probably make a move to the north, an assessment which seemed
to be confirmed when Monmouth moved his army out of Bridgwater on the Sunday afternoon. He had therefore sent Colonel
Oglethorpe with a party of horse to check on any movement on
either of the two roads leading north, one to Bath and the other to
Bristol. Another patrol of a hundred horse and fifty dragoons,
under Sir Francis Compton, was out on the moor directly in front
of the royal position. They had advanced guards and sentries
before them to give notice if anything came that way. Finally there
was an infantry guard out ahead of the guns on the main road to
Bridgwater, who could call for help if necessary from fifty men
who had been sent to occupy a sheepfold quite near the road.

Monmouth could not of course see all this but, as an experienced

The late D. of M & other Rebells
taking shipping for Holland.

The Late D of M entring
Lime with 1500 Men

Rebells Marching out
of Lime

FEAR NOTHING BUT GOD

The late D of M.s
Standard

Contemporary playing cards produced to celebrate the defeat of the
rebellions of Monmouth and Argyll

IV ♠

Severall Officers by Command
of y.^e King going into y.^e West

IX ♦

the Late D: of M: writing
a letter to y.^e D of Albermarl

VII ♣

The D. of Grafton &c: fighting their
way through severall of y.^e Rebells horse
in y.^e lane leading to Phillips Norton

IV ♥

The Battaile att Bridgwater

QUEEN ♣

The Defeat of the Rebells
2000 Slayn & their Canon taken

V ♦

Severall of ẙ Rebells hang'd
upon a Tree

VII ♦

the Lᵈ. Gray taken in Disgvise

KING ♣

Goodenough Coll Holmes
&c: under Examination

Bonfires made the 26 of July att night being the thanksgiving for the Victory 1685

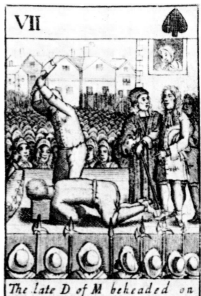

The late D of M beheaded on Tower Hill 15 july 1685

Severall Rebells tryed in the West.

Major Holmes and 2 other Rebells Hanged in Chaines

ABOVE James, Duke of Monmouth

LEFT James II

RIGHT John, Lord Churchill, the future Duke of Marlborough, originally the commander of the King's forces sent to combat Monmouth's rebellion but later superseded in command by the Earl of Feversham

LEFT Judge Jeffreys
RIGHT Bevil Skelton, the Envoy Extraordinary at the Hague who failed to prevent the planning of Monmouth's rebellion and the departure of the rebels
BELOW A present-day view from the Polden Hills across Sedgemoor

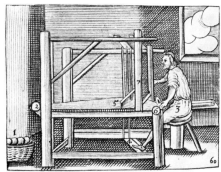

Contemporary illustrations of craftsmen – the shoemaker, the tailor, the blacksmith and the weaver – giving some idea of the costume and appearance of the sort of man who made up the ranks of Monmouth's army

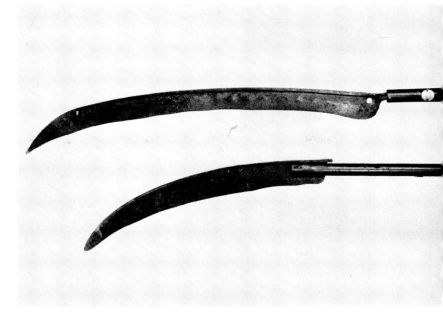

A selection of weapons, most of them recovered from the battlefield at Sedgemoor

soldier, he should have been able to guess where Feversham would place his guards and patrols. If they were wide awake they could hardly fail to hear his proposed night march. He would have to depend on luck and on the royalists' over-confidence if he was going to be able to give Feversham a real surprise. It seemed worth the risk. Anything must have seemed better than marching off to Keynsham Bridge once again. After this inspection, 'he called the field officers together, and demanded of them if they thought it was advisable to fight, if we could surprise them in the night? They all agreed it was, provided the foot did not entrench. Upon which he sent back the spy that brought him the account to see if they entrenched or not, who brought answer that they did not.'[27] This was enough. When he attacked, the royal army would be asleep, possibly drunk, in their tents with no entrenchments to protect them. With any luck at all he was poised to inflict one of the greatest upsets in English military history. The rebel army would march at eleven o'clock that evening.

Rebel security was feeble in the extreme. The news that Monmouth was to fight was soon known in the villages for miles around. A brother clergyman later told Paschall that a man had come to his village, fifteen miles away from Bridgwater, on that Sunday afternoon just as the villagers were coming out of church. 'Neighbours,' he cried, 'the Duke of Monmouth desires you all to hasten in to helpe him, for he hath gotten the Kings Army in a pound at Weston, and is afraid they will gett away from him if you come not speedily to his assistance.'[28] If the news had really spread this far it is a miracle that Feversham had not heard it. His men must have been extremely careless. Feversham himself had a good supper, but he did not forget his duty. He was out on the moor with Compton's patrol till well past midnight, listening for any sound from the rebels and waiting to hear if there was any news from Oglethorpe. It was a very still night, but he did not hear a thing, not even the march of five thousand men. He returned to the village and went to bed, thankfully handing over all immediate responsibilities to the General Officer of the Day, Lord Churchill, who assumed effective command of the army while Feversham slept.

Six

Trial by Battle

'In truth God was not theirs, as they had boasted, nor did then stand neuter.'[1] The Reverend Andrew Paschall was not alone in seeing the battle of Sedgemoor as a remarkable manifestation of God's judgement on the good old cause. For such men Sedgemoor was a trial by battle, the final trial of a view of God and the world which had disturbed the placid life of Englishmen for over forty years. Some might seek to explain the extraordinary events of the morning of 6 July in terms of human error and human weakness. But most men knew that such human agents were but pawns who played out a drama designed by providence. And what a drama! The rebels had come so close to destroying the royal army as they lay asleep in their beds.

We who now try to understand the events of that fateful morning are handicapped by the normal problems of the late-comer, forced to rely on the confused accounts of several men, each of whom could know only part of the whole story. Many of these accounts are themselves second-hand, the memories of survivors taken down by inquisitive local worthies who were themselves not present at the battle. What any single man could know was in any case very little, since most of the events were shrouded in a double darkness, the darkness of night compounded by the heavy ground mist so common in the low-lying moorland where the battle took place. But even if all our witnesses knew exactly what they did and where they did it and if all their accounts tallied with each other to make a comprehensible and logical whole, we today would still have a serious problem in visualizing the drama. For many of the most vital landmarks which delineated its various stages are no longer there. Sedgemoor

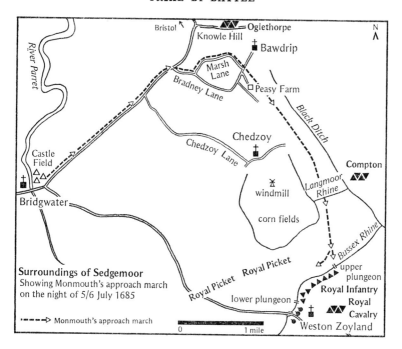

Surroundings of Sedgemoor
Showing Monmouth's approach march
on the night of 5/6 July 1685

••---▷ Monmouth's approach march

0   1 mile

is still a low-lying flat green expanse of land, but it is no longer the
Sedgemoor of 1685. Gone is the Bussex Rhine which half-
encircled the royal encampment. Gone are the Langmoor Rhine
and the Langmoor Stone which marked its easiest crossing-place.
Gone are the windmills, the cornfields, the sheep-pounds, the
lanes and tracks which played their part in the events of that
exciting night. Time, generations of farmers and above all the
civil engineers who built the great King's Sedgemoor Drain a
century after the battle have altered the local scenery beyond
recognition and force us to use our imaginations to the full. Not
everything has vanished. Weston Zoyland still stands where it
did on its thirty-foot eminence above the moor. Chedzoy is still
there, two miles to the north-west with Knowle Hill rising steeply
two miles beyond. And down on the moor, close to where the
Bussex Rhine is thought to have lain, there is a monument to
record the place where so many brave men died nearly three
hundred years ago.

Just a year after the battle King James II paid a visit to the West Country to see for himself the places 'which ye rebellion had signalized'.[2] He came down the road from Bristol to Bridgwater and made a halt on Knowle Hill where one of his companions, Nathaniel Wade, late commander of the Red Regiment in Monmouth's army, was able to give his master a detailed account of what had taken place on the ground that lay beneath him. Knowle Hill is the last outcrop of the Poldens, the line of low wooded hills that form the northern border of the great stretch of flat land known as Sedgemoor. The view from the hill is excellent and King James's advisers chose well. If one crosses the fields below the summit to where the hill descends rapidly towards the Bridgwater-Glastonbury road one gets a superb panorama of the whole battlefield and of the approach that Monmouth took to get to it. Right down below you is the village of Bawdrip with its church tower surrounded by leafy trees. About four to five miles south-south-east is the high and easily recognized tower of Weston Zoyland church on a slight rise that comes out of the flat, green moorland intersected by drainage ditches and now cut right through from north-west to south-east by the King's Sedgemoor Drain. Just beyond the Drain, about half a mile from Bawdrip church, is Peasy Farm, on Monmouth's route from Bridgwater to the battlefield. One mile beyond the farm is the short, square tower of the church of Chedzoy village, which Monmouth had to circle if he was to achieve complete surprise, and beyond the village the cornfields which yielded such a bloody crop in 1685. Finally, right in front of Weston Zoyland, just under four miles from Knowle Hill, is the actual battlefield. In King James's day he would have been able to see the famous Bussex Rhine and with his perspective glass be able to pick out, with Wade's guidance, a number of features now vanished, such as the upper and lower plungeons, the two points in the Bussex Rhine with a hard bottom which made a suitable crossing-place for horsemen. We can imagine the tall, bewigged King nodding as Wade pointed out the various features, before making his way down the hill to have a closer look for himself. We can also imagine the horsemen of Oglethorpe's patrol who stood in the same place on the night of the 5/6 July 1685 and saw nothing at all, but the moonlit night above them and a sea of mist below.

While the royalist army prepared for bed and Oglethorpe's scouts idled the evening away, Monmouth's camp in the Castle Field outside Bridgwater was the scene of excited bustle and preparation for the night ahead. There was much that had to be done in the few hours between Monmouth's final decision to fight and the beginning of his march. Muskets must be checked and powder and ball distributed. Swords, scythes and sickles needed a final sharpening. Equipment must be darkened and muffled, lest a sudden jangle or the glitter of a blade lose for the rebels the vital element of surprise. The greatest danger was likely to come from the unschooled horses of the rebel cavalry, horses who had never even been trained to stand steady at the noise of musket fire, because of the rebels' shortage of powder, let alone to walk silently towards an enemy at dead of night. Fortunately the way that lay ahead was soft, with few stones to clatter under the horses' hooves. With a bit of luck the occasional neigh might be taken for an isolated horseman from a royalist patrol. Nevertheless it seems astonishing that Monmouth should have hazarded his whole enterprise by taking his ill-starred cavalry on a night attack.

Time was found in the rush of preparation to see to the spiritual and material welfare of the soldiers who were so soon to set out on their five or six mile night march to submit their cause to trial. The men were summoned in the evening for a drumhead service where Ferguson preached once more and 'the officers went to prayers for a blessing on their undertaking, some of them praying in red coats and jackboots, a sight which had not been seen in England since the Restoration'.[3] But there were many who needed more than Ferguson to bolster up their courage. Such men could be satisfied from the copious stocks of plundered liquor in the town, so that 'many came forth half drunk. But the valour which this gave them might easily evaporate in the time they spent in the march in so long a way and such narrow lanes.'[4]

At last, at about eleven o'clock, the rebel army marched out along the Bristol road, urged on by the sight of their outwardly confident leader who rode up and down the column 'animating his men with great zeal', and attended by many well-wishers from Bridgwater to speed them on their way. One can hardly believe that this farewell was conducted in mime, but the royalist cavalry scouts on Knowle Hill, only just over two miles ahead on the same road, heard nothing at all. No patrol was sent down the road to check that the rebels had not set out on their half-expected night march to Keynsham until well after one o'clock, two hours after the rebels had started their march and long after they had left the main road.

The departure from Bridgwater may have been a trifle noisy, as men shook hands and waved goodbye to their friends, but a very strict silence was preserved thereafter. Orders were given that 'what man soever that made a noise should be knocked in the head by the next man'.[5] Such orders were obeyed. The five thousand men marched along the Bristol road in two columns, one of cavalry and one of infantry, with no noise at all, past the lane leading to the loyal village of Chedzoy and then turned off to the right into Bradney Lane, less than a mile from the watchers on Knowle Hill. Here they halted to receive their final orders.

Five hundred cavalry led by Lord Grey were now to go ahead of the remainder of the army. Guided by the spy Godfrey, they were to cross the upper plungeon of the Bussex Rhine, which lay some way nearer to the rebel approach than the nearest royalist infantry regiment, and so 'silently get behind the camp, seize the officers in their beds, as also the 18 guns and 160 wagons standing all together and, if occasion were, turn the guns, as they might have done easily, upon the King's Camp and thus give them a terrible alarm on that side'.[6] While the cavalry were causing confusion, the rest of the army led by the three guns escorted by Wade's Red Regiment were to follow and form up in a line along the Bussex Rhine itself, ready to fire into the royal camp and then 'run over the ditch'[7] to 'finish what the horse had begun'.[8] The orders are a little complicated for an unreconnoitred night attack, in which few of the participants had very detailed knowledge of the local geography, but they are clear enough orders and none of the three accounts which mentions them, one by Wade and two based on interviews with members of the rebel army,[9] give the reader any reason to suppose that Monmouth and his officers did not know of the existence of the Bussex Rhine.

When Monmouth had given his final whispered orders, his officers re-joined their regiments and the army set off down Bradney Lane. After only a few hundred yards they struck off to the north into Marsh Lane to avoid going too near to a loyal man's house which lay on the most direct route. Marsh Lane led them very close indeed to the foot of Knowle Hill where Oglethorpe's scouts should have been listening and watching, but still nothing was heard of the tramp of four thousand men and the march of five hundred horses. The lane swung round to the east after half a mile and so past Peasy Farm into the north part of the moor. The rebels had now marched over three miles in complete silence and had two more miles to go across the moor, across the Langmoor Rhine, the first of the two parallel ditches which drained the land in front of Weston Zoyland, and so across the Bussex Rhine into the sleeping royalist camp. As the rebels marched south-east and then south from Peasy Farm they moved away from the supine horsemen of Oglethorpe's patrol into the region watched on the one hand by one hundred horse and fifty dragoons under the command of Sir Francis Compton and on the other by the eight men of the village watch of supposedly loyal Chedzoy. Just how loyal these Chedzoy men were is not too clear. Two men, sympathizers with the rebel cause, had seen Monmouth's army as it made its way into Bradney Lane. They walked directly over to Chedzoy and told the watchmen the exciting news that Monmouth was marching and that there was going to be a fight. They then rushed off to the windmill that stood in the cornfields on the Weston Zoyland side of Chedzoy to get themselves a grandstand seat. They must have had a good view, once the mist disappeared and the rising sun threw its light on the final scene of the drama. But the Chedzoy watchmen, 'whether thinking it might be too late for them to go with safety to give notice to the camp; or from country dullness and slowness, did not, as they might and ought to have done, inform the Royal Army of the extreme danger in which it then was'.[10] Monmouth's army marched safely and silently on.

Andrew Paschall, the Rector of Chedzoy, who recorded this cautious behaviour by his parishioners, knew the lanes and paths by which Monmouth approached the royal camp as well as any man. They were, he tells us, narrow and incommodious, as one would expect of lanes whose only function was to serve isolated farmsteads. They were also probably hedged or raised on causeways above the moor, so forcing the rebel officers to keep to them or lose their way in the dark and mist. This prompts one to wonder just how long Monmouth's column was. We do not have much information. Did the infantry march at the close order, one and a half feet apart, or at the order, a yard apart? Could they march three or more abreast or only two? Close order would make sense in that it would be less likely for each man to lose sight of the man in front in the dense mist. But it would also mean that the men were very close bunched up and thus likely to tread on each other's heels and make a noise. If we assume that the rebels marched at the close order and three abreast, the four thousand men of Monmouth's infantry would have been strung out along nearly half a mile of track. If we assume, as seems more likely in such narrow lanes, that they marched at the order and only two abreast, the column would have been well over a mile long with the rearmost men barely off the Bristol road before the leaders were passing Peasy Farm, and this was just the infantry. The five hundred cavalry were much farther along the route. The soldiers were hardly likely to march faster than two miles an hour under the conditions of a silent night march, so Wade and the vanguard Red Regiment must have been separated from Foulkes with the rearguard White Regiment by more than half an hour. Whatever the actual figures we must imagine Monmouth's army as it made its way towards the royal camp as a long, long column of frightened men, each man peering anxiously through the mist trying to keep touch with the man ahead and the man behind, wondering and worrying about what was happening up ahead of him and able to communicate with each other only by nudges and whispers which as they passed down the column would rapidly become incomprehensible. It was a world of shadows where trees and bushes could be mistaken for men and where the slightest

noise in the darkness beyond the column could arouse an in-
fectious panic down the line. By the time that the rebels moved on
to the moor, the liquor which had stirred them three hours or so
before must surely have lost its effect and even Ferguson's sermon
must have been little more than a dim memory. All that remained
was the sight of the back of the man in front, the muffled trudge of
feet on the soft dirt of the track, the sense of righteousness in the
heart and the twinge of fear in the stomach.

Once we appreciate the length of Monmouth's column it is
clear just how incompetent the royalist patrols must have been.
How could one hundred and fifty horsemen miss a column of men
a mile long marching along well-worn tracks? The answer, of
course, was that they were no longer looking, having long ago
decided that Monmouth would not move that night and having
no desire to patrol across the moorland in the dense mist. Sir
Francis Compton had even withdrawn 'that most necessary guard
at Langmoor Stone and the sentinels that stood near it, before
bedtime'.[11] In fact, this piece of information collected by Paschall
is not quite true. There was one sentry left near this vital crossing-
place, but the general impression of carelessness is quite correct.
The way to the royal camp lay open. In the camp itself all was
silent, save for the occasional snore or the neigh of a horse in the
village. But a few precautions had been taken. Feversham had
ordered all the cavalry horses tethered in the village to be ready
saddled and bridled. And out in front of the village, where the
royal infantry lay 'at rest in the tents, the muskets and pikes
standing up against them',[12] there were some men who expected
an attack that night. Fortunately for Feversham these were mainly
officers of Dumbarton's Regiment, the regiment that Monmouth's
men would first reach. In particular, Captain Macintosh 'believed
overnight and would have ventured wagers on it that the Duke
would come. He, in that persuasion, marked out the ground
between the tents and the ditch where his men would stand in
case of an attack; and gave directions that all should be in readiness; and it was well he did so.'[13]

Captain Macintosh might be sleeping with a clear conscience,
but his readiness could do nothing to check the progress of

Monmouth and the rebel army. Nor could anybody else as far as could be seen. No alarm was raised; no problems were met until the leading horsemen of Grey's cavalry reached the black and muddy waters of the Langmoor Rhine about a mile from the royal camp. So far God was theirs, 'as they had boasted'. But here they were to encounter their first setback. The guide could not find the great Langmoor Stone which marked the crossing-place. He paced up and down the ditch in the darkness, while the horsemen waited restless but silent, ready now to move forward into the last lap.

Then, suddenly, the silence was shattered by a single shot. Some say it was fired by Captain Hucker, a Taunton clothier who commanded a rebel troop of horse. Some say he fired on purpose to warn the royal camp. Other men said that the shot was fired by a royalist trooper who saw the rebel horsemen as he peered through the gloom across the ditch. Whoever had fired the shot the alarm had been given and total surprise was lost. Compton's trooper galloped from the Langmoor Stone back to the royal camp and, riding up and down the infantry lines, cried out 'with all imaginable earnestness, twenty times at least, "Beat your drums, the enemy is come. For the Lord's sake, beat your drums." '14

The drummers awoke, raced barefoot out of the tents and beat to arms. Tousle-haired, their heads thick from the cider of the night before, the regular infantry poured out into the still dark misty night at the drummers' call. They grabbed their weapons where they stood beside the tents and then drew up in the space between their tents and the Bussex Rhine, pulling on their clothes and fixing their arms as they ran. It took only a few minutes from the first beat of the drums for the royal infantry to be ready for a rebel attack. And most of the regiments were unprepared. Dumbarton's were in position even quicker.

Long before Lord Grey could have heard the ominous sound of the royal drums his guide had found the crossing-place and his troopers were filing across the Langmoor Rhine. They now rode hard for the upper plungeon across the Bussex Rhine a mile away, only minutes behind the royal trooper who raised the alarm and still with plenty of time to cause complete chaos in the royal camp. Their path was barred by Sir Francis Compton and his guard of one hundred and fifty mounted men, a small enough obstacle for five hundred horsemen keyed up for a fight. Grey's vanguard charged, fired off their carbines and wounded the royal commander in the breast. But once again it was proved that rebel cavalry were no match for the regulars. At the first reply to their fire the rebels wheeled round and galloped back to Grey and the main body of their cavalry. Captain Sandys quickly took over command from the wounded Compton, counter-charged and, despite his small numbers, threw the rebel horsemen into confusion. He then pulled back behind the Bussex Rhine to take up his position guarding the upper plungeon on the right of Dumbarton's Regiment, who by now stood to arms. Only one troop of rebel horse, under the command of a cabinet-maker and veteran of Cromwell's Ironsides, Captain John Jones, stayed to fight for the vital crossing-place. Jones's charge against Sandys's three troops of regular cavalry earned the admiration of royalist and rebel alike. 'He played his part with so much valour that for the same he was thought not unworthy of a pardon from the General.'[15] But even Jones could not fight his way through alone and the easy way for the rebel horse into the royal camp was now secured.

But all was not yet lost. Grey managed to pull most of the rest of his cavalry together and, now without a guide, rode on eagerly towards the ditch, seeking another way over the wide and miry gulf which was all that lay between him and the royal army. The royalist dragoons were later to ford the ditch with ease, but how was the unguided Grey to know the passage was so simple? Past Dumbarton's Regiment he rode, successfully countering their challenge with the cry that his men were cavalry from the Duke of Albemarle. Then, as he rode past the Guards, he was discovered and Captain Berkeley, who commanded the right wing of the first battalion, ordered his men to fire a volley into the ranks of horsemen who now, as the mist rose, could be dimly seen across the ditch. The other companies of guardsmen followed Berkeley's lead and volley after volley of musket balls crashed into the flanks of the unschooled rebel horses. There was now no holding the terrified horses. The most skilful horseman in the world would not have been able to get such horses to face another second of such terror and the rebel cavalry vanished from the field to play no further part in the battle. Some ran one way, some another, some straight back into the ranks of the rebel infantry who were even now marching on to the field, but none went anywhere near the lower plungeon, and the royal camp and guns were safe.

When Monmouth, who was marching on foot alongside his leading regiment, heard the single shot followed shortly by the beat of the royal drums, he urged Wade to double his pace and get his men on to the field before all should be lost and the royal infantry ready to receive them. Wade covered the last mile from the Langmoor Stone very fast, his march guided by the glow of the slow matches of Dumbarton's Regiment, the only regiment in the royal army still equipped with the outdated matchlocks. Not far behind Wade were the three rebel guns, followed shortly by Matthews's and Holmes's regiments who were second and third in the rebel column. A great gap then opened up between these three leading regiments and the rest of the rebel infantry who were still toiling across the moor and were now totally confused by the crescendo of noise that they could hear ahead of them. The men at the back never arrived in time for the battle and some were still marching forward when the vanguard regiments had been routed and chased from the field.

Wade's men were in some confusion as they came up to the Bussex Rhine, after their rapid march, and some forty yards from the ditch he halted them and put his regiment in order for the assault. Wade thought that he was now opposite the two Tangier regiments on the left of the royal line, leaving plenty of room for the rest of the rebel infantry to form up on his left as they came up, so that they could storm the whole of the royal camp across the ditch. He had in fact not advanced nearly so far and his regiment stood opposite the two battalions on the royal right, Dumbarton's and the first battalion of the Guards. Not that this need have mattered very much. His men, who had behaved so admirably throughout the campaign, seemed ready now to summon up their final strength, to race down to the ditch, through the mud and then up the other side to fall on the waiting Scots and guardsmen with sickle, scythe and pike. One minute of terror lay before them as they ploughed through the mud into the face of the royalist volleys but then, that minute over, what hope had the royalists got against such numbers and such courage?

Wade was just about to give the order to charge when Matthews's men came up on his left and immediately began to fire at some distance across the ditch. The impetus for the assault vanished in a moment. Wade's regiment could not advance into the fire of their own comrades and a moment's reflection deprived his men of the will to storm across a ditch of unknown depth and devilish-looking blackness. They opened fire across the ditch in their turn and nothing that Wade, Monmouth or anyone else could do could recapture that moment when they had so nearly made their assault, an example which would surely have been followed by the other regiments in their turn. Like stalled horses they refused to move either forward or back, but stood where they were, shouting abuse and firing their muskets towards the two royal battalions who lay so near before them. Holmes's regiment came up on the left of Wade and Matthews and they fired too, but 'their men being new, shot too high'[16] and their musketeers did little damage as they wasted their ammunition and dawn drew nigh. The same could not be said of the three rebel guns which were brought up opposite Dumbarton's Regiment and, under the expert eye of Monmouth's Dutch gunner, caused practically all of the casualties suffered by the royal army.

It is difficult to be sure of the length of this phase of the battle in which the rebel musketeers fired across the ditch, while the royalists for the most part lay still, not returning their fire, preserving their ammunition and waiting for the light. Some accounts say half an hour. Wade himself said that his regiment stood for an hour and a half before the rebel regiments on his left were broken and he led his own heroic Red Regiment from their exposed position. Wade's estimate seems more likely, since quite a few preparations had to be made before Feversham and Churchill were ready to move forward for the kill.

The most urgent need was to bring up some of the royal

artillery to counter the rebel guns which were causing such heavy casualties in Dumbarton's Regiment. Now, in the darkness, it could be appreciated just how careless it had been to leave the royal guns so far from the main position. Time was wasted finding horses to drag them into the firing line, time during which a few more Scotsmen were killed. Help was to come from an unexpected source. Sleeping in Weston Zoyland was the Bishop of Winchester, an old soldier who delighted in the nickname of 'Old Patch', who had come down in his coach to watch the destruction of his rebellious tenants from the manor of Taunton Deane and maybe to offer some advice from his store of military knowledge. Now, in the emergency, he sprang into action, harnessing his own carriage horses to six of the royal guns so that they could be brought into action, three on the right of Dumbarton's to fire on the regiments of Matthews and Holmes, three in front of the Guards to fire on Wade. Soon the three small rebel guns were silenced and the royal gunners loaded with caseshot to shatter the files of rebel musketeers and pikemen who still stood firm before them.

As the rebel guns were silenced and the fire from the musketeers became more ragged as their ammunition began to run out, the royal army made ready for a general advance. Lord Churchill led the two Tangier battalions commanded by his brother and Colonel Kirke from the extreme left of the royal line, where they had seen no action, to the extreme right, beyond Dumbarton's, where they could wait ready to advance against Holmes's regiment on the rebel left. His own Royal Dragoons were brought up to what was now the centre of the royal line to reinforce the hard-hit Scotsmen of Dumbarton's Regiment. Oglethorpe, who having finally dis-covered Monmouth's departure from Bridgwater had come directly to the royal camp, was ordered to lead his own patrol reinforced by cavalry from Weston Zoyland across the upper plungeon to threaten the left of the rebel line. Another body of cavalry crossed the lower plungeon to threaten Wade's still un-daunted Red Regiment on their right.

Day was dawning and first light revealed the state of the battle to the two watchers in the windmill at Chedzoy. As friends of the rebels they can hardly have liked what they could see. Three

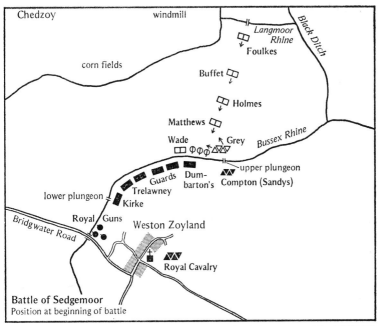

Battle of Sedgemoor
Position at beginning of battle

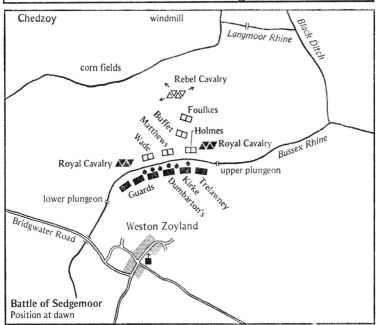

Battle of Sedgemoor
Position at dawn

regiments of rebel infantry still stood firm in a line along the Bussex Rhine. The other two regiments and what was left of the rebel cavalry stood confused behind them and to their left on the edge of the cornfields which surrounded the mill. Many men from these two regiments and most of the cavalry had already run away. But some men were still making their way towards the sound of musket and cannon fire. At each end of the rebel line the two parties of royal horse waited restlessly, eager for the order to charge. And across the ditch lay the royal infantry, tired of being shot at and waiting for the moment when they might cross the ditch and kill. The silent watchers were to catch one last gleam of hope. Oglethorpe, no doubt thoroughly ashamed of his slackness and eager to recover some reputation, charged too soon and 'tried one of their battalions, but was beaten back by them, though they were mingled amongst them, and had several men wounded and knocked off their horses among which was Captain Sarsfield who was knocked down by the butt-end of a musket and left for dead upon the place'.[17]

It was a respite, but a brief one, and it took little imagination to see what was going to happen any moment. The two watchers no doubt climbed down quietly from their mill and quickly left the field, lest they be taken as rebels. They were not alone. The Duke of Monmouth, too, could see when he was beaten. 'All the world cannot stop those fellows,' he said to Lord Grey who had rejoined him after the rout of his cavalry. 'They will run presently.'[18] Stripping off his armour, he took £100 from his servant Williams and rode fast off the field to the north, accompanied by Grey and one or two others. Did Wade and his republicans raise a cheer as they saw their king desert them? Perhaps they did not even notice in the heat of the action, an action in which Monmouth to do him justice had played so far a noble part, standing in the front of the infantry, half-pike in hand to encourage them. Now Monmouth and Grey rode straight for Knowle Hill where, looking back over their shoulders, they were able to watch the last stand of the men who had fought for the good old cause.

The royalist cavalry on the wings of the rebel army had continued to test the endurance of the rebel pikemen, after Oglethorpe's repulse. At last the Earl of Feversham, who had joined the cavalry on the royal right, saw the pikes of Holmes's regiment 'begin to shake, and at last open'.[19] The moment had come for the general assault and Feversham ordered the foot to pass over the ditch to charge the rebels. With a great shout they rose up and led by the dragoons raced through the mud with ease and rushed straight towards the rebel army. The two rebel regiments on the left dropped their arms and fled, pursued by the dragoons and cavalry. Wade's men lasted a moment longer, but soon he found them 'not inclinable to stand' and made 'a kind of disorderly retreat' to the Langmoor Rhine about half a mile to their rear.[20] Here they made a last stand before being charged by a party of horse and dragoons and routed, though even now the remarkable Wade was able to maintain some sort of control and led two or three hundred of his regiment clear away to safety.

Other rebels were far less fortunate as they tried to run away before the pursuing horsemen brutally slashing down at those who tried to escape their fury. The deep and boggy Langmoor Rhine was the grave of many; the cornfields beyond it the grave of many more who had managed to struggle across the ditch. According to a royalist writer the greatest slaughter was of Colonel Buffet's regiment of Taunton men, the fourth regiment in Monmouth's column who had never really got into the battle and must have been caught unprepared when their comrades broke and fled. How many of the rebels were killed altogether at the battle of Sedgemoor is difficult to say. Some accounts suggest between two and four hundred rebel dead on the moor itself and another thousand slaughtered in Langmoor Rhine and the cornfields beyond. Adam Wheeler, a drummer in the Wiltshire militia, who came up to Weston after the fight was over, tells us that the countrymen that 'gathered up the dead slayne in this battell gave an account of the Minister and Church Wardens of Weston of the number of one thousand three hundred eighty and fower; besides many more they did believe lay dead unfound in the corne.'[21] Wheeler himself who had a passion for statistics saw one hundred and seventy-four corpses in a single pile, 'which those that were digging a pit to bury them in gave the number of'.[22] Such figures are not necessarily accurate, but it seems quite likely that a quarter of the entire rebel army were killed in the battle and in the slaughter that immediately followed it. The bloodlust of the royal soldiers was such that they were still pulling fugitives out of the corn and butchering them as they cried in vain for quarter, hours after the battle had been won. Maybe they were just extremely brutal men. More likely they had been badly scared and this was the only way to assuage their fears. How many royalist soldiers would have remained alive if Monmouth's men had actually broken into the royal camp and caught them in their beds? It had been such an unpleasantly close-run thing, where a rebel victory of appalling magnitude had only been prevented by a miracle and 'where Providence was absolutely a greater friend than our own conduct'.[23] But now the trial by battle was over and it was clear that 'God did not then stand neuter.' 'God by a wonderfull victory declar'd the Duke of Monmouth rebell'[24] and the good old cause was dead.

Seven

The Rage of the Adversary

Now did the rage of the adversary increase, and like a flood swell to a great height, insomuch that many poor creatures, yea, many of the Lord's own professing people were constrain'd to hide themselves in woods and corners, where they could find places to shelter from the fury of the adversary, divers being taken captive, some shut up in prison houses, others some hang'd up immediately by the hands of the enemy.[1]

The fury of the adversary was still at its height as the sun rose on the blistering hot July day that followed the battle. The true horror of the carnage in the cornfields before Chedzoy could now be seen, as the royal soldiers trampled through the ripe corn stained red with the blood of the defenceless rebels. 'Our men are still killing them in ye corne and hedges and ditches whither they are crept',[2] wrote one who had had enough by seven o'clock. But the slaughter was coming to an end. Sword arms were tired and swords becoming blunt. Besides it was rather hot and long past breakfast time. The boring business of rounding up the prisoners could be left to the men of the Wiltshire militia, whose colonel had forbidden them to join in the fun of carnage and plunder, lest the beaten enemy should stand and fight and 'every man of them might loose his life.'[3] Adam Wheeler, the Wiltshire drummer, recorded the confinement of two hundred and thirty-eight prisoners in Weston Zoyland church, many of them mocked and abused as they walked or crawled towards it and all of them stripped by the militiamen of any decent clothes which the royal soldiers had not already taken. Altogether some five hundred prisoners, including seventy-nine wounded, were locked up in the roomy village church to spend a long day and a long night, unfed, untended and forsaken by the God of battles, reflecting on the folly of rebellion and their likely fate.

Five men died in the night and one 'got out at the little north door while the watch was asleep, and so escaped with his life.'[4] The rest were to witness in the morning a rehearsal of their own probable fate, for none could be so dull as not to know the punishment in store for men caught in arms, levying war against the King. King James had thought it wise to treat the rebels with a mixture of leniency and terror, a free pardon for those who accepted his proclamation and the utmost severity for those who did not. All men should see what it meant to be a rebel. In reply to an inquiry from the Duke of Albemarle, the King had consulted 'the most able in the law' who had told him that rogues such as those 'who proclaimed the late Duke of Monmouth King may be hanged without bringing them to a formal trial. The King leaves it therefore to your discretion to proceed in the matter as you shall see cause, but would have some of them made an example for a terror to the rest.'[5] The justification for such summary punishment by the military presumably lay in the assumption that, as long as the state of rebellion existed, civilians as well as soldiers could be dealt with under martial law. To satisfy such conditions the rebellion was not regarded as 'ceased' until some time after the battle of Sedgemoor.[6] During this period the King expected the soldiers to make a few examples. Although full records do not exist, it seems probable that about a hundred prisoners were summarily executed in the week that followed Sedgemoor,[7] not counting those who were slaughtered in the immediate aftermath of the battle. Four days before Sedgemoor the King had rebuked Lord Feversham for not being harsh enough to the many traitors in Frome, as he marched through the town. 'His Majesty thinks you might have done well to have hanged any persons you found deserving it there, as he would have you do in other places if you see cause.'[8] No one wanted to disappoint the King and his officers now hastened to hang a few of the prisoners 'for a terror to the rest'. On the morning following the battle the Dutch gunner who had caused such havoc in Dumbarton's Regiment and an officer who had deserted from the militia were dragged out of the church and hanged before the army 'on a tree in Weston Moore'.[9] The church warden of Weston Zoyland recorded the hanging of another twenty rebels that day, four of them in chains, a piece of soldierly justice which was to lead to much grumbling from the loyal men of Chedzoy who later complained that they had been 'at great charge to build gallowses and gibbets, and to make chains or gemmaces to hang up the rebels'.[10]

The royal army marched away the same day from the long line of gibbets and hanging men and the great burial pits which marked the scene of their triumph. Feversham, with the Guards and the Wiltshire militia, set off towards Wells, halting for the night at Glastonbury where six more rebels were hanged from the sign post of the White Hart Inn, 'who after as they hung were stripped naked, and soe left hanging there all night'.[11] The remainder of the prisoners were then taken into Wells where they were confined in the gaol and in the cloisters, while the army received a tumultuous welcome from the loyal city, bells, bonfires and a sermon in the damaged cathedral from Old Patch himself.

The time had come for the forces of law and order to disperse. Many of the volunteers departed cheerfully for London, ready to bore their friends with unlikely tales of their daring exploits. Most of the militia were sent home, before the need to pay them should become an embarrassment to the Government, already a little embarrassed by the problem of deciding just how many days' service could be claimed by the men of the Somerset and Devonshire militia who had fled at Axminster and then turned up again as if nothing had happened. Meanwhile the royal army set off for London, Churchill, Feversham and the Duke of Grafton going ahead to receive their just awards. But not everyone went home. There was still a little business to be done in the West Country.

Three days after the battle a long line of prisoners, manacled together two by two, and two carts full of wounded rebels made their slow and painful way out of a very subdued Bridgwater along the road to Taunton, watched by a cowed and apprehensive crowd. They were escorted by Colonel Percy Kirke in command of five hundred infantry from the two Tangier regiments, together with cavalry and dragoons, the men who had rounded up these prisoners as they fled from the battlefield to the west. Kirke celebrated his arrival in the 'nursery of rebellion' by hanging nine of his prisoners, who were later buried in St James's churchyard. None of these nine seem to have been Taunton men and it is probable that Kirke, like most of the royal commanders, selected for his example of terror some of the men who lay wounded in the carts, men 'who without surgeons (which is not aloud to any) must have dyed however'.[12] The royal surgeons were busy enough looking after their own men, while wounded rebels were not just a nuisance, but a real danger as 'their wounds began to be very noisome' and threatened the whole countryside with infection.[13]

In the next six weeks Colonel Kirke's campaign of round-up and retribution was to earn him, probably unfairly, a reputation as the cruellest soldier in English history. To him was to be attributed every injustice and every brutality, every rape, theft and plunder, every murder and degradation that was to be done or said to be done by all the King's soldiers and loyal subjects in the west. That there was much injustice and brutality there can be little doubt. What more could be expected in a conquered kingdom? A man, who later got abroad after hiding for a long time in the West Country, made a full report on the behaviour of the King's soldiers who paid only what they wished to pay, took the best of everything and had 'made one entire bawdy house of ye West of England, forcing and enticeing the wives and daughters of such as were accounted nonconformists.'[14] There is plenty of official evidence to support such a general condemnation, despite the efforts of those in London to get the soldiers to pay the full price for what they needed and to treat civilians with respect. This is how soldiers behave in a conquered land. Kirke must be responsible for some of this. Many of the culprits were after all his own soldiers. But that it was all done at Kirke's orders or by Kirke's men is unlikely and is certainly not supported by surviving evidence. One wonders exactly what Kirke had written in the letter to Blathwayt, the Secretary at War, to which he got this reply. 'I have received his Majesty's pleasure upon the two particulars mentioned by you, – concerning plundering and murther by soldiers in pay.'[15] Was he asking for permission? In fact, it is clear that Kirke had written to ask what powers of punishment he had over those of his men who had committed such crimes, since the substance of the letter is to pass on the King's order that military criminals should be handed over to the civil arm. Officers were of course reluctant to do this, preferring their own justice or lack of it. In late August Colonel Trelawney was ordered to hand over those of his soldiers who had committed robberies to be tried by the common law. 'You ought not to excuse them upon any account from such a tryall.'[16]

One did not need to have served in Morocco to acquire a taste for plunder and violence. The cavalry troopers, the dragoons, the Scotsmen of Dumbarton's Regiment who in late August replaced the Tangier men as the holding force in the West Country, all behaved in the same way as Kirke's notorious Lambs. They did not all do so with impunity. In December the King ordered a full inquiry into the looting of lace by dragoons from the house of a honest citizen of Colyton, 'intending that the offenders should be punished according to the utmost severity of the law and that full reparation should be made'.[17] In the following month nine grenadiers of Dumbarton's Regiment who had assaulted a Mr William Martin of Exeter were ordered to be secured and handed over to the civil justice, while their leader, Lieutenant Livingston, was required to enter into a recognizance for his appearance at the next assizes.[18] But it has to be admitted that there are not really very many cases of the Government's taking action against the soldiers and one must accept that the West Country was not a pleasant place to live during the long period of military occupation which followed the rebellion.

Officers like Kirke and Trelawney were tough men who commanded equally tough men. What they did in the West Country was nothing to what they would have done in similar circumstances in Africa, or indeed in Scotland or Ireland, but they were certainly not prepared to handle rebels, suspected rebels or their families with kid gloves. They raped, pillaged and bullied if they could get away with it, which they usually could. How many of the stories attributed to Kirke himself have any substance, it is impossible to say. They have the sort of brutal charm which we in our century may find it easier to believe than our forefathers. Did he really have the regimental music play in time to the dancing of his hanging victims? Did he really, as Ailesbury tells us, force an innkeeper's daughter to go to bed with him as the price of saving her father's life? 'She consented, hoping to save her father's life by it, and she getting out of bed in the morning, saw her father hanged on the sign-post.'[19] Maybe he did. Some people do behave like this towards their enemies. All the same, these stories, all of which are based on folklore and gossip, do seem rather unlikely. Would King James have kept such a man in command if they had really been true? He wanted the west to be punished, but not like this. Kirke was to receive several rebukes from Whitehall, but they were on account of his greed, not of his cruelty or licentiousness. His sin in Whitehall's eyes was to release men who had been in the rebellion, 'under pretence of having obtained his Majesty's pardon'. How else was a serving officer to make any money out of a rebellion which yielded so little worthwhile plunder? Sunderland told him not to be so impatient. Pardons could be sold later. 'His Majesty does not think fit to do anything of that kind till they shall be tried before the judges . . . after which I doubt not he will be ready to gratify you in any reasonable request of this nature.'[20]

His Majesty could have had few complaints about Kirke's execution of his main duty, which was to employ the men under his command to hold down the west and to search for the rebels who had fled after the battle. In this latter task he was to have many helpers. Other units of the regular army were detailed to patrol the roads leading into London, sending out 'troops of horse and dragoons in small parties to stop and examine all carriers and passengers and other persons that may give any cause of suspition'.[21] Deputy lieutenants and Justices of the Peace all over the country were ordered to keep their eyes open for suspicious men and many of the militia remained in arms for a few days after the battle, their loyal desire to serve the King sharpened by the thought of the bounty money offered for captured rebels and the enormous rewards advertised for the rebel leaders, £5,000 for the Duke of Monmouth dead or alive, £500 for Lord Grey and up to £100 for many of their lieutenants, such as Goodenough and Nelthrop.[22] Men could live a long time in the seventeenth century on such rewards as these, while those not fortunate enough to capture a leader should be able to make a bit by blackmail and plunder. Such attractions, together with the vindictive hatred that many loyalists felt for the beaten rebels, drew many scores of amateurs into the game, quick to acquire for themselves warrants permitting them 'to search for arms, horses and other furniture of war and apprehend all concerned or suspected of being in J. Scott's rebellion'.[23] Men who had stayed at home or who had fled at the first sign of the rebels now came forth to join in the hunt, a hunt which was not itself without danger, as a Mr Bond was to discover when he tried to arrest some rebels hidden near Lyme Regis. Mr Bond was 'cruelly murdered' and his two companions mortally wounded.[24] The rebels might have been defeated, but they were not prepared to deliver themselves meekly unto the justice of the King.

Searching for rebels was to prove a formidable task as they scattered after the battle to hiding-places throughout the West Country. The group of fugitives led by Wade was one of the very few who remained more than a hundred strong and thus able to fight off any but the most determined pursuit. 'Most of them who did escape were within an hour so disperst that you could not see anywhere ten of their men living.'[25] William Clarke of Sandford found such a flight rather shocking. 'The greatest wonder to mee is that since above 7000 men ran away, and the King's party was not more than 3300 men, that the cowardly roggs (who knew they must be hangd) could not bee prevayled withall to make a stand.'[26] But the time had passed for that. The rebels had submitted their cause to the Lord of Hosts and he had decided against them. Now they must run before it was too late.

The rebel cavalry were the first to flee and of course the best equipped to make their flight effective. Their horses were pressed hard on the morning following the battle as the fugitives strove to stretch the distance between themselves and their pursuers. Soon horses were spent and the rebels had to continue their way on foot, their exhausted mounts providing a welcome gift to many a local farmer. In December, John Martin of Nyland explained to the justices that 'the Tuesday after Weston fight' a stranger had come to his farm and left behind a bright bay nag of about $14\frac{1}{2}$ hands, saying that 'if he did come againe he would pay for the keeping of him; if not that he should take him as his owne.'[27] Since many of the rebels' horses had been stolen in the first place, Martin and many like him were to have some awkward questions to answer.

The rebel infantry had a harder job in fleeing the battlefield, tired as they were after a sleepless night, a five mile march and a fruitless fight. But flee they must or die, and flee fast, away from the questing horsemen, away from the level moorland to the west, the north and the south, where woods and hedges, cornfields and deserted buildings could give them a chance to sleep up for the rest of the day before continuing their journey in the comparative safety of the night. Many were flushed out in these first few hours, too tired or too weak from loss of blood to cover their tracks effectively, some of them betrayed by their fellows or by the formerly friendly countrymen now eager to curry favour with the victors. But well over two thousand of the rebel infantry got clear away from the neighbourhood of Sedgemoor, tended their wounds, slept off their fatigue and pondered the future of the vanquished.

Where were they to go? The instinct of most men seems to have been to run for home, hiding up in cornfields and woods by day and moving by night, uneasily aware that every man's hand was against them and anxiously listening for the parties of cavalry and dragoons that patrolled the whole area. The neighbour-hood of home had many advantages for the fugitive. Nowhere else could he find friends and relations ready to tend him and feed him, ready to warn him of the approach of danger. Nowhere else was he likely to know of a perfect place to hide, the hiding-places of childhood, the secret chamber in his house or the loft in the barn or the concealed meeting-places of his conventicle in the woods and hills that surrounded his home. The West Country is a paradise for the fugitive, a fact which must have encouraged the preachers to carry on their mission in the face of the savage persecution of the early 1680s. Imagine the task of searching for the men from Axminster hidden in the beech and oak woods that crown the high land to the east of the Axe where bracken, gorse and heather provide marvellous cover and where there are in many places great sunken ditches covered by undergrowth, 'secret caves of the earth' where the Reverend Stephen Towgood could still continue to hold services for his Independent congregation. Here he could preach from the twelfth chapter of the Book of Revelations.[28] 'And the woman fled into the wilderness where she hath a place prepared of God that they should feed her there.' Here men might feel safe from the soldiers. But could they feel safe from their former friends and neighbours? Hiding near home might be convenient, but it had its dangers. There were many who had never loved the rebels. Eight of the Axminster fugitives were captured and carried to prison by their fellow-townsmen who got paid at the rate of one pound per rebel and fivepence for the cord to bind them.[29] Nor was it necessarily a former enemy who flushed the rebels out. 'There was also great treachery used by many that were taken by the Adversary, in betraying their fellows,' Towgood tells us.[30]

Even the innocent could betray a rebel. In neighbouring Colyton a fugitive was quietly enjoying the company of his family when a neighbour rushed in to tell him that the soldiers were coming. He just had time to run into the garden and throw himself down among some cabbages when the soldiers entered the house. 'They enquired of his children where he was, and they innocently told them.' Men lurking around their homes must have had many a scare from such parties of soldiers and dragoons, as did the Colyton mercer John Clapp. He managed to get home after the battle and having greeted his family went to bed. Soon he heard the dreaded tramp of soldiers' feet. He hastened to climb through a trap door into the roof. The soldiers came into his bedroom and remarked 'that as the bed was warm its recent occupant could not be far away. But they failed to notice the trap door and gave up their search.' Some Colyton men were not so lucky, like Zachary Drower, a young joiner who hid under the wheel of a water-mill owned by his family. 'The soldiers, having searched the premises unsuccessfully, were moving off, when one of them noticed under the wheel something white, which proved to be his shirt sleeve, and thus led to his discovery.' Zachary's luck was to change. He was later pardoned and was to live nearly fifty more years, no doubt long enough for his neighbours to get thoroughly bored with the repetition of the story of that frightening day when he was only twenty-one.[31]

The fugitives had to live out this cat and mouse existence for nine months before 'the outcasts returned to their habitations' and picked up the threads of their former lives.[32] Not till 10 March 1686 did King James II issue his most Gracious and General Pardon. And even then a large number of rebels were excepted. 'Yet it reach'd our case most of us, and freed abundance of Monmouth's men who had lain about at hide in woods and places, till they were almost starv'd many of them.'[33] The dangers of death from starvation or exposure became serious as autumn and winter replaced the early sunny months of hiding. Cold and hunger forced many rebels to forsake their safe places in the countryside and find new hiding-places in buildings closer to home and closer to the prodding swords of the royal soldiers, who found many a rebel concealed beneath the hay and corn in the lofts of West Country barns. It was a sad and hungry winter for many, only made bearable by the thought that one day there must be a pardon and the persistent rumour buzzing round the villages of the west that Monmouth was yet alive and would return to lead them once more to victory against their persecutors.

While dragoons hunted and soldiers raped, while rebels hid in holes and widows wept, the petty bureaucrats of local officialdom were busy at work. The constables of each parish in the area of rebellion were ordered to produce a list of all those people suspected of being involved in the rebellion, those actually known to have been in arms, those absent from their homes between the relevant dates and thus assumed to have been in arms, those who had supplied the rebels with food and horses and those who had given them succour after they had been defeated. It was a massive task, but not an impossible one in a small parish. Most men knew who had been out with Monmouth or who had actively encouraged the rebels, though the scope for error and dishonesty remained enormous. What a chance to pay off old scores, to put down the name of an enemy or a business rival. What a chance to leave off other names, for love or money. How important the parish officials must have seemed that year, able by a stroke of the pen to make a man a traitor or a loyal subject of King James.[34]

Slowly the lists were completed, each man's name accompanied by a brief account of his crime, 'levying war against the King', 'being out in the horrid rebellion', 'flying from his colours', 'absent from his home in the tyme of the rebellion', 'aiding and assisting James Scott', 'entertaining a rebel', and so on. Listed too were the present whereabouts of the rebels as far as they were known to the parish authorities, 'not taken', 'not returned', 'not come home', 'at large' or the more ominous 'in prison' and the final 'dead'. In some parishes, even in whole hundreds, every single man is listed as 'not taken' or 'at large'. For some lucky groups of rebels this information could be correct, though few villages escaped completely. Over half the rebel army got away from Sedgemoor and were never captured. But often the listing simply reflects the ignorance of the constables who could not know that these men were already lying with their friends under the great mound on Weston Moor or had been taken and imprisoned miles away.

The constables had little time to check their facts. The completed lists were required by the Grand Jury of each county and would theoretically form the basis for the prosecution of the rebels at the assizes. In fact the lists were for the most part of little value to the judges, since the majority of the men whose names were inscribed on them were not available in the gaols to be tried for their lives, being already dead or safely hidden. The men who were actually tried were those available to be tried, whether they appeared on a list or not, the men who had been herded into the prisons and bridewells by the soldiers and their eager helpers. The lists still had a function. They defined in official eyes who was a rebel. Once on the list, a man dared not appear openly in his former village, unless he had some extremely good alibi for his absence at the crucial time. Parish constables were not the only local officials drawing up lists of rebels. For the remainder of 1685 the business of West Country quarter sessions, manorial courts and urban magistrates tended to be dominated by their desire to demonstrate their loyalty and reveal the names of the traitors in their midst. When the jury of the hundred of Taunton and Taunton Deane made their quarterly presentation of offences to the Sessions at Bridgwater on 14 July the foreman apologized to the bench for the absence of normal business. 'As for the matters and offences which are usually presentable att this court, our countrey have been soe much disturbed by a late notorious rebellion that wee could not make inspection therein.' He then humbly presented a list of men from the hundred known to have taken up arms against His Majesty, 'by the reputation of our neighbours'.[35] The list was short. A week was hardly enough to prepare a list of all the men in Taunton and Taunton Deane who had borne arms against their king.

By the time that the Court Leet of North Curry hundred had their semi-annual meeting on 27 October life had calmed down a bit. The tithing-men were able to intersperse an accurate list of the local rebels and their fate with the more familiar business of the court, such as the names of those who had failed to keep their ditches clean.[36] The men of North Curry no doubt needed such homely reminders of normal life that year. So many of their number had vanished since the last meeting of the Court Leet. In North Curry tithing twelve out of a total of fifty-six adult male residents were presented as 'in ye late duke of Monmouth's service', their names coupled with such laconic information as 'killed at norton', 'wounded', 'mort', 'hanged', 'in prison' or 'fled'.

More interesting than such lists with their bald record of dead or fled rebels are the records of the magistrates of Lyme Regis which are preserved in their Misdemeanour Book. This is one of the very few documents that gives us any information about the examination of captured rebels. Here we can find the truth of the Reverend Stephen Towgood's observation of the treachery of some of the former rebels. On 11 July John Bailes of Axminster was examined before the Lyme magistrates, to whom he gave the names of twelve men from Axminster and four from Colyton whom he had seen when he was in Monmouth's camp and 'saith that one Toogood a minister did often use the house of one Bryan a clothier in Axminster before Monmouth's landing'. Weston Hillary, a soapboiler from Hawkchurch in Dorset, was another who gave his friends away.[37] Here too we can find the often pathetic attempts by captured rebels to excuse their behaviour. They often pleaded *force majeure*, like George Salter of Whitchurch who, after twenty-three weeks in hiding, was captured by a company of soldiers at Wotton Fitzpaine. He 'confessed that he came into Monmouth's camp near Lyme Regis and went with the same camp several days, being, as he saith, compelled to drive one of the great guns as far as Phillips Norton'.[38] The Lyme Regis magistrates heard many strange stories, as fugitives were flushed out of their hiding places and brought before them, but the results were usually the same. 'Sent by *Mittimus* to Dorchester Gaol. By Mr. William Way of Bridport and a company of soldiers.'[39]

Many hundreds of the rebels made no attempt to get home after the battle, preferring the chance of a free and open life in a foreign country to hiding, desperate and wanted men, in their own back-yards. Many fled west after the battle, crossing the Quantock and Brendon Hills to friendly Exmoor, where guides could be found to take them across the moor by hidden ways to seek a passage in a small boat from Ilfracombe or Lynmouth.[40] Some of these fugitives ended up in New England, though most of those who evaded the cavalry patrols and waiting frigates probably made for the Low Countries, once again the favoured destination of the exile. Many headed for the ports of south Devon, Dorset and Hampshire which offered a quicker passage to Holland, though the chances of capture on the way or in the ports themselves were greater than in the Bristol Channel. Many rebels chose to lie low until the first and most intense period of search and watchfulness had passed, hiding up in the West Country or in the London area, in Wapping and Redriff, 'skulking and hovering for an opportunity to escape'.[41]

Prominent amongst the group of fugitives seeking to escape abroad were the former exiles and the rebel leaders, men with no home or village to which they could safely run and with no hope of any pardon in the England of James II. Several of the lesser leaders got safely away, but the Government had a remarkably high success rate in rounding up the men who had played key parts in the rebellion. The rewards no doubt helped a bit. Only two of the five rebel regimental commanders at Sedgemoor managed to get away. Perhaps significantly they were the two comparatively young professional soldiers, Matthews and Foulkes, both of whom escaped to the Low Countries and both of whom were later to serve with some distinction in the army of William III, Foulkes leading a regiment against King James at the Battle of the Boyne, a satisfactory revenge for the humiliation of Sedgemoor. The veteran Colonel Abraham Holmes, wounded at both Phillips Norton and Sedgemoor, was captured on the battlefield, a valiant soldier to the last whose courage many thought should earn a pardon. The other Cromwellian colonel, 'that beggar old Buffett', commander of the Taunton men, was taken by one of Kirke's patrols a fortnight later. Wade, after leading his men off the field, recovered his horses in Bridgwater and then with about fifty fellows rode to Ilfracombe and seized a small coasting ship which they victualled and took to sea, only to be forced ashore by two frigates patrolling off the coast. It was now each man for himself. Wade fled for the woods and made his way along the northern edge of Exmoor to the village of Brendon, just south of Lynmouth. Here he remained safely for a couple of weeks, before news got around of his whereabouts and he was shot down trying to escape by a party led by a former rector of Brendon, the Reverend Richard Powell. The romantic must feel dismay that Wade was not killed on the spot by the pistol-toting parson, since his later apostasy was to blacken his reputation as the military hero of the rebellion. The historian can only be grateful that Wade's wound was no worse than it was, for his confession provides by far the best account of the rebellion from the rebel point of view. What Wade thought, after his pardon enabled him to live out his life as town clerk of Bristol, we do not know.

Wade's capture completed a remarkable grand slam by the

Government of all four of the leading republicans and Rye House plotters who had been so active in the planning of the rebellion in Holland. Richard Rumbold, the one-eyed maltster and former owner of the Rye House, had been captured in Scotland, where he had fought for Argyll, after a truly splendid resistance for a man of sixty-one. Richard Goodenough had been one of Wade's party and was taken after they had been forced ashore. Like Wade he turned king's evidence, but was not freed for some time. In July 1686 he was sent to Jersey 'to be kept prisoner during life', but was released at the end of May in the following year.[42] Richard Nelthrop had fled in the opposite direction after the battle and made his way, in company with the notorious fanatic preacher John Hickes, towards the south coast ports. They took shelter on the way at Moyles Court, a house on the outskirts of the New Forest owned by Dame Alice Lisle, the widow of one of Charles I's judges. Here they were betrayed and captured by a party under the command of Colonel Thomas Penruddocke, who took them off to prison together with their elderly hostess who was soon to be the first victim of the Bloody Assizes, an awful warning to all kind people in the West Country of the dangers of harbouring traitors.

Penruddocke had a good record as a rebel-catcher, but the greatest prize of all, five thousand pounds, was to be shared by the men of the Sussex militia under the command of Lord Lumley, who had brought his men up to Ringwood, 'the most westerne part of Hampshire . . . that we might be the reddier if any commands shall come to march more westward . . . I shall carefully wach this part of the countrie,' he wrote to the Earl of Middleton on 29 June, 'through which tis very likely somme of the rebells will endeavour to escape whenever they shall be defeated, which I hartily wish to heare of.'[43] His assessment of the situation was quite accurate. Monmouth and Grey had ridden north to the Mendips, after they had taken their final distant farewell of their doomed army. They had then swung round to travel south-east, riding all day and most of the night, hoping to reach Poole and the safety of a ship before they were discovered. But the flight of Monmouth has little of the romance and none of the good fortune of that of his father after the battle of Worcester. Monmouth and Grey split up in Dorset to make their separate ways to the coast and Grey was soon taken. Monmouth, who now travelled with the Brandenburger Anton Buys, survived a little longer, half-starved and dressed in peasant clothes, until on the morning of 8 July he was dragged out of a ditch covered with undergrowth after a long and well organized search. The approximate location of his final hiding-place had been given away by a peasant woman called Amy Farrant who had seen him creeping towards it for the night. She was later to receive fifty pounds for her information. One cannot help thinking that the same woman would have given Charles II a good meal and a safe hiding-place and spurned the chance of reward. But Charles II was never a rebel. A few days later the chronicler Narcissus Luttrell saw Monmouth and Grey brought up to London, guarded by several troops of horse; 'the former seem'd much dejected, the latter very cheerfully talking of dogs, hunting, racing etc.'.[44] Grey's habit of 'cheerfully talking' was to save his life, but nothing could now save James Scott, late Duke of Monmouth.

King James and his ministers must have been pleased with this haul of rebel leaders, to whom should be added several more of the prominent rebels, such as the only hero of the cavalry, Captain John Jones, the Dorset lawyer Christopher Battiscombe, Major Perrot, the crown-stealer, and the hard-riding Anabaptist preacher from Devon, Sampson Larke. But they waited in vain for one man whom they would dearly have liked to see brought up to London in chains. Ferguson the Plotter escaped the hands of justice once again. At first he was reported to have been killed in the battle, in which he had ridden with the cavalry and is said to have beaten some of the rebel troopers with the flat of his sword in frustration at their cowardice. Then he was reported to have escaped with Wade, but no fellow-parson was to capture him. How he got away no one knows. The next we hear of Ferguson he is back in Amsterdam, making life a purgatory for our old friend Bevil Skelton, His Majesty's Envoy Extraordinary at The Hague.

Life was no less frustrating for Skelton after the rebellion than it had been before. He had, it is true, organized two rather good parties at The Hague to celebrate the news of the victory and the capture of Monmouth. Two thousand guilders had been spent on fireworks, bonfires and a liberal treat of wine for the common people, with 'entertainment both times to several persons of quality'.[45] But if he thought that the drunken cheering of the crowd in The Hague was a sign of a general change in the sympathies of the Dutch people, he was soon to be disillusioned by a letter from a Mr Goddard describing the attempts of the loyalist party in Rotterdam to celebrate the victory. They had taken an English ship out on the river 'and having hung her as full of lights as we could, with trumpetts huzza's and gunns we began His Majesty's health'. But no sooner had they fired off their first triumphal volley than the noise was drowned by factious Englishmen on the banks, who replied 'with curses, healths to Monmouth and titles of papist doggs and such like', fired on the ship and then raised the rabble to attack the loyalists as they tried to get ashore.[46] It seemed that the Dutch were going to be as troublesome as ever and that the English Whigs had learned nothing from the failure of their rebellion.

Such an impression was confirmed when Skelton tried to implement the former proclamation to banish leading rebels from the territory controlled by the States General. Proclamation or no proclamation they were as safe as ever. Even if the magistrates did try to seize them, 'the *canaille*' would stop them, and in any case it was more than likely that the magistrates would give them plenty of warning of any intended arrest.[47] As a result Skelton's secretary was to report from Amsterdam in September that 'severall of the Proclamation blades walke dayly in these streets'.[48] Skelton was to have no better luck when he tried to get another proclamation published to banish some of the new crop of rebellious subjects who had been forced into exile after Sedgemoor. It was not until 21 May 1686,[49] after ten months of effort on his part, that it was eventually printed and the envoy's repeated, and for the most part vain, attempts to get it implemented were to continue until his eventual recall later in the same year.

Skelton was simultaneously involved in a complex enquiry into the financing of the rebellion, a matter of pressing interest to his masters at home, who continued to be worried about the dangers of a new rebellion backed by foreign money. He was able to identify several of the 'rebellion-promoting merchants' and especially the 'two pillars of the cause', Daniel Le Blon of Amsterdam and James Washington of Rotterdam. These were the men who were said to have accepted jewels and plate belonging to Monmouth, his mistress and her mother as security for the loan which had provided most of the cash to equip the expedition. It seemed that the godly merchants had cheated the rebels. Skelton was told that Lady Henrietta Wentworth 'had sent above £9,600 worth of plate to James Washington, to whome she sayd that the late Duke of Monmouth had also sent his, but he denies the ever having received any from either of them ... and disowns all connection'.[50] Yet when Skelton searched Monmouth's trunk, which had been left in Rotterdam, he found inventories of plate, but no plate, and also 'a scheme of his nativitie .... which one Partridge had drawne'.[51] On 18 August he interviewed Lady Henrietta herself on the sea front near Scheveling, 'where she had little to say to me besides complaynts of Washington's having cheated her of above £4000 worth of goodes and plate, and desired my assistance in the recovery of it, but that in a haughty kinde of way ... And in all her discourse I could not discover the least concerne for her lovers death, of whome she spoke, to my thinking, with greate indifference'.[52] Lady Henrietta went to England later in the year to try to convince the world of her innocence. The Earl of Ailesbury saw her 'in the most lamentable condition of health'.[53] She died at her home at Toddington in Bedfordshire in April 1686, but not perhaps of the broken heart attributed to her by romantics, if we can believe Skelton. Shortly before her death Daniel Le Blon was arrested in Amsterdam as a fraudulent bankrupt, greatly to the joy of Skelton's agent, Ezekiel Everest. 'Enfin this pillar of Monmouth's pretended Reformation and elder of ye English Calvinist Church here is now cried out upon as the arrantist cheat and rascall that is in ye world, not only by ye Dutch but by ye Godly fraternity and even by ye fugitive rebels who say that he has cheated Monmouth and ye

Lady Wentworth of severall thousands of pounds upon ye deposited goods that were putt into his hands for to fitt out the Heldernberg.'[54]

Skelton and Everest were to get some light relief from such serious and ultimately insoluble inquiries. The Low Countries were rapidly becoming the favoured asylum of half the lunatics and deluded persons in England. Amsterdam was teeming with former witnesses of Popish Plot days, fled from the wrath of a popish king and now all more than a little mad.[55] In November Everest discovered two new mad women who claimed to be the Duke of Monmouth's sisters. They had, they said, 'a magical sword which in the pomel containes such a potent talismanick spell that when it is once drawn his enemies must have fledd before the bearer'. They had also planned an elaborate scheme to assassinate King James by poisoning his sheets.[56] In the following March there was a further addition to the Duke of Monmouth's growing family with the arrival in Amsterdam of a young man pretending to be his son, who was courted by Captain Matthews, John Trenchard and Monmouth's former chaplain, Hooke, amongst others. Skelton interviewed him at The Hague on 29 March and discovered that he was the only son of a rich yeoman from Leicestershire. 'I take him to be a very foolish raw boy, he sayes that he runne away from his father to take armes with Monmouth but that he came to late, the rebells having been just defeated when he came to the place.'[57]

Meanwhile the defeated rebels had been pouring into Skelton's territory for months. On 28 July he had reported to the Earl of Middleton that Ferguson and sixteen other rebels had fled from England in an open boat and were now in Amsterdam. He expected him to hide in Friesland, 'where the Presbyterian ministers will be ready to shelter him'.[58] Elaborate plans were made to capture him, though to no avail. Skelton had early admitted his apprehension of the hopelessness of the task. 'When I consider how cunningly he hath hitherto escaped I feare he may give us the slip.'[59] Right through August, September and October more and more rebels were to flock over out of England. In early November Everest in Amsterdam grumbled that 'there are so many stranger faces here of our English fugitives . . . this town is become a kinde of purgatory to moderate and peacably inclined men.'[60]

Skelton and his spies kept themselves very busy prying into the affairs of the exiles, anxious to discover the first warning of a fresh rising, eager to discover rifts and jealousies, eager to discover individual rebels who would inform on their fellows still in England in the hope of a pardon. There were many fears to play on, as men like Wade, Goodenough and Grey apostasized in England, and more and more of the detailed organization and background of the rebellion became apparent to the Government. But there were few who were prepared to go so far as to return to England to give evidence against their former friends, however much they now disliked them or disapproved of them.

The godly exiles led by the Reverend Matthew Meade would have little to do with the ungodly, hard-drinking crowd led by Colonel Matthews, who in turn hated Meade for dissuading the pious Londoners from following Monmouth. But such dissensions produced no crop of informers. Meade himself was simply waiting for a holier generation to do the work, as Everest discovered when he heard him preach in the Brownist church in Amsterdam. 'He was pretty moderate till, ye later end in his prayer, he with a foaming mouth prayed that Babylon might be destroyed in England and her brats dasht against ye walls, so that, by the help of an innuendo, you may well inferr whom he meant by Saints, viz ye Rebells and factious reformers, and by ye brats of Babylon all other moderate Christians whether Roman Catholicks or Church of England.'[61]

There was no more hope of suborning John Trenchard, the former Whig Member of Parliament for Taunton, another man much disliked by most of the exiles for his failure to support the rebellion, after drawing 'all their West Country men into Monmouth's faction' and then sailing off to France 'to see as it were a farr off how ye traine would take'.[62] But Trenchard had a much clearer view of the realities of English politics than had the supporters of Monmouth, as he was to explain in November to Everest.

'Why then I perceive'; said I to Mr. Trenchard, 'that you had but mean thoughts of our friend ye D. of Monmouth'. 'So mean', said he, 'that I went out of England four dayes before he landed and did not care to returne to help him', for he says that he knew that ye main gentry of England and ye clearest sighted nobility in the late Parliament when in their clubbs declared they were rather for ye Princesse and Prince of Orange for to succeed, because they saw the line of succession was clearer that way .... though ye comonalty which were ledd by other persons that were angerd, were all together for Monmouth without examining what they did.[63]

Trenchard, who was excepted from the General Pardon of 1686, was prepared to wait until his analysis worked itself out and returned to England with William III who knighted him and later made him Secretary of State.

Everest was to have rather more luck with 'one Peter Parry, a West Country petit gentleman', the son of a Taunton merchant, whose desire to ingratiate himself with the English authorities had made him much hated by the other exiles and who now promised to tell stories against them. By February he had agreed to stand as a witness against men of estate who had been involved in the rebellion and had been so far untouched. Previously he had had qualms 'of being made use of as an evidence which was then a more shameful thing then now'.[64]

While Everest and Skelton tried to probe their secrets and foment divisions amongst them, the rebels themselves were faced with the serious problem of earning a living in the Low Countries. With so many of them to be fed this was by no means an easy task and at one time starvation in a foreign country seemed to be the likely fate of many of the humbler followers of Monmouth. Their leaders saw it as their responsibility to do something to avert such a calamity. Everest reported a meeting of a rebel club in Amsterdam who considered means of providing for 'nine or ten shoemakers and other tradesmen fled from ye rebellion' and 'other factious brethren that are ruined for the holy cause'.[65] One idea was to make use of the rebels' newfound military skills to form a company or regiment under the Switzers 'where they hope to be well entertayned'. The Elector of Brandenberg, the Prince of

Luneberg and the Duke of Neuburg were also mentioned as potential employers 'who shall keep up the Protestant spirit', though Everest caustically observed that 'such serpents when they grow warme may come to bite their landlords one day.'[66]

Many rebels certainly did become mercenary soldiers for various European princes, but a much more ingenious scheme was being prepared to employ most of the exiles, a scheme which at the same time would make use of their basic skills and embarrass Skelton and the English Government to the utmost. Before the rebellion most of the rebels had been employed in the West Country cloth industry, one of whose main markets was the Low Countries. 'By a modest computation', wrote one of the exiles, 'there are about 400,000 men, women and children in England whose livelyhood depend upon the makeing of serge, bayes, kerseys etc. and of those commodities there is transported yearly above £800,000 into Holland.'[67] What better idea than to employ the rebels in exile to make the same cloth as they had previously exported? The Prince of Luneberg and the Estates of Friesland were very interested in this unexpected opportunity to improve the manufacturing base of their provinces and reduce their import bill. One of the leading English projectors of the scheme was Joseph Tiley, the Bristol clothier who had proclaimed Monmouth king at Taunton and later repaired the bridge at Keynsham. He entered into an astonishingly favourable contract with the Estates of Friesland to produce cloth in the city of Leewarden. 'They are so fond and transported to bring the manufactory into the province that I believe they would have refused nothing that could with any colour of reason have been offerred to them to oblige the English.' He was granted twenty years exemption from taxes, rent-free houses for himself and his fellow-exiles, a workhouse sufficient for sixty looms and fulling mills built at the expense of the State, an interest-free loan of 25,000 guilders for ten years, a guaranteed market for army uniforms, customs exemptions on all imported raw materials and a supply of trainee labour in the form of three hundred children of ten years old at least, 'ye first year free, ye second year at 10d a week', and eighty children of fourteen years at least on the same conditions. All that the exiles had to supply was skill and working capital. Few clothiers can have ever had such an offer. 'That one article of ye children is worth £1600 a yeare, one yeare with another,' observed Tiley, 'and ye said 380 children are to be provided only by ye City of Leeuwarden; but should this manufacture have been continued, as the trade increased the Lords would have obliged all the towns and villages in the province to have delivered children in proportion upon the same termes.' Tiley reckoned that with all these concessions he could produce cloth fifteen per cent cheaper than in England and with virtually no transport costs at all.[68]

Such a scheme, which was repeated on similar terms at Luneberg, was attractive to capitalist and worker alike among the exiled rebels. Leading investors included Joseph Hilliard, Monmouth's 'harbinger and avantcourier', a clothier with business in both Taunton and Exeter, the merchant Hugh Crosse of Bishop's Hull near Taunton, Christopher Cooke of Wilton who before the rebellion had regularly employed six or seven hundred men in the woollen manufactory, Colonel Danvers, John Trenchard, who was said to have drawn £10,000 from his estate for the purpose, many of the long-term exiles in the Low Countries, such as the two Locks, father and son, as well as several Dutch merchants.[69] The exiled workers hastened to get jobs in the new enterprise. In early February 1686 it was reported that so many of the outlawed had gone to Leewarden that Amsterdam was quite rid of them. Five hundred more families of English sergeworkers were expected in the spring.[70] Luneberg was reported to be just as flourishing. Mr de Hoog, the chief director, told Everest in May that they had a capital stock of their own of 36,000 guilders and as much again from their friends at interest and a work force of four hundred persons. The finished cloth was as good as any English. Some of it was even bought by Amsterdam merchants to be sold at high prices as genuine English cloth.[71] The example was being taken up elsewhere. In March some other rebels under Major Manley were seeking to establish yet another centre of the cloth manufacture at Groningen.[72]

Few things worried English governments in the seventeenth century as much as a threat to their cloth industry, the major employer and the major earner of foreign currency, and a state of near panic ensued as the scale of this challenge by the rebels became apparent. Some encouragement could be found in a series of reports by Everard that there was much dissension among the investors and that things were not going as well at Luneberg and Leewarden as was imagined. The Luneberg manufactory was undercapitalized and 'some of ye rebelling weavers that went up thither are come hither again for want of haveing their wages paid.'[73] The Leewarden project had been held up because there was no carpenter who knew how to make the mills and looms in the English way. They did not have enough woolcombers, the spinners found the German wool difficult to spin and the fullers were not sure whether the water was good enough.[74] But each problem seemed to be solved in turn and, in fact, Tiley later claimed that he had deliberately leaked stories of disappointment and difficulty in order to discourage his competitors.[75]

On 10 February Everest had written to Skelton suggesting a more subtle motive for these mushrooming enterprises than simple gain. 'I am apt also to think that the bustle and flourish they make about this manufatory in Friesland is partly as a kinde of stratagem for to frighten as it were ye King for to give them a pardon.'[76] But when, in the following month, the news of the General Pardon reached the Low Countries there seemed to be no lull in activity. On the contrary the capitalists had successfully managed to persuade 'the common sort of ye English rebels that were concerned in ye Lewarden manufactory of workmen; weavers, tuckers etc.' that it was not safe to trust the General Pardon and that they would still be called traitors by their insulting neighbours or enemies; 'neither could they hope for such a liberty of conscience in England as in that place and that this raigne could not last long.' This was subtle propaganda and a lawyer called Mr Hunt was engaged by Everest to try to show the rebel workers their error in believing it.[77]

A pardon for the workers was not going to be enough to save England from this dangerous competition. It was their employers, nearly all of them excepted from the General Pardon, who had to be wooed. As the agent Captain Slater wrote to Skelton on 29

April, 'noe better expedient (I conceive) can be found then to permit the cheife undertakers to returne home who will take with them all the inferior workmen, and by this meanes the hectoring parte of the rebells will come to starve.'[78] This seemed indeed to be the only answer. His Majesty bowed reluctantly to the pressure. Some of the investors, such as Manley and Danvers, belonged to the 'hectoring parte of the rebells', men who would never make terms with King James II and 'curse those who seeke for pardon'.[79] But most of the West Country clothiers were prepared to accept the King's terms. Christopher Cooke was pardoned on 5 May on condition that he 'forthwith breake of his designs, and returne himself, with his estate and servants and mechanicks into England'.[80] On the thirteenth Skelton was informed that old Joshua Lock had already withdrawn all his effects from Luneberg and Leewarden and was ready to return to England the moment he recovered from the gout. Three days later both he and his son were pardoned.[81] On the 2 June Hugh Crosse was pardoned on the same terms as Cooke, as were a number of other West Country sergemakers and clothworkers, including that 'petit gentleman' and intending informer Peter Parry, now described as a mercer.[82] In the end there remained of the major investors only Joseph Tiley, a man whom the King was reluctant to pardon but the chief undertaker, and Joseph Hilliard who had unfortunately already been pardoned on 27 March and had returned to England to sell his estate in Taunton in order to invest the proceeds in Leewarden.[83] The business was that good. However Tiley wanted a pardon and he was eventually to get it, on condition that he dishonour his contract with the Estates of Friesland and break up the manufactory at Leewarden. Once Skelton and Everest had Tiley's active co-operation the business was rapidly brought to a close and when Everest went to Leewarden at the end of July he found the doors shut and was told that the last workman had left a fortnight previously.[84] The Estates of Friesland had seized Tiley's goods as some compensation for his poor faith. Was there any chance that King James might reimburse him?

It is difficult to say just who won this last round of the rebellion; the King, Skelton and Everest who bowed to blackmail to save

England from a dangerous competitor or Tiley, Cooke and Crosse who got their pardons at the expense of a little honour and a flourishing business. When one considers just how difficult it was to make James II change his mind, it seems fair to say that Tiley, who had actually proclaimed Monmouth as king in Taunton, won on points. One thing is clear. The good old cause had moved forward into a new phase that was to sustain it for the next hundred years. It was to be business, not religion, that both motivated and supported the Dissenting Whigs in years to come. They had had enough of rebellion and in the future they would make money, not war.

Eight

Confess and be Hanged

The Lord Chief Justice told us that if we would acknowledge our crimes by pleading guilty to our indictment, the King, who was almost all mercy, would be as ready to forgive us, as we were to rebel against him...

And now was that common saying verified 'Confess and be hanged', for notwithstanding his large promises of grace and favour, we were all condemned to be hanged, drawn and quartered and by his order there was 230 executed, besides a great number hanged immediately after the fight. The rest of us was ordered to be transported to the Caribee Islands.[1]

There was no room for mercy in the hearts of the Tory nation in the aftermath of Sedgemoor. They had been too frightened for that. Relief at the completeness of the victory was coupled with a desire for the most terrible vengeance against these men who had come so close to upsetting the apple-cart of privilege. All of them must suffer as an unforgettable warning to their kind never to rebel again. Later some of the Tories were to demonstrate the same disgust which nearly all subsequent writers have employed to describe the punishments inflicted by the Bloody Assizes. But in 1685 there was hardly a whisper of criticism of Judge Jeffreys's campaign of revenge in the west. Men who levied war against their king were guilty of high treason and deserved to suffer the punishment for high treason, a 'punishment rejoiced at by all good men', as Sir Edward Seymour was to remark in the House of Commons later in the year.[2]

There were many to punish. Colonel Kirke, ably assisted by his many eager helpers, had done a good job of rounding up the rebels after the battle. By the time that Lord Chief Justice Jeffreys arrived at Dorchester on 5 September to begin the trials of the rebels, over a quarter of Monmouth's army, between fourteen and fifteen hundred men, had been herded into the prisons, bridewells and other places of detention in the West Country to await their fate. The conditions in prison were appalling. The standard allowance for the maintenance of prisoners was three halfpence a day, much less than it cost to maintain a man in a workhouse and, out of this, gaolers and other officials expected to make a profit. Even the three halfpence seemed too much to the local ratepayers, who had to find the money, and there were numerous complaints made at Wells Quarter Sessions at the 'considerable chardges in supplyeing the poore prisoners taken in the late rebellion in the West'.[3] Not all the prisoners were poor. But even those who were wealthy enough to provide their own food and to buy a few privileges had to suffer. The main problem was overcrowding. There simply was not sufficient prison accommodation in the west to take all these men, on top of the usual prison population of Quakers and other unfortunates. The worst place seems to have been the Somerset county gaol at Ilchester where four hundred rebel prisoners were packed in, so that at night 'there was no room for us to lie down.'[4] Such conditions naturally bred disease, and gaol fever and small-pox was to save many of the captured rebels from the attention of the executioner. The parish register of St Mary Magdalen, Taunton, records the burial of twenty-two unnamed rebels who had died in prison, and this was just one parish. Altogether, hundreds must have died of disease or from their wounds, which were for the most part left unattended by the authorities. The sickly stench of festering wounds in Ilchester gaol made local loyalists fear an epidemic, a danger which was increased by the frequent visits paid to the prisoners by friends and relations from all over the country. A local surgeon, Joseph Winter, was asked to dress the wounds of the rebels, in order to reduce the risks of disease and also to ensure 'that they might be preserved to suffer the condign punishment that their wretched treason deserved'. Winter seems to have been an excellent surgeon and his attention was indeed to save many men for the gallows, or at least for transportation, who might otherwise have died.[5]

The general overcrowding, the venality of prison officials and the fact that many of the prisons were not really suitable for holding men awaiting trial for their lives, provided opportunities for many rebels to escape from prison, both before and after the Bloody Assizes. Some escaped before they even got to prison by bribing their guards, as did Peter Parry of Taunton whom we met preparing to inform on his friends in Amsterdam. Others escaped by ganging together and overpowering their guards. The *London Gazette* of 17 September carried an advertisement offering a reward of a pound for the recapture of any of a large number of rebels who had broken out of their prison in a workhouse near Exeter.[6] Another man claimed to have escaped with six friends after making their gaoler drunk by putting brandy into his wine.[7] But most prisoners had no such opportunities and they waited day after awful day in their filthy prisons to see just how much mercy there was in the heart of the good King James.

For the time being King James took little interest in his rebellious western subjects. They could stay in their prisons to await their fate. There was important business to be done in London. The early capture of Monmouth provided the King with the opportunity for a dramatic execution of the attainted rebel leader on Tower Hill. Monmouth spent much of his last few days on earth penning abject letters to the King, the Queen, the King's brother-in-law the Earl of Rochester, and anyone else he could think of, begging for mercy or asking for an intercession with the King, offering to betray his friends, convert to Catholicism, anything to save his life. King James even granted him an interview, a favour which was normally thought to be a sign of clemency. But there was to be no mercy for Monmouth, grovel though he might at the feet of his rival. Sir John Bramston was told that the King had asked Monmouth how he could expect pardon after the way he had behaved. 'To make me a murderer and poisoner of my dear brother, besides all the other villainies you charge me with in your declaration.'[8] The King himself described his meeting with Monmouth to the Prince of Orange. 'The Duke of Monmouth seemed more concerned and desirous to live, and did not behave himself so well as I expected nor as one ought to have expected from one who had taken upon him to be King. I have signed the warrant for his execution tomorrow.'[9]

Now that death was certain Monmouth pulled himself together and behaved with the courage and sangfroid which generations of Englishmen have managed to achieve in the face of public execution. On 15 July he was brought out onto Tower Hill where, before a large and sympathetic crowd, he resisted manfully the nagging bishops who tried to get him to make a public acknowledgment of his sin in rebelling against the King. The execution itself was an unpleasant botched affair. Monmouth jokingly asked the executioner, the famous Jack Ketch, to make a quick job of it, and gave him six guineas to do his business well. But when he placed his head on the block and spread his arms as a signal for the axe to fall, the executioner only managed to gash his neck. Several assistants held Monmouth down while Ketch took four more strokes and still failed to sever the head. In the end he had to finish off the job with a knife. Monmouth's head was then put into a red silken bag, placed next to his body in the coffin which was brought back to the Tower and buried in the chapel.[10] 'Thus ended this quondam duke', wrote Evelyn, 'darling of his father and the ladies . . . debauch'd by lusts, seduc'd by crafty knaves . . . He failed & perished.'[11]

Lord Grey had also failed, but he did not perish. He, too, was prepared to betray his friends to save his life, but he did so in a 'more resolute and ingenious' way than Monmouth and 'never so much as once asked for his life.'[12] He also had a powerful advocate at Court in the person of the Earl of Rochester, who had a financial interest in Grey's continued existence, since Grey's estate was entailed and would pass with his death to his blameless brother, and Rochester had been given a life interest in it when Grey was outlawed. Rumours of Grey's possible execution led Rochester to indulge in a flurry of tree-felling on his estates in Northumberland. Rochester's intercession was to save Grey. On 21 July instructions were given for him to have pen, ink and paper brought to his cell in the Tower. He was to make good use of them, writing a full and witty, if not totally honest, confession which was later to be published as *The Secret History of the Rye-House Plot*. He was also required to give evidence at the trials of the Cheshire peers Lords Delamere and Brandon. On 12 November his pardon passed the Great Seal and he was set at liberty, being given back his estates at Upp Park in Sussex in the following June. Grey's quiet life in the country was interrupted in November 1688 by a letter from his Catholic neighbour and kinsman John Caryll inviting him to join the royal army against William III. In a charmingly tactful reply Grey declined the invitation, which his 'inclinations, as well as duty' supported, by referring to an unfortunate riding accident which had so discommoded him 'that tis with greate difficulty I now write to you'.[13] Despite his reputation as seducer, coward and informer, Lord Grey was to do well in the new world of the 1690s, playing a full part in the business of the House of Lords and holding important offices in the public administration. In 1695 he was created Earl of Tankerville, 'being a town in Normandy, at the siege of which place one of his ancestors performed a wonderful piece of gallantry'.[14] He died in 1701.

Grey's confession deals mainly with the Rye House Plot and with the planning of Monmouth's rebellion in Holland and says little about the rebellion itself. King James and his two Secretaries of State were soon able to supplement this information with material gathered willingly or unwillingly from the more important prisoners who were brought up to London to be interrogated after their capture. Nathaniel Wade was to make the fullest confession of all these men, but many other rebel leaders, such as Goodenough, Battiscombe and Colonel Holmes were interrogated and gave the Government information of varying importance. Masses of information must also have been sent up to London by the local justices, by the regular army and militia officers through whose hands the captured rebels passed on their way from capture to prison and by the gaolers, informers and stoolpigeons who gathered information from the rebels while they were actually in prison. However, surprisingly little of this material has survived. In the official State Papers Domestic for the month following the collapse of the rebellion at Sedgemoor there is not a single information or desposition, though there are a number of copies of letters from the Secretaries of State thanking people in the West

Country for collecting information and giving them further instructions. The absence of such material is in striking contrast to the period immediately following the discovery of the Rye House Plot and one can only assume that papers have been deliberately destroyed. The files of State Papers are suspiciously thin for the whole reign of James II and it is probable that following the Revolution of 1688 many public officials attempted to destroy as much evidence as they could of their collaboration with the former king. No one would be more likely to do this than King James's two Secretaries of State. Fortunately for us, both Sunderland and Middleton had servants who kept some of the relevant material in their own possession and this has enabled a few depositions and examinations to filter down through time to give the historian some information.[15] But even this source is disappointing. We have, for example, an account of the examination of Sampson Larke, the Anabaptist preacher from Combe Rawleigh in Devon, by all accounts one of the most important local leaders of the rebellion. This tells us virtually nothing about the local organization of the rebellion, the main fact emerging from the examination being Larke's confession that he was in fact out with the rebels.[16] All that most of the prisoners seem to have been asked were questions about the overall leadership of the rebellion, about the possible connections of members of the Whig gentry and aristocracy with the rebellion and, in particular, about the financing of the rebellion. These are important questions and one can understand why the Government wanted to know the answers, even though most of their informants knew, or said that they knew, very little about such matters. But one would have thought that a government that was proposing to try the fourteen hundred men in the western prisons would have wanted to know something about their various degrees of guilt – who were the leaders at the village level, who had a long history of opposition to the Government – as well as their comparative status in local society. A rich man might well be deemed more guilty than a poor man. He would at least have an estate worth plundering after he had been attainted. Such information was certainly collected after the punishments of the assizes had been inflicted, but no papers survive to establish whether the Government knew such things beforehand.

The man who most needed to have such information was Lord Chief Justice Jeffreys who, together with four other judges, had been given a special commission to try the rebels at the next assizes. Jeffreys, who was still only forty in 1685, was a man of striking good looks, much loved by his friends for his wit and good fellowship, which was only impaired by the agony he often suffered from a stone in the kidney. Such agony sometimes led to a savage brutality in his manner, but it was a savagery which he normally reserved for the courtroom. Jeffreys had had a brilliant career based on an intense loyalty to the King at whose pleasure he was appointed and a reputation for using his gift for bullying cross-examinations to get the verdict that the King wanted. He had no love for Dissenters or rebels and the news of his appointment can have done little to cheer the prisoners in the gaols of the West Country. On 20 August Jeffreys returned to London from Tunbridge Wells where he had spent the previous month taking treatment for the stone and then set out towards Winchester, together with his legal colleagues and an armed escort.

Jeffreys's task was formidable. He had little more than a month to try all the rebels, as well as to carry out the normal business of the assizes. This would clearly be impossible if many of them pleaded not guilty and it was his first task to demonstrate that such a plea would be extremely unwise. In this he was almost totally successful, and he was able to despatch the cases of 1,336 rebels in just nine days actually spent in court. Death was the only possible sentence which a judge could give to a man convicted of high treason, but this could be commuted to transportation for life or the King could use his prerogative of mercy to pardon the convicted man. Since most of the rebels had been caught in arms they were quite clearly guilty of high treason and few commentators have queried the fact that they were sentenced to death, though many have criticized the methods used by Jeffreys and the other judges to secure a guilty verdict in the many doubtful cases. Where Jeffreys has been criticized is in the large number that were actually executed. There seems to have been considerable doubt whether it was Jeffreys or James who made this decision. Some historians put all the blame on the King, pointing out reasonably enough that Jeffreys was in correspondence with the King throughout the period of the assizes and was assured by Sunderland that the King was pleased with the way that he was carrying out his business. Other writers put the blame mainly on Jeffreys. The confusion of responsibility is not helped by the fact that the two main contenders were later to blame each other for the severity of the assizes, once this had been seen to be a bad thing. In his memoirs King James stated that a commission was issued to Jeffreys, 'to go down into the West and inflict such punishments as the example of former reigns and the security of the present seemed to require. But imprudent zeal, or some said avarice, carried him beyond the terms of moderation and mercy, and he drew great obloquy upon the King's clemency, not only in the number but in the manner too of several executions and in showing mercy to so few . . .'[17] The truth is difficult to determine. Contemporary documents are themselves ambiguous. On 14 September Sunderland wrote to Jeffreys about 'such persons as you shall think qualified for transportation', implying that it was up to Jeffreys who was actually executed.[18] But on 19 September Jeffreys wrote to the King referring to the rebels 'your Majesty designs for transportation', implying the reverse.[19] The argument is perhaps rather an academic one, in any case, since at the time practically nobody except the rebels thought the punishments too severe and in most cases there would have been time for the King to send down orders to commute sentences of death to transportation if he wanted to. What probably happened was that the fate of most of the rebels was decided in London on the basis of information which no longer exists and that Jeffreys was given a wide degree of latitude as to how he should deal with the rest.

The actual conduct of these most famous of all assizes is shrouded in mystery. The assizes were always an event of great interest to the local gentry and one would have thought that these particular assizes, with the dramatic appeal of so many local men being tried for their lives, would have given rise to many colourful accounts in letters and diaries. But the only colourful accounts of the assizes which exist were written by Whig propagandists after the Revolution of 1688 specifically to blacken the memory of King James and his administration. All the information in these 'Western Martyrologies', as they were called, needs to be treated with suspicion.[20] They include trials of men who were never tried, lengthy cross-examination of men who pleaded guilty and absurd expressions put into the mouth of Judge Jeffreys. Above all, by giving the impression that single trials were conducted at great length, they make a nonsense of the very crowded timetable faced by the judges at the Bloody Assizes. There simply was not time for all the speeches and fulminations which they attribute to Judge Jeffreys. Unfortunately, no contemporary descriptions of the assizes which could refute the propaganda of the 'Western Martyrologies' are known to survive, if they were ever written. Nor do we have later descriptions of the trials from those few rebels who have left us accounts of their various sufferings. All we have is a verbatim account of one single trial, written a very long time after the event and almost certainly heavily embroidered for political purposes, a few more or less formal accounts in newspapers and newsletters and the very formal record of the incomplete Gaol Delivery Books for the Western Circuit. The result is that we just do not know how the assizes were conducted. We know only the formal facts of the pleas offered by the defendants, the verdicts given and the sentences imposed. For the rest we simply have to use our imaginations.

The one trial for which we do have a supposedly verbatim account was not of a rebel at all. This was the trial held at Winchester Castle on 27 August of Dame Alice Lisle, the elderly lady who had entertained John Hickes and Richard Nelthrop at her home when they fled after the battle. The Government clearly wanted to make an example of her. Harbouring a rebel was itself high treason and it was important that people throughout the West Country, and indeed in London, should realize just how awful the consequences of such behaviour were likely to be. Nothing would bring the gravity of the crime home more quickly than the execution of a lady of quality. Unfortunately for the

Government the propaganda effects of the trial backfired. Public sympathy for the plight of a woman who was seventy years old, deaf and apparently rather dim-witted gave the assizes a bad name and quite overshadowed any cautionary effects which the trial may have had. Dame Alice pleaded not guilty and rested her defence on the allegation that, although she knew Hickes, she did not know that he had been out with the rebels. This seems inherently unlikely, unless she really was incredibly stupid. All the same, the bullying cross-examination of the defendant and witnesses from the bench and the uncompromising instructions to the jury which finally ensured a guilty verdict leave a bad taste in the mouth, even if the account is clearly heavily embroidered. Dame Alice was condemned to be burned at the stake, the normal punishment for a woman convicted of high treason, a sentence which was commuted to execution by the King. 'She was old and dozy and died without much concern',[21] the first and best known victim of the Bloody Assizes.

Jeffreys and his colleagues then set off for Salisbury where six men were tried for seditious words and were all sentenced to be fined and whipped. Some effort seems to have been made to make the punishment fit the crime. One man, who had said 'that he would never go to church till Monmouth was King' was sentenced to be 'whipped from the end of the town to his parish church, and a second time from the farthermost part of the City to the Cathedral'.[22] There were no captured rebels to be tried in Salisbury and the judges now moved on to Dorchester, whose gaol was packed with rebels, and the important business of the Bloody Assizes began.

Several witnesses have left accounts of the preparatory work carried out before the trials of the rebels in order to secure as many guilty pleas as possible. The gossipy and not too reliable Ailesbury tells us that the prosecuting counsel, a great Whig lawyer called Henry Pollexfen, employed the deputy clerk of the assizes to speed up proceedings against the Whiggish rebels. 'This fellow, by Mr. Pollexfen's orders, went in to the prisons and made the poor people believe they had nothing to save their lives but by pleading guilty, on which each strove who should be the first.'[23] Ailesbury's information, though not his culprit, is confirmed by the Quaker John Whiting who, although not a rebel, was in the crowded Ilchester gaol.

There came David Trimm of Wells, and took account of the prisoners (which perhaps was his place, as county-clerk to do) with the causes of their commitment, but not only so, but wheedled them to confess how far they were concern'd, pretending if they would confess, they would do them all the kindness they could at the Assizes, so drew out of them what they could, under hopes of favour and then went in, and writ down their examinations . . . which if they had denied at the Assizes (or pleaded not Guilty) would have been produced as evidence against them, and as reported was.[24]

A similar story is told by the very creditable witness the surgeon Henry Pitman, who was also in Ilchester gaol. Pitman, however, takes the story a bit further and gives us an inkling of what must have happened in the small and not very distinguished courtroom at Dorchester on Saturday, 5 September, the first day of the Bloody Assizes proper.

But seeing our former confessions were sufficient only to find the [True] Bill against us by the Grand Jury; and not to prove us 'Guilty'; the Petty Jury being obliged to give their verdict according to the evidence in Court: the Lord Chief Justice (fearing lest we should deny what we formerly confessed and, by that means, put them to the trouble of proving it against us) caused about twenty-eight persons at the Assizes at Dorchester, to be chosen from among the rest, against whom he knew he could procure evidence, and brought them first to their trial.[25]

Jeffreys was to try ninety-eight rebels that day, an apparently formidable task in itself, but one which was made more so by the fact that the first thirty of them pleaded not guilty. It seems inconceivable that thirty men could be tried for high treason in one morning, if they were prepared to defend themselves. The trial of Alice Lisle at Winchester took six hours, well into the evening, and in one of the most dramatic scenes a candle was held close to the face of a hostile witness while Jeffreys cross-examined him. A long time was needed to conduct any criminal trial. The reading of the indictment, the swearing in of the jurors, the presentation of evidence by prosecuting counsel and by the defence, the cross-examination of witnesses and the summing-up were all normally conducted in great formality and often at great length. Single speeches often cover several pages in the *State Trials* series. How then could thirty men pleading not guilty be tried in a morning? To secure a verdict of guilty on a charge of high treason the Crown had to call two witnesses to prove the defendant's guilt, while each man presumably had a defence, had witnesses to swear that he was nowhere near the rebel army at the relevant time, witnesses to swear to his character and his former good behaviour or to say that he was in bed with the gout and so on. Clearly such a process would have been impossible in the time and one can only assume that the trial of these thirty men was a put-up job, as Pitman suggests, that they were tried without being given a chance to call witnesses in their defence, probably on the evidence of a single witness and the 'confession' which had been extracted in gaol. All the same, one man, William Saunders, must have had a convincing defence or a smooth tongue, since he was acquitted. The other twenty-nine were found guilty. Sentence was passed on them the same day, the awful sentence for high treason:

That you be carried back again to the place from whence you came, and from thence be drawn upon an hurdle to the place of execution, where you shall be hanged up by the neck, but cut down alive, your entrails and privy members cut off your body, and burnt in your sight, your head to be severed from your body, and your body divided into four parts, and disposed at the King's pleasure. And the Lord have mercy upon your soul.

Orders were given to the Sheriff for the men to be executed on the following Monday, 7 September. In fact, only thirteen of the twenty-nine men condemned in this first batch were actually executed, because Jack Ketch, who had been brought down from London with a butcher to help him do his work, claimed that it was physically impossible to carry out any more butcherings in one day. These first victims were 'all inconsiderable fellows', except for Matthew Bragg, an attorney from Dorchester itself who was thought to have 'put them upon that plea'.[26] Bragg's defence was that he was forced by a party of Monmouth's cavalry to ride with them as a guide, but that he went home as soon as he possibly could 'and was no more concerned in the affair'. His hagiographer claimed that the witnesses called by the Crown were a Roman Catholic 'and a woman of ill fame to whom the L. Chief Justice was wonderfully kind', while Bragg called more than twenty witnesses to prove his innocence.[27] But, in view of what we have already said about the timetable of the morning session of the first day at Dorchester, this must seem rather unlikely.

After lunch things began to move along a bit quicker. Sixty-eight more prisoners were brought into the courtroom. All pleaded guilty and they were sentenced to death, though only a few of them were actually executed, most having their sentence commuted to transportation. In the evening Jeffreys dictated an account of his day's work to the Earl of Sunderland. 'I this day began the trial of the rebels at Dorchester and have despatched 98; but am so tortured with the stone that I must beg your inter-cession to his Majesty for the incoherency of what I have ad-ventured to give him the trouble of, and that I may make use of my servant's pen to give you a relation of what has happened since I came here.'[28] Poor Judge Jeffreys! No wonder that he sometimes shouted at the fanatic rogues who stood in court before him. And this was only the first day.

The tactics used by the bench on that first Saturday morning's session were to pay off. 'The sudden execution of these men so affrighted the rest', wrote Henry Pitman, 'that we all, except three or four, pleaded "Guilty" in hopes to save our lives.'[29] For one thing now seemed certain. Those who pleaded not guilty and were convicted would definitely be executed. Those who pleaded guilty had a fairly good chance, though no guarantee, of receiving the comparative mercy of a passage to the West Indies as a transported convict. When the court reconvened at Dorchester on Monday one hundred and three rebels were tried and only two pleaded not guilty. And so it was to go on. Altogether in the five days of trials at Dorchester nearly three hundred men were sentenced to death, of whom seventy-four were actually executed and the rest either transported or later pardoned.

The judges then went on to Exeter where the comparatively small number awaiting trial were disposed of in a single day. Twelve men were later executed. After this respite the judges moved over into Somerset whose prisons were bursting at the seams with rebels awaiting their arrival. By now the process of trial had become formalized. Very few rebels pleaded not guilty and the judges were able to get through the vast number of cases very quickly. In two days at Taunton over five hundred men were tried, whilst on 23 September, the last day of the assizes, all records were broken in the Market Hall at Wells when five hundred and forty-two men pleaded guilty and 'one Will Mangell, who was Matthews's servant, pleaded not guilty, was tried in the morning and executed in the afternoon'.[30] Jeffreys might well feel that he had honoured the promise made the day before in a letter to Sunderland. 'I will pawn my life and loyalty that Taunton and Bristol and the county of Somerset too shall know their duty before I leave them.'[31] His business finished, he returned to London, stopping off at Windsor on the way to see the King, who expressed his thanks by handing over to his hard-worked servant the Great Seal of the office of Lord Chancellor which had become vacant in the course of Jeffreys's campaign in the west.

No one knows exactly how many rebels were actually hanged, drawn and quartered as a result of the Bloody Assizes. We can be fairly sure that eighty-six were executed in Dorset and Devon, but it is impossible to get accurate figures for Somerset. Three days after the end of the assizes, Jeffreys signed a warrant for the execution of two hundred and thirty-nine rebels condemned at Taunton and Wells. However the executions were not carried out immediately on receipt of the warrant. Indeed they were still going on months later, a fact which meant that they rapidly lost their novelty value and were not always recorded by news-writers. It is clear, however, that not all the condemned men were executed. Many died in the prisons, where smallpox seems to have been a serious scourge that autumn and winter. Some escaped. Others were later pardoned or had their sentences commuted to transportation. One or two answered to the names of dead men on the lists of transportees and so got carried away out of the country in their place. About a third may have avoided execution in one of these ways, making a grand total of about two hundred and fifty rebels executed as a result of the assizes. This is a large number, larger still if one adds to it the hundred or so executed by the soldiers after the battle. Altogether we can conclude that, very roughly, about 7 per cent of the rebel army were executed. Execution on this scale seems excessive but, as we have seen, it aroused little comment at the time and was only really used as a black mark against Jeffreys and King James as part of a later propaganda campaign, when they were being criticized for many other things. Simply as a deterrent it was certainly effective. The west did not rebel again.

What perhaps made these executions most awful both in contemporary and modern eyes was the fact that the full sentence for high treason was inflicted on all the victims. If they had simply been hanged or shot and then buried there would probably have been much less adverse comment. No one would expect a seventeenth-century government to take a serious rebellion lightly. But the Government was not prepared to behave in this tidy, if still vengeful, way. They wanted the whole West Country to be reminded every day of the awful nature of what their fellows had done. The executions were carried out in batches in towns and villages throughout the area, ten here, two there, five there. Everyone was to have the chance to see the men hang, to smell their entrails burning, to admire the skill of the butchers who carved them up. And many took the chance, often walking several miles to see the execution of a friend or relation.

Perhaps the greatest crowd was at Lyme Regis, the place where it had all started, where on 12 September twelve of the more famous rebels, including Holmes, Battiscombe and Sampson Larke, were executed. They were brought from Dorchester gaol, six in a coach and six in a cart, and then left for two hours in an inn at Lyme Regis, 'until the butchers had prepared every thing for their slaughter'. All twelve then walked to the beach where Monmouth had landed, on the west side of the Cobb. The gallant

Colonel Holmes, who was the first to be executed, had to be helped up the ladder by the sheriff, 'having but one arm, and the gallows higher than ordinary'.[32] He died bravely, like the good old soldier that he was. Next came the Anabaptist preacher Sampson Larke, who as he mounted the ladder was able to identify several members of his congregation in the crowd and offer them words of comfort before being 'turned off'. How long the business of execution and the subsequent butchery took we do not know, but it must have been a fairly lengthy process. Much time was also spent by each man in prayer as he made ready for his ordeal. It was traditional, too, for the condemned man to make a last speech, either from the ground or from the pulpit eminence offered by the ladder to the gallows. Sometimes these speeches could be very long, eloquent and moving to their friends gathered below them, moving even now, despite the garbled, stilted form in which they have been printed. Altogether there may well have sometimes been a whole hour between executions and one can imagine only too well the feelings of John Marders, constable of Crewkerne, last but one to die at Lyme, who 'seemed to the spectators to be somewhat unwilling to die' or the last man of all, John Kidd, the head gamekeeper of Longleat. 'Do you see this?' he said as he pointed to the dismembered carcasses in front of him. 'Do you think this is not dreadful to me, that eleven of twelve of us, that but a few hours since came down together, are dead and in eternity? And I am just going to follow them, and shall immediately be in the same condition.' Then, after addressing some improving words to the crowd, 'he prayed some small time very devoutly, and with seeming great joy and comfort; and the executioner did his office'.[33]

What happened at Lyme and has been recorded by devoted pens was to happen in every important town and many small villages in the West Country and it was not something that anyone who had seen it was ever likely to forget. If anyone should miss the sight of the actual executions they could hardly avoid the two hundred and fifty pickled heads and the thousand quarters of corpses which were even more widely distributed than the executions themselves, being stuck on spears and poles at cross-roads, bridges and other prominent places throughout the area. Here they were to stay till the summer of 1686 when the King made his tour of inspection of the West Country. Now he was to see what his subjects had had to see for nearly a whole year and, sick at the sight, he ordered the rotting heads and quarters to be taken down and buried.

Preparing the relics for exhibition must have been a full-time job for several people that autumn and winter. This prosaic side of the drama is well illustrated by the surviving warrant of the Sheriff of Somerset to the constables of Bath, where four men were to be executed.

These are therefore to will and require you immediately on sight hereof to erect a gallows in the most public place of yor said cittie to hang the said traytors on, and that you provide halters to hang them with, a sufficient number of faggots to burne the bowels of fower traytors and a furnace or cauldron to boyle their heads and quarters, and salt to boyle therewith, half a bushell to each traytor, and tarr to tarr them with and a sufficient number of spears and poles to fix and place their heads and quarters, and that you warne the owners of fower oxen to bee ready with a dray or wayne and the said fower oxen at the time hereafter mencioned for execution, and yourselves togeather with a guard of fortie able men att the least, to be present on Wednesday morning next by eight of the clock, to be aiding and assisting to me, or my deputie, to see the said rebells executed.

This was thoughtful planning but the careful sheriff had forgotten something. In a postscript he added, 'you are also to provide an axe and cleaver for the quartering of the said rebells'.[34]

We have little information to tell us on what grounds it was decided whether a man should be executed, transported or pardoned. As we have seen, those who pleaded not guilty and were convicted could be singled out for execution, though not all of them were. For the rest it is difficult to say. Some leaders were executed, but several were not. Many were pardoned because, like Goodenough, Grey, and Wade, they were prepared to give evidence against their fellows. One man for instance, Mallachi Mallack, a wealthy clothier of Axminster who was condemned to death at Dorchester, was later pardoned as a reward for giving evidence against an even wealthier man, Edmund Prideaux of Ford Abbey, the son of Cromwell's attorney general and a leader of the Whig gentry on whose assistance Monmouth had so foolishly depended. Mallack swore that Prideaux had provided Monmouth with money and horses, and Prideaux was 'given' to Jeffreys, in order that the new Lord Chancellor could get some financial reward for his loyal services by selling him a pardon. A bargain was finally settled for the princely sum of £14,500, the only clear evidence of Jeffreys's making money by selling pardons. Still, evidence or not, one must assume that many other men were able to acquire a pardon through passing money in the right places. Even a poor man might find he could raise quite a bit of money to stay alive, much more indeed than his estate would be worth once he was dead. These considerations apart, it is not easy to determine how the judges chose whether a condemned man should be executed or transported. Luck must have played an important part, though one feels that there must have been some rational mode of selection. The most likely hypothesis is that the decision probably often rested on the rebel's age. It made much more sense to transport a young man, since one of the main objects of the exercise was to make some money by selling the prisoners to planters, and young men were clearly likely to live longer and thus be more valuable. For all that, there is plenty of evidence of young men being executed and old men sent off to the West Indies in the hope that they might survive the ten years' servitude that awaited them.

Young or old, about eight hundred and fifty rebels were sentenced to transportation. From a financial point of view this was a much more attractive punishment to the Crown, even if it lacked the dramatic deterrent value of execution. Whether he was transported or executed, the rebel's estate was forfeit. But transportation involved none of the expense in ropes and firewood, tar and salt of an execution for high treason, while a second profit could be made by selling the convicted rebel to a planter. Jeffreys reckoned that each prisoner would be worth £10, if not £15. The main question, then, was who should benefit from them. The Crown had been at considerable expense in putting down the rebellion. If Jeffreys's lower estimate was correct it would take the sale of five hundred convicts to pay off the reward to Monmouth's capturers alone. Nor had the Crown finished paying out. As Jeffreys pointed out in a letter from Taunton, 'your Majesty will be continually perplexed with petitions for re-compences for sufferers as well as for rewards for servants'. His suggestion was that the money from the convicts could be used as a fund to pay off these petitioners.[35] But James was a Stuart and a king and not the man to think in such a petty way. He gave a hundred of the convicts to the Queen as a present and a further hundred to her ageing Italian secretary, Geronimo Nipho, who promptly sold then to George Penne, 'a needy papist'.[36] The rest were given, presumably at a price, to various people connected with the trade or administration of the West Indies, such as Sir Philip Howard, the Governor of Jamaica, who received two hundred. Orders were given that these people or their agents should take the prisoners off the Government's hands as soon as possible, 'his Majesty intending to be at no further charge about them but for guarding them to the ports where they are to be embarked'.[37]

Now was the time for prisoners with money or good connec-tions to try and buy themselves a better life in the West Indies than the servitude which the King had planned for them. There was plenty of scope for this. George Penne, for instance, was so needy that he did not have enough cash to pay the shipmasters for his convicts' passage and tried to raise it by getting some of them to buy their freedom. They would still have to go to the West Indies, but could live there as free men. Similar activities were undertaken by the shipmasters themselves. Some of these trans-actions were plainly fraudulent, since the money was paid in England and, in the circumstances, it was difficult to get a satisfactory guarantee that the terms of the contract would in fact be carried out in the West Indies. And indeed King James had prepared a very nasty surprise for such people, having ordered the general assemblies of the various West Indian islands to pass laws binding the convicts to ten years' servitude, 'and that they be not permitted in any manner whatsoever to redeem themselves by money or otherwise'. No ship's captain, no importer, no planter or other master was to be allowed to discharge or redeem a prisoner before he had served his full term, on pain of a fine of £250 for any infringement.[38] Some prisoners seem to have got round these orders. The sister of Azariah Pinney, a young rebel from Dorset, paid £65 to Penne for her brother's ransom and he did in fact live in the West Indies as a free man. Indeed he laid the foundations of the family fortune while he was there. But Pinney's case is rather special, as he had earned some relaxation of his sentence by giving evidence, probably against his neighbour Edmund Prideaux. The surgeon Henry Pitman, whose relations paid Penne £60 for his and his brother's freedom, was to suffer the indignity of enslavement when he arrived in Barbados, though he was later to make a dramatic escape in an open boat with seven other men and eventually returned to England. Here he discovered that he and his brother had been pardoned several months previously, 'without any condition of transportation', two of a group which included at least one man, John Marders of Crewkerne, who had already been executed, and Daniel Defoe, the only evidence that the author of *Robinson Crusoe* was in fact 'in arms under the Duke of Monmouth', as he was later to claim.[39]

Many of the rebels destined for transportation never reached the West Indies. They seem to have been very slackly guarded on the roads to the ports. Maybe the soldiers sympathized with their plight. Thirty of Sir Philip Howard's batch escaped between Wells and Sherborne and another three escaped from Sherborne gaol. When the remainder finally reached Weymouth many were sick and some of them for whom 'there is no hope of their recovery' were left behind when the ship sailed.[40] Many more rebels were to die on the convict ships which carried them to the West Indies. Eight of the eighty Monmouth men who sailed on the *Betty* from Weymouth to Barbados died at sea and another died on arrival. The mortality on the ship which carried the carpenter John Coad and ninety-eight other convicts to Jamaica was even worse. Conditions were similar to a West African slaver with the rebels crammed between decks with very little air, food, water or sanitation. Fever broke out and twenty-two prisoners, as well as many of the crew, died on the passage.[41] Many more rebels must have died in their first year in the West Indies, subject to the appallingly high rates of mortality faced by all immigrants to the sugar islands.

On arrival in the West Indies the prisoners were sold to planters or dealers and then set to work. The rebels, who were mainly artisans, were an invaluable asset to the islands which were chronically short of skilled labour. Most of them seem to have been employed in skilled work and were probably fairly well treated compared with the blacks, though there are many records of brutality. After the Revolution of 1688, representations were made to William III to free the transported Monmouth rebels but, although ultimately successful, this process was to take a long time. In January 1690 William ordered that the laws made by the island assemblies condemning the Monmouth men to ten years' servitude be disallowed and that provision be made for pardons to be issued 'for such as desired the same'.[42] But this was by no means the end of the matter, as William's orders were for a long time resisted by the West Indian authorities, anxious as they were about their future in the midst of the war with France. The newly arrived Governor Kendall of Barbados put the planters' point of view very clearly in a letter dated 26 June 1690.[43]

To my grief I find the militia very thin, the island having sent 600 men to the relief of the Leeward Islands, without which they had probably been lost [to the French]. There has been great mortality among the white servants here, and by reason of the war the planters have been unable to supply themselves with white servants. For this reason I have not announced the repeal of the Act concerning the Monmouth rebels to the Council and Assembly. It seems that, when they arrived, the Lieutenant-Governor received positive orders from King James that their servitude should be fixed by Act at ten years. The planters accordingly bought them, and thinking themselves secure of them during that time taught them to be boilers, distillers and refiners, and neglected to teach any others as they would otherwise have done. If these men are freed, the loss to the planters will be great, and since we are at war and so thinly manned I think it would be a great kindness to the Island if the King ordered an Act to reduce their servitude to seven years. But if the King adhere to his original orders no injustice will be done to these rebels, for by law of the country if they come without indentures they must serve for five years, which period will expire next Christmas.

In the end the Government compromised. The rebels must be freed, but the islands could impose 'such restrictions as are requisite to prevent them from leaving the island without the royal permission'.[44] On 17 March 1691, the Bill repealing the Monmouth rebels' Act passed the Barbados Assembly. Even now the attainder on the rebels had not been lifted and their estates were still forfeit. How many of the rebels survived this long and how many actually returned to England we do not know. Some certainly did, but it seems probable that the majority stayed in the West Indies and used their new skills to earn their living as free men for the rest of their lives.

The attainder of well over a thousand men meant that there was a good haul of forfeit estates in the West Country which could be used to satisfy the horde of petitioners whom Jeffreys had correctly predicted would perplex the King. Commissioners were appointed to inquire into the value of the rebels' estates. Amongst them was Gregory Alford, the loyal Mayor of Lyme whom we met earlier so alarmed at the sight of three strange ships in Lyme Bay. Alford and his colleagues held inquisitions before juries of local men and the information received was solemnly recorded in the archaic Latin of the exchequer clerks who had been sent down from London to assist them.[45] The haul was not really very satisfactory, scarcely enough in some places to pay the considerable fees and expenses of the commissioners, though some rebels were wealthy enough, such as the Taunton sergemaker John Hucker, whose estate was granted to Lord Churchill.[46] Once in possession of the facts, the commissioners were empowered to take over the rebels' property, leasing or selling their lands and selling off their goods and chattels. The whole business seems tedious enough, though it tells us a lot about the sort of people who were rebels, but presumably it was attractive to the commissioners who were in a position to get some good bargains for themselves or their friends, though they were specifically forbidden in the terms of their commissions from taking up the leases of rebel lands themselves.

Meanwhile the petitioners were busy, hoping for the grant of an estate, a job in the government service or just a hand-out in return for their past sufferings or endeavours in the loyal interest. It is nice to know that Samuel Dassell won promotion in the customs service for his brave if foolish attempt to do something to stop the rebels when they landed at Lyme Regis.[47] Here, too, is George Alford, vintner and mariner of Lyme and presumably a relation of the Mayor, who claimed to have been the last man that 'stood to his arms in opposition to Monmouth landing there, for which he was afterwards condemned to be hanged'. He was asking for a government employment to make up for his loss of business and was granted the post of tidesman in the port of Bristol.[48] William Dryer, gunsmith of Taunton, was another loyalist condemned to death by Monmouth who was now asking for some 'allowance or consideration'. He had raised and armed fifteen men at his own expense to oppose the rebels, 'for which he had his doors broke open and arms taken away to the value of £130 and being afterwards taken by the rebels was condemned to die'.[49] So many people claimed that they had been condemned to death by the rebels that one's suspicions are aroused. Why did the rebels not get on with the job of hanging them? Were they so short of rope?

Then there were the soldiers with a special claim on the Government's bounty. Captain Murdo McKinzie of Dumbarton's Regiment claimed to have captured a rebel standard at Sedgemoor with his own hands and was now asking for reimbursement of his and his men's losses in equipment and horses on that bloody day.[50] Hatton Wolrich, who was captured by the rebels at Keynsham, had lost 'his horse, arms and all other necessary accoutrements' and now prayed 'His Majestie's royal bounty towards his remounting and equipping again for His Majestie's service, or to be continued in pay and not discharg'd ye troop, untill he may be able to refitt himself within some convenient time.'[51] As the man who deceived Monmouth about the size of the royal army outside Bristol he deserved some recompense.

Several petitions came from the relatives of rebels, eager to dissociate themselves from the rebellion, and even more eager to grab some of the family property for themselves. It is only now that we hear of Peter Battiscombe, praying for a grant of his executed brother's estate, 'petitioner having been always faithful and having been much impaired in his credit by the wicked and traiterous practices of his said brother'.[52] Then there was Daniel Moody, a master gunner in the royal train of artillery, whose sister Elizabeth was the wife of the rebel preacher John Hickes, who 'by sinister and clandestine artifices did so far prevail upon the weaknesses of petitioner's father as to make a will unfavourable to petitioner, his only son . . . although petitioner never displeased his father but often opposed Hick's fanatical principles'.[53] Could he please have a grant of Hickes's estate? And so it went on. The Government was to be busy handling all these claims throughout the short reign of James II and indeed for many people the hope of getting something out of it was their only real interest in either the rebellion or the judicial holocaust that followed it.

What was the impact of the rebellion and the assizes on the West Country towns and villages which provided the recruits for Monmouth's army? The pattern of nemesis varied enormously from community to community, depending mainly on the ability of the local rebels to avoid capture after Sedgemoor. Few places can have suffered more than Colyton in Devon, whose rebels we studied in some detail in the first chapter. According to the lists prepared by the constable, Colyton provided eighty-six recruits for Monmouth's army. No less than thirty-three of these men were captured after the battle. Two of them, Edward Barber and William Blackmore, were amongst the group whose escape from the workhouse at Exeter was advertised in the *London Gazette*. Despite the reward offered for their recapture, both these men survived and returned to Colyton where each had a child baptized in the summer of 1688. Two other men were lucky enough to be pardoned. The other twenty-nine were convicted, twenty at Dorchester, four at Taunton, three at Exeter and two at Wells. Thirteen were executed, two of them in the group of 'inconsiderable fellows' who suffered at Dorchester for their unwise plea of not guilty, two in Poole, two in Sherborne, two in Colyton itself and the rest scattered through the West Country from Phillips Norton to Weymouth, where the leader of the Colyton men, Roger Satchell, met his end. The execution of the two men in Colyton itself might have been symbolic, though on the whole the judges do not seem to have troubled themselves overmuch about ordering their victims to be executed and their quarters exposed in their home towns. It would presumably have increased the deterrent effect of the slaughter. But it could equally well have led to a martyr cult and it is perhaps significant that the sufferings of both these men, William Clegg and John Spragg, appear in the 'Western Martyrologies'.[54]

The other sixteen convicted men were transported, ten of them being in the group given to the Queen's secretary. At least two of these men, Edward Venn and Philip Cox, died at sea in the *Betty* on their way from Weymouth to Barbados. Others who are in the list never appear to have reached Barbados and may have died or possibly escaped on the way. Two who definitely did escape were Peter Bagwell and John Whicker who were amongst the eight men who got away in an open boat with Henry Pitman. After an amazing run of adventures, including being forced to work as slaves on a Spanish pirate ship under the guard of negro overseers, they returned to England in 1688. There is record of only one other convict from Colyton returning home. This was John Skiffes, perhaps significantly the youngest man to be transported. He was sent to Jamaica in Sir Philip Howard's batch, but must have been back in Colyton by 1693 since he had a child baptized in the following summer. We can calculate the ages of nineteen of the convicted men. Most of them were fairly old, even compared with the generally high age of the Colyton rebels. Only two were under twenty-five, while twelve were thirty-five or over, a fact whose main significance is probably that they were unable to run fast enough to avoid capture.

We have evidence then of the permanent loss of twenty-six men from Colyton, thirty per cent of those recorded by the constable. But this is unlikely to be the end of the toll. For it would have been extraordinarily good luck if no man from Colyton had been killed at Sedgemoor or died later from his wounds or in prison. No record exists of the names of men who died in these ways. Still, we can guess at some of them. Several of the married rebels can be discovered in the baptismal register going through the process of building up a young family in the years before 1685, at which date the process abruptly stops and is not re-started after the General Pardon of March 1686. The example of Humphrey Mitchell probably sums up their experience. He was born in 1658 and in 1680, at the age of twenty-two, he got married. There follows in the register a regular string of young Mitchells, Humphrey, Elizabeth and Ann who was baptized early in 1685. But then no more and in February 1686, Elizabeth Mitchell, now described as a widow, dies and we hear no more of the family. We do not know what happened to the families of dead or convicted rebels, but they must have suffered immense hardship and many must have shared the experience of the widow and daughter of Philip Cox who were reported in 1687 begging for bread in the streets.[55]

It would be wrong to give the impression that all the men who left Colyton to greet the Duke of Monmouth with such high hopes were killed, executed or transported as a result of their foolishness. There is clear evidence that at least twenty-one of the rebels, nearly a quarter, survived and returned to Colyton to carry on the business of life. Some did not survive very long. The veteran Bartholomew Butter, who was fifty-eight in 1685, only lasted another eighteen months. But many had a whole life in front of them and time no doubt softened the horrors of the rebellion and its aftermath.

The experience of Lyme Regis offers a striking contrast to that of Colyton. One would have thought that the small Dorset port would have been singled out for exemplary punishment as the place which first welcomed Monmouth and one of the very few towns to produce more than a hundred recruits for the cause. This may well have been the Government's intention, but there could be no vengeance on absentees and very few Lyme rebels were ever tried. One reason for this is suggested by a report by the customs officer Thomas Tye, who wrote on 8 July, two days after Sedge-moor, that 'vast company of the rebels of this town and of the adjacent parts flock here daily with as much confidence as if they had served His Majesty faithfully all the time.'[56] Many of them had probably accepted the King's proclamation of pardon for those who laid down their arms. The deadline was in fact on the day that Tye made his report. Whatever the reason there is definite evidence of only six men from Lyme Regis being tried at the Bloody Assizes. Five of them were executed and one was trans-ported.

The fortunate survival of a population listing of 1694 enables us to state with some confidence that almost exactly half the Lyme rebels were still living in the town nine years after the rebellion, apparently none the worse for their experiences.[57] Three of them belonged to the group of comparatively wealthy men singled out by the tax for which the list was originally prepared. None of them appeared amongst the eighty-seven persons in receipt of alms. Lyme Regis, in fact, seems to have got off rather lightly, as did many other towns and villages in the area of rebellion. But no man or woman in the West Country was likely to forget Monmouth's rebellion and the Bloody Assizes, whether the local toll of victims was low or not. Nobody in the West Country has forgotten it yet, nearly three hundred years after the event, as the author of this book was to discover in the course of his researches. There are some things which can never be forgotten.

Nine

The End of Rebellion

The kind message you sent to the King by Mr. Bentinck, and your good wishes, I believe brought us good luck, for, God be thanked, here is the end of all troubles and in such a manner as that we may never hope to see the like again as long as we live.

Queen Mary of Modena to William of Orange. 19 July 1685.[1]

The west was to be a quiet place after the fury of the rebellion and the assizes. The Government continued to keep an eye on the area, fearful of another rising to avenge the humiliation of 1685. Many reports were sent in relating to pseudo-Monmouths or people like the deluded youth we met in Amsterdam who claimed to be his son. It is always difficult to get people to believe fully in the death of a king or indeed any very famous man. Many people in the West Country shared the delusions of John Bragg of Lyme Regis who told Solomon Andrews, JP, in February 1686 'that Monmouth was no more dead than he was, and that we should see other manner of doings here'. When asked whom he thought had been beheaded on Tower Hill he said that it was 'an old man with a beard in his place'.[2] This sort of rumour was slowly to die away. Monmouth was never to acquire the glamour of Owen Glendower, who some say still lies asleep in a cave in the Vale of Gwent, waiting for another day to sally forth against the English.

There was some unpleasantness when the rebels who had avoided capture were able to return openly to their homes after the General Pardon of March 1686. Former rebel and former loyalist made uneasy neighbours and there were many injustices and violent acts to avenge. Some rebels even threatened to sue loyalists for trespass during the rebellion and its aftermath. But this was soon quashed. Sunderland instructed the local justices to assure the loyalists 'that they shall not want his Majesty's protection against all such and the like malicious attempts and endeavours'.[3] The only really serious trouble was to occur in the neighbouring Somerset villages of Huntspill and Burnham. The Huntspill men had been loyalists and had 'assisted at ye takeing of severall of ye rebells at Burnham'. Earlier troubles culminated in a great fight at Huntspill fair, 'where a group of self-declared Monmouth men with severall whom they gott together from other parishes went to Huntspill in a tumultuous manner and fell upon ye loyall partie at Huntspill in such a manner that many of them had like to have been killed.'[4]

That hatred should spill over into violence was to be expected, though there seem to have been very few examples of this sort of thing. Much more remarkable is the apparently friendly way in which the West Country greeted the King when he came down to visit his formerly rebellious subjects in the summer of 1686. There appear to have been no unpleasant incidents at all, though the King was taking no chances. When he visited the battlefield, the churchwardens of Chedzoy laid a plank bridge across one of the rhines but James, fearing a booby trap, refused to use it and jumped his horse across.[5]

Enthusiasm for the King was to increase in the following year when, in April, he issued his first Declaration of Indulgence, granting toleration to both Protestant Dissenters and Roman Catholics. The King was to receive two hundred addresses of thanks in the course of the next fifteen months, including one from 'the combers, weavers, and other workmen in the serge manufacture about Taunton'.[6] Perhaps this should not surprise us too much. King James was a papist, but his actual policies as a papist king may well have blunted the fears of the Taunton weavers who fought against him in 1685. The Earl of Ailesbury has summarized what he thought were King James's hopes for the nation. 'Trade he had much at heart, and his topic was, liberty of conscience and many hands at work in trade', a programme which could hardly fail to appeal to a Dissenting artisan.[7] Considerable efforts were to be made in the last year of James's reign to persuade the Dissenters that toleration was but a mask to conceal the

King's efforts to remove all civil liberties and dragoon the nation into popery. This may be true though, since he had no opportunity to complete his programme, this assessment of the King's motives must remain pure conjecture.

True or not, the western Dissenters were not prepared to oppose their king again. When William of Orange invaded the country in November 1688 he landed in Torbay and his march took him through part of the area which had risen in 1685. But there were few signs of enthusiasm for the new deliverer, 'most of our western people having ever since Monmouth's time been much troubled with dreams of gibbetts, etc.'.[8] The men who flocked to William were ironically those who had suppressed the rebellion, not the rebels. It was men like Lord Churchill and the Duke of Grafton who deserted their king and their military commands to come into the camp of this second nephew whose invasion finally put an end to the Catholic cause of James II. The King was later to give some advice on the subject to his son, the 'Old Pretender', whose birth in 1688 was one of the proximate causes of William's invasion. 'Be never without a considerable body of Catholick troopes without which you cannot be safe. Then people will thanke you for Liberty of Conscience.'[9] The fact that there were several Catholics in the royal army was one major cause of the growth of opposition to the King, but there were not enough to outweigh the effects of the defection of his former friends and servants.

Largely because of the success of the Revolution of 1688, historians have tended to dismiss Monmouth's rebellion as an irrelevant episode, whose main significance was to lull King James into a mood of false confidence and give him an excuse to increase the size of his army. Monmouth is treated as a romantic but very silly Stuart, worth a couple of tears but little more. The rebels are dismissed as a rabble of fools who should have realized that all that they desired would be granted by their true deliverer only a few years later. Such writers feel sorry for their sufferings, of course. Who could fail to be moved by the horrors of the Bloody Assizes? But really the rebels were very stupid not to wait for 1688.

Such a view does scant justice to the rebels of 1685. They may have been foolish, but they were certainly not fools. Throughout this book I have tried to stress the sort of men who became rebels, serious family men who thought hard before taking the final decision to leave their homes to fight for the cause that they believed in. They were the last rebels of their kind in English history, indeed almost the last of any kind, and as such they deserve serious consideration, if not respect. Never again was such an army to rise against the English Crown, an army composed of shopkeepers and artisans, an army officered for the most part by men from these same social groups or men who shared the same ideals. Never again was there to be a rebellion in which republicanism played an important part. Men who believed, as did Richard Rumbold, that 'no man comes into the world with a saddle on his back, neither any booted and spurred to ride him',[10] could hardly be satsified by the Revolution of 1688, a revolution whose result was to replace the present threat of autocracy by the future rule of oligarchs in London and Tory squires in the countryside. Nor did the revolutionary settlement satisfy the full desires of the Dissenter. Toleration was granted and persecution for conscience sake was brought to an end. But the Dissenters still did not recover the civil liberties which their fathers had enjoyed in the 1650s. The Test and Corporation Acts which debarred true Dissenters from most positions of civic power were not repealed till 1828 significantly close to the date when the First Reform Act gave substance to the sort of franchise which the rebels of 1685 would have introduced if they had won.

Contemporaries knew what sort of men were out with Monmouth in 1685. They might despise them because of their lowly origins, but they feared them for the same reason. There were too many men like them who might rejoice if they were successful. And, although that success had been denied to them, it had been too close for comfort. That, surely, is why the repression was so savage. These were not poor deluded men following a romantic charmer, but men who posed a real threat to the established form of society. It must never happen again. It never did. The gentlemen who closed ranks to welcome the autocratic William in 1688 also closed ranks to express their contempt of lower-class rebellion and the enthusiastic religion which fuelled it. Even the gentlemen who rejected the new régime of William III, the republican gentlemen who feared that William's autocratic ways and his liking for a large army were a poor replacement for James II, refused to associate themselves with the rebels of 1685. Indeed, even in 1683 aristocratic republicans like Algernon Sidney had finally bauked at rebelling in the company of lower-class levellers like the maltster Richard Rumbold. For Sidney and those who followed him saw their ideal in the example of the Roman republic whose history they read in Latin, the prerogative of their class. Men like Rumbold looked to the levelling texts of the Bible for their inspiration and it was this mixture of religion and radicalism which gave them the courage and determination to do what they did. Recent research has demonstrated that the gentleman republicans of the 1690s consciously sought to remove the enthusiastic element from the history of English republicanism, rewriting the memoirs of the fanatic gentleman Edmund Ludlow in such a way that the future world would know him as a gentleman like them, but no fanatic.[11] The rebels of 1685 knew better, for they sought Ludlow as their leader, a wise choice even if unsuccessful, for Ludlow must have been one of the few Englishmen alive who at the same time had the social distinction and military experience to lead them and the sort of mind which could have understood their motivation.

The reinterpretation of Edmund Ludlow was not the only gloss to be produced in the 1690s. Other pens were producing a slanted and subtle picture of the events of 1685 which has been the basis of interpretation from that time to the present. Indeed the historiography of the whole decade of the 1680s is a propaganda job that would have done credit to a modern revolutionary régime. This is not particularly surprising. The Revolution of 1688 marked an extraordinary break in English history, the removal of a legitimate monarch and a simultaneous revolution in the relationship between executive and legislature. Such changes require careful handling by both journalists and historians. One event which required handling particularly carefully was Monmouth's rebellion.

Both Whig and Tory wanted to belittle the rebellion, though

for different reasons. The Tories, of course, deprecated any challenge to divinely instituted authority, the Established Church and the existing hierarchy in society. Monmouth's rebellion was just such a challenge and the picture which the Tories wanted to make clear, both to contemporaries and to future generations, was the wickedness and hopelessness of rebellion, the contemptuous ease with which a well ordered society could put down such a rebellion and the inevitability of an unpleasant fate for those who had been so foolish as to take part in it. At the same time they were prepared to sacrifice a Tory victim in the interest of healing the breach in society, and so did little to undermine the Whig view of an almost incredibly evil Judge Jeffreys. Jeffreys died in the Tower shortly after the flight of James II and so made an ideal scapegoat for a repression which it is difficult to imagine horrifying many Tories.

The Whigs needed to be rather more subtle. It was clear that Monmouth's rebellion was a Whig rebellion, but it was also clear that it was a rebellion by the sort of Whigs whom the men of 1688 did not want to encourage. Whiggery was always a somewhat uneasy coalition of Whig aristocrats, City money, Dissenters and the genuinely radical elements in English society, which survived as a potentially dangerous underswell in English politics from the Civil War till the reign of Queen Anne. Monmouth's rebellion was a rebellion by these last two elements, Dissenters and radicals, and as such was an embarrassment to the Whig politicians who were drawn from the landed classes. As a Whig rebellion it had to be seen as a good thing, a revolt of the worthy, if poor, elements of West Country society against the intolerable oppression of a Catholic and absolute prince. But it must not be seen to be too worthy, since it must not upstage the far more noble, and of course successful Revolution of 1688. Even more to the point, it must not be given too much praise, since it was very much a rebellion of lower-class and left-wing Whigs without the physical or moral support of the Whig gentry. Indeed it is clear that many rebels felt that they did not need such physical or moral support and could establish a new levelling régime which ignored the existing hierarchy in society. Such ideas were dangerous indeed, but Whig historians have been competent to deal with all problems. The rebels were praised for their courage, their loyalty and their virtue, but were condemned for their folly, poor timing and support of such a clearly unsuitable leader as James Scott, Duke of Monmouth. At the same time it was emphasized that the rebellion failed because it was not supported by the rebels' social betters. The message is clear. No Whig rebellion can ever be successful unless it is supported and officered by the Whig gentry. And there can be no republic which ignores the existing hierarchy in society, a convenient doctrine which seems never to have been forgotten by the English people.

The greatest exponent of such an approach to Monmouth's rebellion was not a contemporary but a man who wrote a century and a half after the event. Macaulay's account of the rebellion in his *History of England* remains the most stirring and memorable even today. It is an interesting combination of the careful use of the surviving evidence in central government records and the imaginative development of his own preconceptions. This can perhaps be illustrated best by Macaulay's comments on the sort of people who were rebels. When he described the recruits coming in to join Monmouth at Lyme Regis he mentioned 'the yeomen, the traders of the towns, the peasants, and the artisans' and at Taunton he noted that they were composed of 'day labourers, small farmers, shopkeepers, apprentices and dissenting preachers . . . . but not a single peer, baronet, or knight'.[12] This is a moderately accurate description of the sort of people to be found in the rebel camp, though it has a rather different emphasis from my description in the first chapter of this book. Nonetheless it is clear that Macaulay was not too happy that even such moderately elevated people as yeomen, shopkeepers or even artisans should be in Monmouth's army. For when we come to his famous description of Sedgemoor whom do we find fighting? 'Five or six thousand colliers and ploughmen . . . . the Somerset clowns . . . . the hardy rustics . . . . the Mendip miners.'[13] The urban element has vanished, to be replaced by farm labourers and peasants, people of virtually no account at all in Victorian England. Hardly surprisingly, most later writers have followed Macaulay's majestic lead. David Ogg, for instance, tells us that Monmouth's army consisted mainly of peasants and his cavalry were mounted on cart-horses,[14] a fact which seems inherently unlikely and does not square with descriptions of rebel cavalry patrols made by royalist officers. Monmouth's cavalry was not much good, but it was not that bad. Other writers pick up Macaulay's earlier reference to apprentices, put it together with a comment from the confession of Nathaniel Wade and then infer that Monmouth's army was an army of young fellows out on a spree.

In other words the overall impression of the rebel army is that it was composed of ploughboys, apprentices and various other types of young fool who were carried away by hero-worship, misplaced idealism or simply a lust for a little excitement. Such an analysis of the rebels makes the repression look particularly savage. Surely it was not necessary to crush so mercilessly a rebellion which consisted mainly of simple-minded young hay-seeds? One or two hangings as an example would have been enough. From this viewpoint Jeffreys appears as a savage, sadistic brute who gloried in the shambles that he made of the West Country.

My analysis of both the rebels and the rebellion differs in many respects from the Whig stereotype. I think that it would have been quite possible for the rebels to win at Sedgemoor, even without Whig gentlemen as their officers, an opinion which was clearly shared by many contemporaries. I also think that, if the rebels had won, many men would have flocked to their standard from all over the country, though I think that their divisions of interest and lack of experience would have prevented them from making a great success of civil government. The argument of this book is that both Jeffreys and King James thought correctly that they had good reason to do what they did, that the rebels were neither young nor peasants, that the rebellion laid bare a very dangerous threat to the existing state of society and that the Bloody Assizes was a necessary and extremely effective part of government policy which not only taught the West Country its duty, but has taught all Englishmen from that day to the present the folly of armed rebellion.

Appendix

The Rebels of 1685

The purpose of this appendix is to give some substance to comments which have been made in the book about the age, the place of origin and the social and occupational background of the rebels. The starting-point for any such analysis is the document in the British Library known as the Monmouth Roll.[1] This is a copy of the lists of rebels sent by the constables of the parishes in the area of rebellion to the Grand Jury of each of the three counties most involved. Such lists should theoretically have formed the basis for the presentation of rebels to the Bloody Assizes. But, as we have seen,[2] they were not much use for this purpose, since so many rebels on the lists had fled or were already dead. However, they remain invaluable for our purpose, since they include a far greater number of names of rebels than can be found, for instance, in the records of the assizes or Treasury which naturally were only interested in those rebels who were captured and tried.[3]

However, they are certainly not complete lists of all the rebels. They do not even cover the whole area from which rebels are known to have come. In particular, a considerable part of Somerset, mainly in the north and east but including such important rebel centres as Bridgwater, is omitted. Even in the area they do cover they are incomplete, people known to be in the rebellion from other evidence not being on them.[4] Nor can we presume that all those listed in the presentments were necessarily rebels. When we read in the indictments at Bridgwater Sessions of two men 'accused for idle persons and wandering upp and downe the country and suspected for being in James Scott's army', we may suspect upper-class prejudice.[5] Many men accused of being rebels had good stories or excuses. A common one was that they were forced to march with the rebels.[6] Others admitted going to the rebel camp, just out of interest. It must have made a good show. Malicious neighbours might well have a part to play in the appearance of a man's name on the list. Hugh Crosse, a wealthy tradesman from Bishop's Hull, near Taunton, declared later in Holland that he had taken no part in the rebellion. He thought that he must have been accused by some envious neighbour in his own line of business, 'with a malitious design to ruin him'. He decided not to test the fairness of the King's justice. Once he heard that he was enquired about he 'thought it high time for him to flye'.[7] Such evidence could be multiplied and it would be naïve to suggest that incompetent and often partial local authorities would know exactly who did and who did not go out with Monmouth. But this is no reason to dismiss the Monmouth Roll as a source. In the vast majority of cases where there is a reference in another source to a man being involved in the rebellion, his name can be found in the Monmouth Roll, if the rebels from his parish are listed. It therefore seems quite reasonable to use these lists as the basis for analysis of the rebels. Two important assumptions will obviously have to be made, first that the degree of errors and omissions is the same from village to village, and secondly that analysis based on the towns and villages which appear in the list is valid for those towns and villages that do not. Bearing these assumptions in mind what does the list tell us?

The names of a total of 2611 rebels or suspected rebels are given in the list. The names are listed by parishes and occasionally are followed by supplementary information, such as their occupation or their fate (e.g., 'dead', 'in prison' or 'at large'). It is clear from the lists that the general impression gained from literary sources that the rebellion was geographically concentrated is correct. For Devon and Dorset, where the presentments are complete, virtually all the rebels came from parishes in the extreme east and west of the counties respectively. In Somerset, on the other hand, it seems clear that the whole county was involved to a greater or lesser extent. As a result, despite the fact that a considerable number of

Somerset parishes were not listed, there are 1811 names for Somerset and only 488 for Devon and 312 for Dorset.

Within the area of rebellion there was further geographical concentration. Particular places or regions were particularly rebellious. As a general rule there were proportionately far more rebels in towns and industrial areas than there were in rural areas. This is difficult to prove conclusively because of the lack of adequate population figures. The best source for the relative population of parishes at a date near the rebellion would be the ecclesiastical census of 1676, known as the Compton Census,[8] which gives figures for the number of Conformists and Non-conformists in most of the parishes of the Province of Canterbury. However, the document is of little use for our purpose since in the two dioceses with the greatest number of rebels, Bristol and Bath and Wells, the Census gives only a summary of the totals in the whole diocese and does not break down the figures by parishes. The only area covered in detail in the Census which was an important centre of rebellion is the Deanery of Honiton in the Diocese of Exeter. The relative participation of individual parishes within this Deanery* is shown in Table I opposite.

There were four small towns or large villages in this area and it can be seen that they produced a high proportion of rebels relative to their population. Colyton and Axminster were particularly rebellious with just over a quarter of the total population of the area and very nearly half the rebels. Only three of the smaller villages produced many rebels but two of these, Axmouth and Musbury, were very rebellious indeed.

One other piece of information which the Compton Census should tell us is the number of Nonconformists in each parish. This was in fact the purpose of the Census. But it seems clear that these figures are woefully inadequate, incumbents producing the small numbers which they thought that their superiors would like to receive.[9] It is difficult to believe, for instance, that there were only nineteen Nonconformists in Colyton. The only two places in

---

* *Excluding* Uplyme whose rebels are included in the Lyme Regis list and *including* Colyton and Shute which were within the peculiar jurisdiction of the Dean and Chapter but geographically belong to Honiton Deanery.

Honiton Deanery which seem to have a realistic figure are Thorncombe and Axminster, with 162 and 175 Nonconformists respectively.

In order to compare some other areas with Honiton Deanery I have used what seems to be the next best source for the relative population of parishes. This was the return of people swearing to a loyalty oath in 1641, known as the Protestation Returns.[10] These

TABLE I

RELATIVE PARTICIPATION OF PARISHES IN HONITON DEANERY

	A	% total population	B	% total rebels
Honiton	1436		53	
Axminster	1064		79	
Colyton	1019	59%	86	76%
Thorncombe	885		38	
Membury	454		18	
Musbury	252	13%	23	21%
Axmouth	243		32	
11 other parishes	2159	28%	11	3%
Total	7512		340	

A. Conformists, Nonconformists and papists in the Compton Census, MS Salt 33.
B. Rebels in the Monmouth Roll. Add. 30,077.

are probably the best guide to relative population of any seventeenth-century source, since there was no advantage in being left off the list and a positive incentive to make sure that one's name was on it. The Returns are however over forty years old by the time of Monmouth's rebellion and it will be necessary to assume that relative population had not changed much in the intervening years. This is probably a reasonable enough assumption for the very crude analysis which will be done here. Three hundreds in Somerset have records both of the Protestation Returns and of Monmouth rebels and the material is analyzed in Table II below:

TABLE II

RELATIVE PARTICIPATION IN THREE SOMERSET HUNDREDS

	A	% total population	B	% total rebels	$\frac{A}{B}$
TAUNTON DEANE					
Taunton	780	28%	356	66%	2
Pitminster	270		43		6
Bishop's Hull	115	21%	31	22%	4
Wilton	76		24		3
Trull	123		23		5
20 other parishes	1423	51%	61	12%	23
Total	2787		538		5
ABDICK & BULSTONE					
Ilminster	581	35%	54	53%	11
Ashill	109	18%	11	24%	10
Curry Rivell	188		13		14
13 other parishes	801	47%	24	23%	33
Total	1679		102		16
MILVERTON					
Milverton	408	45%	60	79%	7
8 other parishes	502	55%	16	21%	31
Total	910		76		12

A. Names in the Protestation Returns.
B. Rebels in the Monmouth Roll.

This table shows that the urban concentration of rebels was even greater in Somerset than in East Devon. In each of the three hundreds the largest town provides a very high proportion of all the rebels from the hundred. The table also confirms the overall importance of the Hundred of Taunton Deane, the area reckoned by nearly all commentators to be the heart of the rebellion. The participation ratio ($\frac{A}{B}$) is far higher than in the other two hundreds. But we can see that by no means all of Taunton Deane was rebellious. Just five places produced 88 per cent of the rebels – Taunton itself, Trull, Bishop's Hull and Wilton all immediately contiguous to Taunton on the south of the river Tone and Pitminster, the second largest town in the hundred. At the other end of the scale there were eight parishes which produced no rebels at all and another four which had three rebels or less. This general trend of analysis does not mean that there were no small villages which supported the rebellion strongly. We have noted Axmouth and Musbury in Devon. A similar scale of participation can be found in a number of Somerset parishes, particularly in the Hundred of South Petherton where the small villages of Knowle St Giles, Cudworth, Lopen and Barrington all contributed a very high proportion of their population to the rebellion.[11] But these are exceptions, and the obvious conclusion to be drawn from the two tables above is that Monmouth's rebellion was basically an urban and not a peasant rebellion.

Such a conclusion is supported if we consider the occupations of the rebels. The constables of nineteen parishes sent in the occupations of most of the rebels on their list, including those from the important centres of Taunton, Frome and Lyme Regis. They are analysed on p. 202 under various subheadings.

These figures cannot be taken as typical of the whole rebel army, since they are heavily weighted by the occupations of three towns, Taunton, Lyme Regis and Frome, which account for over seventy per cent of the total. However, in view of the urban concentration of the rebels which we have already noted, it seems possible to make a few general points. The social composition of the rebel army is immediately striking. In 1709, Daniel Defoe was to divide the population of the country into seven groups, depending on their ability to live more or less comfortably. Nearly all the people in the Monmouth Roll fall into his middle three groups. There are none of 'the great, who live profusely' and very few of 'the rich, who live very plentifully'. But, on the other hand, there are very few of 'the poor, that fare hard', by which he meant labourers, or 'the miserable that really pinch and suffer want'. What remains are 'the middle sort, who live well . . . the working trades, who labour hard but feel no want, and the country people, farmers etc. who

TABLE III

ANALYSIS OF OCCUPATIONS IN NINETEEN PARISHES

		%
Gentlemen	6	1
Professionals[1]	10	2
Food, drink, groceries[2]	36	6
Clothing[3]	70	12.5
Building and metal[4]	60	11
Carrying[5]	19	3
Clothmaking[6]	296	53
Agriculture[7]	60	11
Labourers	2	—

1. Apothecary, surgeon, cleric, merchant, goldsmith.
2. Victualler, chandler, baker, tobacconist, maltster, butcher, brewer, innholder, miller, tobacco-cutter, soaper, cooper, pipemaker.
3. Tailor (30), shoemaker (17), cordwainer, glover, haberdasher, cobbler, tanner, hosier, mercer, pointmaker, barber.
4. Carpenter (16), wiredrawer (11), smith, bricklayer, mason, cutler, glazier, blacksmith, sawyer, brazier, joiner, locksmith, thatcher.
5. Carrier, porter, mariner, collier, ostler, coachman.
6. Weaver (119), comber (77), fuller (27), clothworker (16), serge-maker (12), cardmaker (10), feltmaker (10), tucker, clothier, combmaker, dyer, carder, twister, clothdrawer, woolbroker.
7. Husbandmen (34), yeomen (26).

fare indifferently'.[12] This concentration in the middle ranks of society is very clear and helps us to get an idea of the sort of people involved in the rebellion. The absence of labourers is particularly noticeable, there being only two in the whole sample.

Most writers on Monmouth's rebellion have noted the comparative absence of gentlemen from the rebel ranks and indeed have considered this to be one of the main reasons for the failure of the rebellion. This may be true, but it is an analysis that in my opinion misses the point of the rebellion. For what these writers mean when they say gentlemen are the representatives of the great Whig gentry families of the West Country – the Drakes, the Youngs, the Prideaux and so on. But once we see the rebellion as mainly urban rather than rural the emphasis rapidly changes. For the social leaders of a town like Taunton were not country gentlemen but successful merchants, shopkeepers and industrialists. Taunton and Lyme Regis, despite their architectural beauty and attractive surroundings, were not places where many of the country gentry chose to live. They were not 'gentry towns', as Defoe was to call places like Bury St Edmunds or Maidstone. Indeed the only two places in the area of rebellion which were gentry towns, Bath and Wells, were both conspicuously loyal.

The distinction between country gentlemen and successful town-dwellers who called themselves or were called by others gentlemen is an important one and can be seen quite clearly if we look at the four men in the Taunton list who were called gentlemen. Only one of them, Dick Slape, who was the son of a loyalist army officer, fitted the conventional idea of the gentleman. John Hucker was a successful sergemaker, William Savage was an innkeeper and Peter Parry was the son of a merchant. Many other men in the Taunton list had sufficient social status to have called themselves gentlemen if they felt like it, such as James Whetham, a maltster with extensive trading links in Bristol, London and the Low Countries, or Abraham Carie, a successful brewer. The longer such people lived and the nearer they were to retirement, the more likely they were to be called gentlemen. All we need do here is to conclude that the urban élite of the towns in the area of the rebellion was well represented in the Monmouth Roll, as we might expect.

When we look at the main body of the rebels several points are immediately obvious. First, as we have seen, they were drawn almost exclusively from the shopkeeping and artisan classes, and not from the class of general labourers. Within this group there seems to be a reasonable spread of the types of trade that one would expect in small towns and villages, with one or two exceptions. It is perhaps rather surprising that there are so few purveyors and processors of food and drink. There are only six bakers, three butchers and three millers, for instance, compared with thirty tailors, seventeen shoemakers and sixteen carpenters. One would not expect such a striking difference in a random sample and it would be interesting to know the reason. At a hazard I would suggest that butchers and millers with their strong links to their sources of supply in the countryside were traditional Tories, with a very different view of life and society from that radical stereotype, the shoemaker.

The most obvious fact which emerges from Table III is the very high proportion of clothworkers in the rebel army. This is exaggerated to a certain extent, since both Taunton and Frome were well known centres of the West Country cloth industry, but the general emphasis is correct. Nearly all places which list occupations have some clothworkers amongst their rebels. The question which has to be considered is whether this concentration of workers from one industry merely reflects the enormous importance of cloth manufacture to this particular part of the West Country or whether there were problems in the cloth industry which themselves determined the decision of so many weavers, combers and fullers to rebel. The latter explanation seems very unlikely. There is not a hint of economic motivation in Monmouth's Declaration nor in any other document connected with the rebellion. It is difficult to see how a rebellion could be expected to help clothworkers in any case. If men were unemployed and wanted work they would have done better to join the royal army where they would at least have been paid. Finally, there is no evidence of problems in the cloth industry in 1685, nor is there any sign of a slump in the exports of cloth going through the two main ports of the area, Exeter and Lyme Regis.[13]

The last point to note in a discussion of occupations is the comparatively small number of husbandmen and yeomen in our sample. This was certainly affected by the fact that the sample is dominated by parishes which were largely urban. In many rural parishes one would expect all rebels to be farmers, as is the case in

Langport, Broomfield and Stoke-under-Hamden, though even in these places it should be noted that they were described as yeomen or husbandmen and not labourers. But, even in the countryside, it would be wrong to assume that there was no selection process taking place. This can be seen very clearly by looking at the four West Somerset parishes of Stogursey, Dunster, Carrhampton and Minehead where rebel occupations are listed. None of these parishes could be called urban or industrial in the seventeenth century and one would have thought that at least half the adult male population would have been engaged in agriculture. And yet the analysis of rebel occupations in these parishes was as follows:

TABLE IV

ANALYSIS OF OCCUPATIONS IN FOUR PARISHES OF WEST SOMERSET

Professional	2 (both surgeons)
Food, drink, groceries	5
Clothing	8
Building, metal	6
Clothmaking	10
Agriculture	2
	—
	33
	—

The pattern is very much the same as in Lyme Regis or Taunton. One can conclude that Monmouth's army was not an army of peasants.

In view of the urban tendency of this analysis it was decided to take three towns as samples in order to see if it was possible to find out any more about the rebels as a group. The towns chosen were those that had the largest number of rebels in the three counties, Taunton, Colyton and Lyme Regis. Taunton was a fair-sized place by late-seventeenth-century standards with a population of six or seven thousand.[14] Lyme Regis was much smaller with a population of only thirteen hundred in 1694, when a complete listing was made.[15] Despite its small size Lyme Regis was very much a town, with its own corporation and an important role as the port for much of the area in which the rebellion took place. Although Colyton was slightly larger than Lyme with a population of fifteen hundred in the same year,[16] it was really more like a large village than a town. But, for all that, it was the most rebellious place in Devonshire and indeed provided the fourth largest contingent of rebels of any place listed in the Monmouth Roll.

One interesting question would be to determine the proportion of the total adult male population that was listed as rebels in these three very rebellious places. This poses an immediate problem. We know the number of rebels and we know the population of two of the towns and have a fair idea of the population of the third, but we do not know the proportion of adult males in the total population. However, as a rough guide, demographers often suggest that the number of men over sixteen is about a quarter of the total in pre-industrial populations. On this basis the proportion of rebels to adult males was as follows:

TABLE V

PROPORTION OF REBELS TO ADULT MALES

	A No. of rebels	B Approx. population	C Approx. adult males	D A as % of C
Colyton	86	1500	375	23
Lyme Regis	116	1300	325	36
Taunton	350	6000	1500	23*

These figures are of course very rough approximations, but they give some idea of the scale of the rebellion in its greatest centres. The high percentage for Lyme Regis is probably partly a reflection of the fact that, when Monmouth landed there, people got rather carried away. On reflection, nineteen of the Lyme Regis rebels decided not to march out of the town with him. So, if we say that in the centres of rebellion somewhere about a quarter of

* The proportion was much greater in the parish of St Mary Magdalen than that of St James (roughly 33 per cent and 11 per cent respectively).

adult males joined the rebellion we should not be too far out.

What were the special characteristics of this quarter? We have already seen that they were distinguished by their occupations and social status. There were very few labourers. We can also assume that a high proportion of them were Dissenters, though there is no direct evidence which could be used to prove this. But they also seem to have been distinguished by age. Determining the age of an individual rebel is not easy, but it is not completely imposs-ible to do.

The method which was used was to search for the rebels in the relevant parish registers. Such an exercise, known as nominal linkage analysis, is fraught with considerable problems. Spelling was far from consistent in the seventeenth century, registers are far from complete, many names are duplicated and so on. But, for what it is worth, the method was as follows. The age of a rebel whose name and Christian name was found only once in the baptismal register was determined by his date of baptism. Where there were two people of the same name and Christian name as the rebel it was sometimes possible to eliminate one of them by checking the burial register. Where this was impossible those under the age of thirteen and over sixty have been eliminated, as unlikely to have been in the rebel army. But if both people lie within this range both ages have been included, hence the 'old' and 'young' choices in Table VI below. Where the baptismal registers show three or more people of the same name and Christian name as the rebel, he has been relegated to the 'unknowns'. Where no baptism for a person of the same name and Christian name as the rebel could be found, it was often possible to estimate ages by finding either his date of marriage in the marriage register[17] or the date of baptism of his first recorded child in the baptismal register. These have been converted to ages by adding twenty-three to the period between marriage and 1685 or twenty-five to the period between the baptism of the first recorded child and 1685.[18] The results of the analysis are on p. 208.

The most striking feature of this analysis is the extremely high age of the rebels. If we adopt the 'old choice' then over 80 per cent of the rebels in all three towns are over the age of twenty-five, in

TABLE VI

AGE DISTRIBUTION OF REBELS IN THREE PARISHES

Taunton St Mary Magdalen

	'Old' choice			'Young' choice	
Age	Number	% of no. known	Age	Number	% of no. known
50 and over	7	3.5	50 and over	4	2.0
40 ,, ,,	31	15.5	40 ,, ,,	19	9.5
30 ,, ,,	111	55.5	30 ,, ,,	93	46.5
25 ,, ,,	160	80.0	25 ,, ,,	147	73.5
20–24	30	15.0	20–24	39	19.5
19 and less	9	4.5	19 and less	13	6.5
Total known	199		Total known	199	
Unknown	81		Unknown	81	
	280			280	

Lyme Regis

	'Old' choice			'Young' choice	
Age	Number	% of no. known	Age	Number	% of no. known
50 and over	7	10.0	50 and over	5	7.1
40 ,, ,,	21	30.0	40 ,, ,,	14	20.0
30 ,, ,,	45	64.3	30 ,, ,,	37	52.9
25 ,, ,,	58	82.9	25 ,, ,,	51	72.9
20–24	9	12.9	20–24	11	15.7
19 and less	3	4.3	19 and less	8	11.4
Total known	70		Total known	70	
Unknown	46		Unknown	46	
	116			116	

Colyton

	'Old' choice			'Young' choice	
Age	Number	% of no. known	Age	Number	% of no. known
50 and over	6	9.1	50 and over	5	7.6
40 ,, ,,	16	24.3	40 ,, ,,	13	19.7
30 ,, ,,	41	62.2	30 ,, ,,	35	53.0
25 ,, ,,	57	86.4	25 ,, ,,	51	77.2
20–24	6	9.1	20–24	9	13.6
19 and less	3	4.5	19 and less	6	9.1
Total known	66		Total known	66	
Unknown	20		Unknown	20	
	86			86	

other words are mature, responsible men more likely to have a wife and children. Many of the rebels are of course much older with about a fifth of them born before the end of the first Civil War in 1646.

The greatest difficulty in accepting this picture at face value is the large number of unknowns. The proportion ranges from 23 per cent in Colyton to nearly 40 per cent in Lyme Regis. Many reasons can be put forward for not finding a particular person's name in a seventeenth-century parish register. Human error is certainly one. Proper names are extremely difficult to read in some cases and once a name has been transcribed incorrectly from one source it will obviously be much harder to find it in another. In any case many people may have been born or got married in a different parish from the one in which they found themselves in 1685. This would be particularly likely to happen in a place like Taunton where there were two parishes in a single town. Then there is the problem of Nonconformity. If we can believe contemporary comment practically all of the rebels were Dissenters who would presumably not be too happy about getting married or having their children baptized in an Anglican church. The fact that many did so, despite any misgivings they may have felt, has enabled this analysis to be done at all. But churchwardens' presentments make it clear that many Dissenters did not conform to the law and so one can expect a fairly high degree of non-registration throughout the area of rebellion. In the days before 1662, when most of the rebels were born, the churches of the West Country had ministers who had the respect of their prospective congregations, and one might expect registration to be more complete than in the period of Anglican conformity. Unfortunately it is in just the years of unrest between 1640 and 1660 that English parish registers are worst kept, so that it is impossible to find the baptismal registration of a very high proportion of the rebels. Finally, as was mentioned earlier, many rebels had to be ignored because they were called John Smith or some other common name which appeared too often in the register to enable their age to be identified with any certainty.

Would the ages of the 'unknown' rebels duplicate, reinforce or

destroy the pattern shown in Table vi? There is no way of
determining this. The most harm to my assertion that most rebels
were mature men over the age of twenty-five would be caused
by assuming that all the 'unknowns' were under twenty-five.
If we accept this assumption and adopt the 'young' choice for
the rest of the rebels the proportion of rebels over the age of
twenty-five falls to 59 per cent for Colyton, 52 per cent for Taunton and 44 per cent for Lyme Regis, which makes the average age
of rebels still fairly high but of course very much lower than I have
assumed in the discussion above. A reasonable hypothesis could
be put forward for this assumption. The reason that rebels' ages
are unknown could be because they came into the parish as
servants or apprentices and had not yet married or had children.
Unfortunately we do not have records for the registration of
apprentices in any of these places which might establish the truth
of such an assumption one way or the other. But what little
evidence we have makes it unlikely.

In Lyme Regis, for example, it would seem that there would
simply not be enough people for all forty-six unknowns to be
immigrant servants or apprentices. In the population listing of
1694 there were only sixty-seven males who were neither husbands or widowers nor sons living with their parents and so might
satsify the requirements of the assumption made above.[19] One
third of this group were described as servants, but the rest were
simply listed as unattached to any household. One could hardly
expect every one of these people to be immigrants. But if only a
third of them were natives, there would have had to have been a
hundred per cent turnout from the rest, if the assumption were to
be true. For Taunton it is possible to make a much clearer statement about the likelihood of an immigrant to the town being a
rebel. The parish of St Mary Magdalen kept a register of immigrants and their parish of origin in order that those named might
be sent home if they ever looked like being a charge on the rates.[20]
Only five of these men, out of a total of 188, were definitely in the
rebel army which makes the immigrant component of rebels from
this parish about 2 per cent. One can only conclude that the age
distribution in Table vi is reasonably accurate, that rebels were

relatively old people and that most of them were probably natives of the town from which they went out to fight.

One other fact which an analysis of the family background of rebels can tell us is that it was rare for two brothers or for father and son to be in the rebel army. This can be partly determined by analyzing the surnames of rebels, as is done in Table VII below.

TABLE VII

ANALYSIS OF REBELS' SURNAMES

	Taunton St Mary Magdalen			Lyme Regis			Colyton		
	No. of surnames	No. of rebels	% of total rebels	No. of surnames	No. of rebels	% of total rebels	No. of surnames	No. of rebels	% of total rebels
Surname unique	179	179	64	80	80	69	51	51	59
2 rebels with same surname	30	60	22	8	16	14	12	24	28
3 „ „ „ „	6	18	6	4	12	10	2	6	7
4 „ „ „ „	2	8	3	2	8	7	—	—	—
5 „ „ „ „	3	15	5	—	—	—	1	5	6
		280			116			86	

This table shows that a high proportion of the rebels were the only men with their particular surname in each town's contingent. But people with the same surname are not necessarily closely related, and it is necessary to examine their relationship in more detail if the degree of individual family involvement in the rebellion is to be established. To identify relationships from a parish register is a laborious business, so the exercise has been done only for Taunton St Mary Magdalen. The relationships of the hundred and one rebels with duplicate surnames are on p. 212.

Only fifty-four of the rebels from Taunton St Mary Magdalen had very close relationships with other rebels from the same parish, though it is quite likely that several others were the brothers or sons of rebels in other parishes. The proportion still seems rather small and justifies, I hope, my hypothesis that it may often have been deliberate family policy to send out only one rebel.

The writer would be the first to admit the fragility of the sort of analysis carried out in this Appendix. All the same I felt reluctant to write about a rebellion without knowing anything very much about the rebels who fought in it. For all its imperfections, the foregoing analysis tells us a little more about the sort of people who were rebels than we can find out from the often hysterical or prejudiced views of contemporaries and the often preconceived ideas of historians. It is my belief that it justifies my description of the rebels in Chapter One and gives support to my general hypothesis about the nature of the rebels' motivation. But that is something which the reader must judge for himself.

TABLE VIII

ANALYSIS OF THE RELATIONSHIP OF REBELS WITH DUPLICATED SURNAMES FROM TAUNTON ST MARY MAGDALEN

	Number of instances	Number of rebels	% of total rebels
Two brothers	11	22 ⎫	8 ⎫
Father and son	11	22 ⎬ 54	8 ⎬ 19%
Father and 2 sons	2	6 ⎪	2 ⎪
Father and 3 sons	1	4 ⎭	1 ⎭
No close relationship	18	31	
No evidence	7	16	
		101	

Notes

The historiography and sources for Monmouth's rebellion are well known to historians and there is no need to repeat the bibliography here. Good lists can be found in Bryan Little, *The Monmouth Episode* (1956) and Charles Chevenix Trench, *The Western Rising* (1969). The most important sources which I have used in addition to those listed in these works are:

B.L. Add. MSS. 41803–41846. The Middleton Papers, especially 41,812–14 and 41,817–19 which are letters from the Envoys Extraordinary at The Hague, mainly to the Earl of Middleton.

B.L. Add. MS. 25,370. The correspondence of Francesco Terriesi, Florentine minister in London, vol. xiii (April–September 1685).

B.L. Add. MS. 34,508. English translation of letters from the Dutch envoys in London, 1685.

Somerset Record Office. Sanford MSS (DD/SF) 3109. Letter from William Clarke to Edward Clarke, dated 29 July 1685, on the battle of Sedgemoor.

Standard local and demographic history sources have been used as the basis of the analysis of the rebels which appears in the Appendix.

The following abbreviations have been used in the notes, which are confined mainly to references for quotations in the text. Place of publication, unless otherwise stated, is London.

Add.	British Library, Additional Manuscripts.
B.A.	J. G. Muddiman (ed.), *The Bloody Assizes* (1929).
B.L.	British Library.
Bodl.	Bodleian Library.
C.C.P.A.	Calendar of Colonial Papers, America and the West Indies.
C.S.P.D.	Calendar of State Papers, Domestic.
C.T.B.	Calendar of Treasury Books.
D.R.O.	Dorset Record Office.
Dummer	'Edward Dummer's narrative of the Western Rebellion', in John Davis, *The History of the Second Queen's Royal Regiment* (1895).

Ecclesiastica *Ecclesiastica or the Book of Remembrance of the Independent Congrega-tion of Axminster*. Edited transcript (Exeter, 1874).

Grey *The Secret History of the Rye-House Plot and Monmouth's Rebellion, written by Ford, Lord Grey in 1685* (1754).

Harl. British Library, Harleian MSS.

Heywood 'An account of the rebellion of the Duke of Monmouth in a letter to Dr. James from the Rev. Mr. Andrew Paschall of Chedsey', in Samuel Heywood, *A Vindication of Mr. Fox's History of the Early Part of the Reign of James II* (1811).

H.M.C. Historical Manuscripts Commission.

James II 'King James's account of the battle at Sedgemore' (Harl. 6845, fos. 289–96), in *Hardwicke State Papers* (1778), vol. ii, pp. 304 ff.

Lans. British Library, Lansdowne MSS.

Paschall 'The Rev. Andrew Paschall's second narrative', in *Somerset and Dorset Notes and Queries*, xxviii (1961–7).

Pitman Henry Pitman, *A relation of the Great Sufferings . . . of Henry Pitman* (1689), reprinted in C. H. Firth (ed.), *Stuart Tracts, 1603–93* (1903).

P.R.O. Public Record Office.

S.R.O. Somerset Record Office.

S.R.O.Q. Somerset Record Office, Quarter Sessions Records.

Stopford Sackville H.M.C., *Stopford Sackville Report* (1904), vol. i.

S.T. T. B. Howell, *A Complete Collection of State Trials* (1809–28).

Wade 'Mr. Wade's further information' (Harl. 6845, ff. 274–82), reprinted in *Hardwicke State Papers* (1778), vol. ii.

Wheeler *Iter Bellicosum, Adam Wheeler his account of 1685* in Camden Society, 3rd series, vol. xviii (1910).

Whiting John Whiting, *Persecution Expos'd* (1715).

CHAPTER ONE

1. *Ecclesiastica*, p. 80.

2. Add. 25,370, fo. 217.

3. For evidence for the age, occupations and social status of the rebels see the Appendix, pp. 196–211.

4. *S.T.*, xi, 881. Speech of Richard Rumbold at his execution in Edinburgh.

5. Add. 41,819, fo. 19.

6. S.R.O. DD/HP 17. From the minutes of the Taunton Monthly Meeting of (Men) Friends, 1691–2.

7. *God Save the King* (1660), pp. 30–31.

8. Bodl. Tanner 129, fo. 87.

9. J. Toulmin, *History of Taunton* (1822 ed.), p. 423.

10. Harl. 6845, fo. 286.

11. Harl. 6845, fo. 285r.
12. *C.S.P.D.*, 8–9 July 1683.
13. *C.S.P.D.*, 19 July 1683. Also the Mermaid. *C.S.P.D.*, 4 August 1683.
14. *C.S.P.D.*, 23 August 1683.
15. *C.S.P.D.*, 11 August 1683.
16. The evidence for this can be found in the burial registers of St Mary Magdalen and St James parishes in Taunton.
17. *Ecclesiastica*, pp. 77–8.
18. S.R.O.Q. Indictments 186.
19. *C.S.P.D.*, 29 July 1683, and other letters to same effect.
20. *Ecclesiastica*, p. 78.
21. *Ecclesiastica*, p. 81.
22. For more information see the Appendix, pp. 197–8.
23. e.g., S.R.O. DD/CC 113586; D.R.O. A/30, p. 15; Add. 41,804, fo. 103.
24. *B.A.*, pp. 121–2.
25. Evidence for the value of convicted rebels' estates can be found in P.R.O. E.178/6676 (Devon and Somerset) and E.178/6677 (Dorset).
26. *B.A.*, p. 82.
27. *B.A.*, p. 93.
28. Turner, *Pallas Armata* (1683), p. 281. Actually he is describing an army of fifteen thousand men, but I have divided his figure by three.
29. Add. 41,812, fo. 117v, 9 June 1685.
30. Add. 41,812, fos. 44–5.
31. Grey, p. 95, reporting the messenger Robert Cragg.
32. Wade, p. 322. The gentleman was John Speke.
33. Whiting, p. 142.
34. B.L. Egerton MS. 1527.
35. Add. 41, 804, fos. 16–17.
36. Add. 41,819, fo. 19.
37. *C.S.P.D.*, 7 July 1683.
38. Add. 41,812, fos. 59–62; Add. 41,817, fos. 31–2, 60.
39. Add. 41,819, fo. 19v.
40. S.R.O. DD/SF 3109, 29 July 1685. This is presumably Colonel Richard Bovett.

CHAPTER TWO

1. P.R.O. S.P. 31/2, fo. 27.
2. Harl. 6845, fos. 256–9 is an interesting draft of the Declaration.
3. C. J. Fox, *A History of the early part of the reign of James the Second* (1808), p. xxxii.
4. *The Memoirs of James II, his campaigns as Duke of York* (1962), p. 266.
5. John Miller, *Popery and Politics in England, 1660–1688* (Cambridge, 1973), p. 113.

6. Peter Fraser, *The Intelligence of the Secretaries of State* (Cambridge, 1956), p. 85.
7. *S.T.*, ix, 625.
8. Bodl. MS. Carte 81, fo. 572.
9. *S.T.*, x, 307–20.
10. C. Price, *Cold Caleb* (1956), p. 139.
11. *S.T.*, x, 9.
12. *C.S.P.D.*, 2 February 1685.
13. Add. 41,803, fo. 128.
14. Add. 41,803, fo. 158.
15. Quoted in F. C. Turner, *James II* (1948), p. 240.
16. *C.S.P.D.*, 17 February 1685.
17. Add. 41,812, fo. 51.
18. Add. 41,812, fo. 9v.
19. Add. 41,812, fo. 17.
20. *C.S.P.D.*, 25 April 1685.
21. Add. 41,817, fo. 13, 6 May 1685.
22. Add. 41,812, fo. 74.
23. *C.S.P.D.*, 27 April 1685.
24. Add. 41,812, fo. 93v.
25. *C.S.P.D.*, 21 May 1685; see also *S.T.*, ix, 357 ff. and Bodl. MS. Tanner 31, fos. 22–3 for the story of this publication.
26. Anchitel Grey, *Debates*, viii, 345–6.
27. Sir John Dalrymple, *Memoirs of Great Britain and Ireland* (1771), ii, App. ii, 128.
28. Harl. 6845, fo. 284.
29. Harl. 6845, fos. 284–5.
30. Add. 41,817, fo. 142.
31. Add. 41,803, fo. 292.
32. P.R.O. W.O. 5/1 Marching orders, fos. 37–8.
33. *C.S.P.D.*, 20 June 1685.
34. Add. 25,370, fo. 216v.
35. For examples of such rumours see Add. 29,561, fo. 159; Add. 38,012, fo. 13; Sir John Reresby, *Memoirs* (1875), p. 338.
36. Add. 41,803, fo. 322.
37. *Observator* 1 July 1685. The article is mocking those who believe such stories.
38. Ezekiel 21: 25–7.
39. Add. 25,370, fos. 156, 161, 167v, 174, 197, 201v, 216v–217.
40. *Ecclesiastica*, p. 81.
41. Add. 41,818, fo. 159.
42. E. M. Thompson (ed.), *Correspondence of the family of Hatton, 1601–1704* (1878), ii, 57.
43. Add. 25,370, fo. 168v.

CHAPTER THREE

1. Add. 41,812, fo. 106v.
2. Add. 41,812, fo. 106.
3. Gilbert Burnet, *History of his own Times* (1823 ed.), iii, 12.
4. Add. 41,812, fo. 121v.
5. Add. 41,812, fo. 30.
6. Quoted by Charles Chevenix Trench, *The Western Rising* (1969), p. 72.
7. Add. 41,812, fo. 43.
8. Add. 41,812, fo. 138.
9. Add. 41,812, fo. 44.
10. Add. 41,812, fo. 15.
11. Add. 41,812, fo. 30.
12. Add. 41,812, fos. 122v, 128.
13. Add. 41,812, fo. 2.
14. Add. 41,812, fo. 33.
15. Add. 41,812, fos. 48v, 68v, 81v.
16. Add. 41,812, fo. 121v.
17. Add. 41,812, fo. 20.
18. Add. 41,812, fos. 36–56.
19. Add. 41,817, fos. 122–3.
20. Add. 41,817, fos. 120–1.
21. Add. 41,812, fo. 82.
22. Add. 41,812, fo. 114v.
23. Add. 41,812, fo. 114.
24. Dalrymple, *Memoirs of Great Britain and Ireland*, ii, App. ii, 126.

CHAPTER FOUR

1. Duchess of Albemarle to her husband. Quoted by Estelle Ward, *Christopher Monck, Duke of Albemarle* (1915), p. 210.
2. Godfrey Davies, 'The Militia in 1685', *English Historical Review*, xliii (1928).
3. P.R.O. S.P. 31/2, fo. 4.
4. P.R.O. S.P. 31/2, fos. 2, 3v.
5. *Ecclesiastica*, p. 81.
6. Wade, p. 321.
7. *Ecclesiastica*, p. 81.
8. S.R.O. DD/PH 238.
9. Add. 25,370, fo. 184.
10. C. T. Atkinson, *History of the Royal Dragoons, 1661–1934* (1934).
11. Bryan Little, *The Monmouth Episode* (1956), p. 120.
12. Add. 25,370, fo. 198.
13. Edward Hyde, Earl of Clarendon, *Correspondence and Diary* (1828), i, 141.

14. Quoted in Ward, *Christopher Monck*, p. 208.
15. Wade, p. 324.
16. Whiting, p. 143.
17. P.R.O. S.P. 31/2, fos. 13v–14; Add. 38,012, fos. 3–3v; Dummer p. 46.
18. Stopford Sackville, pp. 4–5.
19. Bodl. Tanner 31, fo. 131.
20. Wade, p. 324.
21. For rather confused and contradictory accounts of this action see Wade, p. 325; Stopford Sackville, pp. 13–14; H.M.C. 12th Rept., App. v, ii, 89; C. R. L. Fletcher and Montagu Burrows (eds.), *Collectanea*, 3rd series (Oxford, 1896), pp. 265–6; H.M.C. *Ormonde* N.S., vii, 343–4 and Bodl. Rawlinson C 421, fo. 183.
22. Bodl. Rawlinson C 421, fo. 183.
23. Wade, p. 325.
24. H.M.C. *Ormonde* N.S., vii, 343–4.
25. H.M.C. *Ormonde* N.S., vii, 343–4.
26. Stopford Sackville, p. 14.
27. Add. 38,012, fo. 12.
28. Wade, p. 326.
29. Wade, p. 326.
30. Stopford Sackville, pp. 6–10.
31. Quoted in Garnet Wolseley, *The Life of John Churchill* (1899), i, 304.
32. Wade, p. 327.
33. Add. 38,012, fo. 13.
34. Wade, p. 327.
35. Wade, p. 328.
36. Stopford Sackville, p. 10.
37. Stopford Sackville, p. 11.
38. Stopford Sackville, p. 9.
39. Add. 25,370, fo. 217v.
40. Stopford Sackville, p. 16.
41. Stopford Sackville, p. 16.
42. Dummer, p. 48.

CHAPTER FIVE

1. Churchill to the Earl of Clarendon, 4 July 1685. Quoted in Wolseley, *Life of John Churchill*, i, 305.
2. P.R.O. S.P. 31/2, fos. 25, 28v.
3. P.R.O. S.P. 31/2, fos. 26v, 27.
4. Ward, *Christopher Monck*, p. 211.
5. Stopford Sackville, p. 12.
6. S.R.O. DD/X/DEA C/1374.
7. Whiting, p. 143.

8. Add. 34,508, fo. 63v.
9. P.R.O. W.O. 5/2, fo. 125.
10. Add. 34,508, fo. 66v; Add. 41,823, fo. 114v.
11. P.R.O. W.O. 89/1, fos. 86–8.
12. S.R.O. DD/PH 211, fo. 248.
13. S.R.O. DD/PH 211, fo. 249.
14. Add. 30,077.
15. D.R.O. A 3/2a, p. 23.
16. D.R.O. A 3/2a, pp. 24–5.
17. Wheeler, p. 161.
18. Add. 30,277, fo. 30.
19. Wade, p. 328.
20. Paschall, p. 16.
21. Wade, p. 329.
22. Information on individual rebels from the sources discussed in the Appendix.
23. Heywood, pp. xlii–xliii.
24. John Oldmixon, *An History of England during the reigns of the Royal House of Stuart* (1730), p. 703.
25. S.R.O. DD/SF 3109, 29 July 1685.
26. Oldmixon, *History of England* . . . , i, 703.
27. Wade, p. 329.
28. Add. 30,277, fos. 33–32v [*sic*].

CHAPTER SIX

1. Heywood, p. xxxix.
2. Add. 30,277, fo. 34.
3. Oldmixon, *History of England* . . . . , p. 703.
4. Heywood, p. xliii.
5. H.M.C. 12th Rept., App. v, ii, 90.
6. Paschall, p. 19.
7. Paschall, p. 19.
8. Wade, p. 329.
9. Wade; Paschall; Wm Clarke in S.R.O. DD/SF 3109, 29 July 1685.
10. Paschall, p. 18.
11. Paschall, p. 18.
12. Paschall, pp. 18–19.
13. Heywood, p. xxxix.
14. Paschall, p. 19.
15. Heywood, p. xl.
16. James II, p. 310.
17. James II, p. 311.
18. Heywood, p. xliii.

19. James II, p. 312.
20. Wade, p. 330.
21. Wheeler, p. 164.
22. Wheeler, p. 164.
23. Dummer, p. 49.
24. S.R.O. DD/SF 3109, 29 July 1685.

CHAPTER SEVEN

1. *Ecclesiastica*, pp. 82–3.
2. Quoted in Allan Fea, *King Monmouth* (1902), p. 294.
3. Wheeler, p. 163.
4. Whiting, p. 144.
5. *C.S.P.D.*, 1 July 1685.
6. When exactly it did cease is not clear, but see the letter from Blathwayt, the Secretary at War, to Colonel Kirke, dated 21 July. P.R.O. W.O. 4/1, fos. 12–13.
7. Narcissus Luttrell, *A Brief Historical Relation of State Affairs* (1857), i, 354; S.R.O. DD/SF 3109.
8. P.R.O. S.P. 31/2, fo. 26.
9. Wheeler, p. 165.
10. H.M.C. *Dean and Chapter of Wells*, ii, 458.
11. Wheeler, p. 166.
12. S.R.O. DD/SF 3109, 29 July 1685.
13. See the comments of the surgeon, Joseph Winter, on the wounded prisoners in Ilchester gaol. S.R.O. DD/PH 212, fo. 45.
14. Add. 41,818, fo. 235.
15. P.R.O. W.O. 4/1, fos. 12–13.
16. P.R.O. W.O. 4/1, fo. 15.
17. *C.S.P.D.*, 3 December 1685.
18. P.R.O. W.O. 4/1, fos. 26–7.
19. Thomas Bruce, Earl of Ailesbury, *Memoirs* (1890), i, 123.
20. *C.S.P.D.*, 25 and 29 July 1685.
21. P.R.O. W.O. 5/2, fo. 135.
22. J. Y. Akerman (ed.), *Moneys Received and Paid for the Secret Service of Charles II and James II* (1851), pp. 110–11.
23. S.R.O. Q.163, 9 December 1685.
24. Add. 34,508, fo. 73v.
25. Stopford Sackville, p. 18.
26. S.R.O. DD/SF 3109, 29 July 1685.
27. S.R.O. Q.163, 7 December 1685.
28. *Ecclesiastica*, pp. 87–9.
29. George P. R. Pulman, *The Book of the Axe* (1975), p. 648.
30. *Ecclesiastica*, p. 83.

31. Pulman, *Book of the Axe*, pp. 807–9 for the stories. Further detail on the Colyton rebels from the sources in the Appendix.
32. *Ecclesiastica*, p. 87.
33. Whiting, p. 157.
34. These lists are in Add. 30,077.
35. S.R.O.Q./Indictments 199.
36. S.R.O. DD/CC 113586.
37. D.R.O. A 3/2a, pp. 11, 15.
38. D.R.O. A 3/2a, p. 19.
39. D.R.O. A 3/2a, p. 17.
40. Add. 41,804, fo. 270.
41. Add. 41,812, fo. 235v.
42. *C.S.P.D.*, 10 July 1686 and 30 May 1687.
43. Add. 41,803, fo. 333.
44. Luttrell, *Relation of State Affairs*, i, 353.
45. *C.T.B.*, viii, 619–20.
46. Add. 41,817, fos. 249–50.
47. Add. 41,812, fo. 195.
48. Add. 41,812, fo. 118.
49. Add. 41,813, fo. 141.
50. Add. 41,812, fo. 156.
51. Add. 41,812, fo. 156v.
52. Add. 41,812, fo. 177v.
53. Ailesbury, *Memoirs*, p. 118.
54. Add. 41,818, fo. 242.
55. Add. 41,819, fo. 20.
56. Add. 41, 812, fos. 236–236v.
57. Add. 41,813, fo. 95.
58. Add. 41,812, fo. 150.
59. Add. 41,812, fo. 174v.
60. Add. 41,818, fo. 126.
61. Add. 41,818, fo. 125v.
62. Add. 41,818, fo. 249.
63. Add. 41,818, fo. 136.
64. Add. 41,818, fos. 230, 234.
65. Add. 41,812, fo. 235.
66. Add. 41,812, fo. 248.
67. Add. 41,819, fo. 122.
68. Add. 41,819, fos. 121–2.
69. Add. 41,818, fo. 235v; Add. 41,813, fo. 112.
70. Add. 41,818, fos. 229, 234.
71. Add. 41,819, fo. 64.
72. Add. 41,818, fo. 269v.
73. Add. 41,813, fo. 15v.

74. Add. 41,818, fo. 234, 234v, 269v, etc.
75. Add. 41,819, fo. 123.
76. Add. 41,818, fo. 234v.
77. Add. 41,804, fo. 158.
78. Add. 41,813, fo. 114.
79. Add. 41,813, fo. 129. Also Colonel Matthews.
80. *C.S.P.D.*, 5 May 1686; Add. 41,813, fo. 128.
81. Add. 41,813, fo. 128v; *C.S.P.D.*, 16 May 1686.
82. *C.S.P.D.*, 2 June 1686.
83. *C.S.P.D.*, 27 March 1686; Add. 41,813, fo. 156v.
84. Add. 41,813, fo. 203.

CHAPTER EIGHT

1. Pitman, p. 435.
2. *Parliamentary History of England*, iv, 1374, quoted by Turner, *James II*, p. 280.
3. S.R.O.Q./Sessions Minute Book (1676–87), fos. 456–7.
4. Whiting, p. 145.
5. S.R.O. DD/PH 211, fo. 45.
6. *London Gazette*, no. 2069, 17 September 1685.
7. Add. 41,804, fo. 210.
8. Sir John Bramston, *Autobiography* (1840), pp. 187–8.
9. Quoted in Turner, *James II*, p. 279.
10. Add. 34,508, fo. 66.
11. William Bray (ed.), *The Diary of John Evelyn* (1895), 15 July 1685.
12. Dalrymple, *Memoirs of Great Britain and Ireland*, ii, App. ii, 125.
13. Quoted in Price, *Cold Caleb* (1956), p. 213.
14. Price, *Cold Caleb*, p. 219.
15. e.g. Lans. 1152a. Papers of Mr Bridgeman, secretary to Sunderland. And Add. 41803, 41804. Papers of Owen Wynne, secretary to Middleton.
16. Lans. 1152a, fo. 238v.
17. J. S. Clarke (ed.), *Life of James II* (1816), ii, 43.
18. *C.S.P.D.*, 14 September 1685.
19. *C.S.P.D.*, 19 September 1685.
20. For a general discussion of this material see J. G. Muddiman (ed.), *The Bloody Assizes* (1929).
21. *B.A.*, p. 28.
22. Quoted in *B.A.*, p. 29.
23. Ailesbury, *Memoirs*, i, 122.
24. Whiting, pp. 152–3.
25. Pitman, p. 435.
26. *B.A.*, p. 29.
27. *B.A.*, p. 79.

28. *C.S.P.D.*, 5 September 1685.

29. Pitman, p. 435.

30. *B.A.*, p. 34.

31. *C.S.P.D.*, 22 September 1685.

32. *B.A.*, p. 86.

33. *B.A.*, p. 98.

34. Quoted in *B.A.*, p. 40.

35. *C.S.P.D.*, 19 September 1685.

36. Pitman, p. 436.

37. *C.S.P.D.*, 14 September 1685.

38. Pitman, pp. 436–41.

39. *C.S.P.D.*, 31 May 1687; for Defoe see *An Appeal to Honour and Justice* (1715), p. 28. The document actually describes him as Daniel Foe, the name which he used as a young man. I missed this piece of evidence in my recent book on Defoe, for which omission I now apologize to his memory, as I also do to Brian Fitzgerald whom I criticized for believing a boast by Defoe which was unsupported by any other evidence.

40. P.R.O. C.O./1/58, fo. 280.

41. John Coad, *A Memorandum of the Wonderful Providence etc.* (1849), pp. 23–31.

42. *C.C.P.A.*, 9 January 1689/90.

43. *C.C.P.A.*, 26 June 1690.

44. *C.C.P.A.*, 20 November 1690.

45. The inquisitions are in P.R.O. E.178/6676 (Devon and Somerset) and E.178/6677 (Dorset).

46. *C.T.B.*, viii, 1090.

47. *C.T.B.*, viii, 257, 436.

48. *C.T.B.*, viii, 1244, 1874.

49. *C.T.B.*, viii, 1960.

50. *C.T.B.*, viii, 686.

51. Bodl. Rawlinson C 421, fo. 183.

52. *C.T.B.*, viii, 1032.

53. *C.T.B.*, viii, 404–5.

54. *B.A.*, pp. 92–3. The editor of *The Bloody Assizes* suggests that the John Spragg, Sprague or Sprake executed at Colyton was a man from Winsham in Somerset, but I think he is wrong. The martyrologist describes the execution at Colyton of John Sprague and William Clegg, 'both of that town', and both names appear in the list of rebels presented at Colyton.

55. *C.T.B.*, viii, 1820. The evidence for this section on the Colyton rebels is drawn from the material discussed in the Appendix and the sources on the general fate of rebels which have been used earlier in this chapter.

56. Bodl. Tanner 31, fo. 154.

57. D.R.O. B7/H2. Assessments for tax on births, marriages and burials.

CHAPTER NINE

1. Dalrymple, *Memoirs*, ii, App. ii, 23–4.
2. D.R.O. A 3/2a, p. 29.
3. *C.S.P.D.*, 29 May 1686.
4. Add. 41,804, fo. 307.
5. Quoted by Little, *Monmouth Episode*, p. 239.
6. Luttrell, *Relation of State Affairs*, i, p. 415. See also i, p. 404.
7. Ailesbury, *Memoirs*, i, 103.
8. B.L. Sloane 4194 fo. 404, quoted by Little, *Monmouth Episode*, p. 249.
9. J. S. Clarke, *James II*, ii, 621.
10. *S.T.*, xi, 881.
11. Blair Worden, 'Edmund Ludlow: the Puritan and the Whig', *Times Literary Supplement*, 7 January 1977.
12. Macaulay, *History of England*, i, 571, 582.
13. Macaulay, *History*, i, 606, 608. Note that these miners, who appear conspicuously in most later accounts of the rebellion and seem to derive from a comment in John Evelyn's diary, are also mainly myth. The contingents from the mining villages of the Mendips were quite small. Little, *Monmouth Episode*, p. 132.
14. *England in the Reigns of James II and William III* (1969), p. 147.

APPENDIX

1. Add. 30,077.
2. See pp. 144–6 above.
3. For assize records see the Gaol Book of the Western Circuit. P.R.O. ASSI/23/3. For Treasury records see *C.T.B.*, vol. viii.
4. A vast range of local evidence exists which could be used to add to the number of known rebels' names, e.g. Quarter Sessions and manorial courts; further names can be found in the Treasury records and in general comment on the rebellion.
5. S.R.O.Q./Indictments 199.
6. e.g. D.R.O. A 3/2a, pp. 19–20.
7. Add. 41,813, fos. 112v–113.
8. A copy of this is in the William Salt Library, Stafford, MS Salt 33.
9. For a general discussion of the value of the Compton Census as a guide to the level of Nonconformity see C. W. Chalklin, 'The Compton Census of 1676 – the dioceses of Canterbury and Rochester', *Kent Records* XVII (1960) and T. Richards, *The Religious Census of 1676* (1927).
10. For a discussion of this source see Joan Thirsk, 'Sources of information on population, 1500–1760', *Amateur Historian*, iv (1959).
11. Bryan Little points out that South Petherton was the only area covered by Monmouth's tour of 1680 which produced many rebels. *Monmouth Episode*, p. 133.

12. *Review*, vi, 142.
13. Nearly all exports through the port of Lyme Regis were of cloth. The table below gives the figures from the port-books for the export subsidy.

1679–80	£308	1683–84	£398
1680–81	£343	1685–86	£364
1681–82	£310	1686–87	£451
1682–83	£346		

    For exports of cloth from Exeter see W. B. Stephens, *Seventeenth-Century Exeter* (1958), pp. 103–4.
14. I calculated this by multiplying the average baptisms per year in the two parishes of Taunton by a factor of 30, i.e. assuming a crude (very crude) birth rate of 33 per 1000. This gives for Taunton St Mary Magdalen 113 × 30 = 3390 and for Taunton St James 88 × 30 = 2640. Total = 6030. In 1683 the Mayor, Stephen Timewell, reported to Secretary Jenkins that nearly three thousand men over the age of eighteen had sworn the oath of allegience (*C.S.P.D.*, 3 September). This suggests a total population of between ten and twelve thousand which seems far too high.
15. D.R.O. B7/H2.
16. Gregory King's figure. See T. H. Hollingsworth, *Historical Demography* (1969), p. 190. The figure is of course considerably higher than the figure of 1019 on p. 212, since King's estimate was of the total population while the Compton Census referred only to adults.
17. In all three towns marriages were very seriously under-registered. For example, in Taunton St Mary Magdalen a total of forty-nine rebels can be found in the marriage register but another sixty-four are recorded as the fathers of children born in the parish. No one has suggested that Taunton was famous for illegitimacy and St Mary's was a very popular church for marriages, drawing in couples from a wide area. Cf. Hollingsworth's comments on the marriage register at Colyton, *Historical Demography*, p. 190.
18. The median of the thirty-six instances where I found date of baptism and date at marriage of the same man in Taunton was twenty-three and the median of the forty-five instances where I found date of father's baptism and date of baptism of first recorded child was twenty-five.
19. D.R.O. B7/H2.
20. S.R.O. D/P/tau. m. 13.3.9.

Index